KT-529-094

APPRENTICESHIP IN THINKING
Cognitive Development in Social Context

Barbara Rogoff

FALKIRK COUNCIL
LIBRARY SUPPORT
FOR SCHOOLS

New York   Oxford
OXFORD UNIVERSITY PRESS

Oxford University Press

Oxford   New York   Toronto
Delhi   Bombay   Calcutta   Madras   Karachi
Petaling Jaya   Singapore   Hong Kong   Tokyo
Nairobi   Dar es Salaam   Cape Town
Melbourne   Auckland

and associated companies in
Berlin   Ibadan

Copyright © 1990 by Barbara Rogoff

First published in 1990 by Oxford University Press, Inc.,
198 Madison Avenue, New York, New York 10016-4314

First issued as an Oxford University Press paperback, 1991

Oxford is a registered trademark of Oxford University Press

All rights reserved. No part of this publication may be reproduced,
stored in a retrieval system, or transmitted, in any form or by any means,
electronic, mechanical, photocopying, recording, or otherwise,
without prior permission of Oxford University Press, Inc.

Library of Congress Cataloging-in-Publication Data
Rogoff, Barbara.
Apprenticeship in thinking: cognitive development in social context
Bibliography: p.   Includes index.
1. Cognition in children.   2. Social interaction in children.
3. Cognition and culture.   4. Children and adults.
I. Title.   [DNLM: 1. Cognition—in infancy & childhood.
2. Interpersonal Relations—in infancy & childhood.
3. Thinking—in infancy & childhood.
WS 105.5.C7   R735a]
BF723.C5R64   1990   303.3'2   89-8697

ISBN 0-19-505973-5
ISBN 0-19-507003-8 (pbk.)

19 18 17 16 15 14 13 12 11
Printed in the United States of America
On acid-free paper

Dedicated to
Esther and William Rogoff
and
Agnes and Oscar Magarian
with deep appreciation for their guidance and support
during critical periods of development

Preface

Children's cognitive development is an apprenticeship—it occurs through guided participation in social activity with companions who support and stretch children's understanding of and skill in using the tools of culture. The sociocultural basis of human skills and activities—including children's orientation to participate in and build on the activities around them—is inseparable from the biological and historical basis of humans as a species. The particular skills and orientation that children develop are rooted in the specific historical and cultural activities of the community in which children and their companions interact. In this book, I examine how individual thinking processes relate to the cultural context and the social interactions of children that provide guidance, support, direction, challenge, and impetus for development.

In presenting my concept of guided participation in cultural activity, I draw heavily on the theory of Vygotsky and refer also to that of Piaget. I focus on literatures in cognitive development, communication and social interaction in infancy and childhood, education, and cultural psychology and anthropology. References to my own research on these topics in the United States and Highland Guatemala appear throughout the book, and part of one chapter summarizes research that I have done with my colleagues on the role of children's social interaction with adults and peers in learning to plan and remember. However, my aim is to integrate the available work from a wide variety of sources to provide a coherent and broadly based account of cognitive development through guided participation in sociocultural activity.

This book is addressed to my colleagues and their students—researchers and scholars in the fields of developmental, cognitive, and social psychology, and those in related areas of communication, anthropology, and education. My hope is that the ideas expressed here will assist in shaping our efforts to understand human thinking and development and will elucidate a sociocultural approach to cognitive development.

The style of the book is intended to make it both provocative and clear to readers who are already embedded in scholarly work in the area, as well as engaging and informative to readers who are new to the topic. From trying to explain the aims of my research to Mayan Indian farmers and weavers, I learned that accessible explanations are not only important for communication, but also essential for scholars to be able to examine assumptions and goals for developing theory and research. I supplement the discussion with illustrations of children's routine guided participation in sociocultural activity, to give readers a picture of the evidence available from observation of children.

Setting the stage for the book is a discussion of how children's cognitive development has until recently been considered a solitary endeavor, with little examination of the contexts in which and about which children learn. With an increasing commitment to understanding the context of development, there have been varying approaches to conceiving of the relationship between the individual and the social world.

In Part I, I argue that the roles of the individual and the social world are mutual and not separable, as humans by nature engage in social activity with their contemporaries and learn from their predecessors. To elaborate how individual thinking processes relate to societal practices developed by previous generations, I discuss how societal practices provide definitions, tools for problem solution, and particular tactics of solution. Primary examples of the societal context of cognitive development are the Euroamerican institution of schooling and the cognitive skills involved in school literacy, arithmetic, reasoning, classification, and remembering.

Part II of the book focuses on the processes by which children's thinking and development are supported and stretched in the immediate social contexts in which children are involved in problem solving, in collaboration with others or in social arrangements of children's activities. Communication between children and their social partners provides a medium for new members of society to participate in more skilled problem solving with the guidance of their partners.

Guided participation involves interpersonal communication as well as stage-setting arrangements of children's activities. It includes explicit efforts to guide children in development as well as tacit communication and arrangements that are embedded in the practical and routine activities of daily life that do not explicitly focus on instruction or guidance. Guided participation is jointly managed by children and their companions in ways that facilitate children's growing skills and participation in the activities of mature members of their community.

The processes of guided participation—building bridges between what children know and new information to be learned, structuring and supporting children's efforts, and transferring to children the responsibility for managing problem solving—provide direction and organization for children's cognitive development in widely differing cultures. At the same time, cultural variation in the lessons to be learned and in the means by which children learn them underscore the importance of children's roles in observing and participating in social activity, the tacit arrangements of children's roles, and the multiple roles of parents and other companions in guiding children's development.

In Part III, I consider speculations and evidence of how social interaction may contribute to children's cognitive development. Vygotsky's and Piaget's views vary in their differing emphasis on the role of a partner's expertise as compared with equality of status as features of social interaction that promote cognitive development. Research on the role of adult–child interaction in children's skill with language, object exploration and construction, and remembering and planning suggests that both task expertise and communication are influential. Shared problem solving, in which children can participate in collaborative thinking processes, appears central to the utility of social interaction for children's development. Peers may be less skilled partners than adults in some activities, but may offer unique possibilities for discussion and collaboration when they consider each other's perspective in a balanced fashion. Peers also serve as highly available and active companions, providing each other with motivation, imagination, and opportunities for creative elaboration of the activities of their community.

In concluding, I argue that children make use of guided participation in sociocultural activity through appropriation of shared thinking for their own uses—an active and ongoing process inherent to communication. I consider the relation of guided participation and creativity, and the roles of challenge and sensitivity of other peoples' support of children's efforts. I stress that the responsibility for learning is often asymmetrical, with children and their families varying in their relative efforts to promote learning. Finally, I argue that our cultural stress on the individual must be balanced with recognition of the interdependence of children and their social partners in cultural contexts, in order to understand the processes and goals of cognitive development.

Stanford, California   B. R.
April 1989

Acknowledgments

I am grateful for the intellectual atmosphere provided by my colleagues and students over many years at the University of Utah. I also gained from the stimulation of Fellows and staff at the Center for Advanced Study in the Behavioral Sciences as a Fellow during the completion of this book, supported by the Spencer Foundation, the National Science Foundation (#BNS87-00864), and a Faculty Fellow Award from the University of Utah. The direction of my thinking was facilitated by these sources and by a Fellowship from the Kellogg Foundation, which I deeply appreciate.

For research funding, I am thankful to the National Institute of Child Health and Human Development (#16793), the National Institute of Mental Health (#41060), the National Institute of Education (#G-80-0060), the University of Utah Research Committee, and the National Institutes of Health Biomedical Research Support Grant (#507-RR07092) through the University of Utah.

It is only appropriate in a book using a metaphor of apprenticeship to acknowledge those who have both guided and challenged me, especially Mike Cole, Jerry Kagan, Jean Lave, Ben and Lois Paul, Sylvia Scribner, Colwyn Trevarthen, Jim Wertsch, Shep White, Bea Whiting, and the Mayan parents and children of San Pedro. I appreciate the intellectual rigor and efforts of my collaborators in the research presented in this book: Pablo Cox Bixcul, Marta Navichoc Cotuc, Shari Ellis, Bill Gardner, Mary Gauvain, Jamie Germond, Artin Göncü, Jayanthi Mistry, Gilda Morelli, Christine Mosier, Barbara Radziszewska, Judy Skeen, Jon Tudge, and Kathy Waddell.

The preparation of this book was greatly facilitated by comments and discussion on a variety of earlier drafts by Bob Calfee, Mike Cole, Denise Fitz, Saul Feinman, Alan Fogel, Mary Gauvain, Donna Gelfand, Artin Göncü, Nancy Hazen, Gilda Morelli, Barbara Radziszewska, Mark Reimers, Bradd Shore, Jon Tudge, and Jaan Valsiner, who naturally are likely to disagree with many of the points expressed. The writing was also aided by excellent advice from Oxford University Press editor J an Bossert and reviewers Margery B. Franklin and Dennie Wolf.

Last, but most important, I thank my husband, Salem Magarian, for his enthusiasm and view on life, and our children, Luisa, Valerie, and David, for giving me an in-depth course in child development with a warm, active, practical perspective.

Contents

APPRENTICESHIP
IN THINKING

1

Cognitive Development
in Sociocultural Context

Little David, at 7 months, sits in his rolling walker in the kitchen as his mother cooks. His big sister Luisa, age 3½, sits on the floor beside him, telling him, "Stay away from the stove. . . . Hot! . . . Hot! . . ." Then she begins to push David across the kitchen, past the oven, in his walker, and says, "Come here, David." Luisa comments to her mother, "I'm teaching him to go past the oven."

Then in a sweet motherese voice, Luisa says, "David, I'm teaching you to go past the oven. Let me show you." She pushes him across the kitchen past the oven again. "See? . . . See? . . . Go *past* ovens. . . . You remember? . . ." She pauses, as if waiting for a response. But David just sits in his walker, looking around. Luisa pushes him across the kitchen again, saying, "Now try again!"

Four short years later, while getting dressed one morning, David comments to his mother, "You know, I thought I'd be a grownup by now. . . . It sure is taking a long time!"

As humans, we progress across the span of a few years after birth to remarkable ability to communicate by means of language, to use and devise tools to solve problems, to engage in flexible cooperative actions with others, to profit from the experience and inventions of our ancestors, to teach and learn from others, and to plan for distant future events. We ruminate about the perspectives of other humans, analyze our past and current situations, and feel proud of our differences from other animals.

To investigate what accounts for our specifically human skills and activities, along with those we may have in common with other animals, scholars have for centuries considered questions of human development. How do the immature skills and characteristics of newborns transform so quickly to those of a being with impressive human capacities?

Answers to these questions have to do with the nature of human nature, the nurture of human nature, and the nature of human nurture. The study of human development has wrestled with the issue of how to conceive the relationship between individuals' activities and features of the environment, yielding a variety of views. All theories recognize that both nature and nurture are necessary, although most attempts to conceptualize the process of development have focused on one aspect and simply assumed the other.

In recent decades, the study of children's cognitive development has been dominated by perspectives that focus on the role of the individual in constructing reality. As Dennie Wolf (personal communication) puts it,

> Since psychology began in this country, the dominant metaphor for a learner has been something between Rodin's thinker and Huck Finn heading off to the territories—a singular, lone figure arm-wrestling the world, some conundrum, or a conceptual matter to the table. We are at long last learning to question the singularity, even the isolation, of that figure.

The stress on the individual undoubtedly derives from a variety of sources, including the focus of American culture on the independent individual conquering a new land (having left relatives behind) and competing with others, and the efforts of social scientists to achieve the objectivity they attribute to advances in the physical sciences (demonstrating "physics envy," as Shep White puts it). As researchers, we have only recently begun to notice the social context of individual achievement and to develop methods for studying the real complexity of life rather than trying in vain to isolate human specimens for study. (Interestingly, this has been the direction taken in the physical sciences as well.)

An emphasis on the individual has characterized decades of research carried out by American investigators studying children's intellectual milestones, IQ, memory strategies, and grammatical skills. It has also been characteristic of the incorporation of Piaget's theory into American research as a dominant influence on the study of children's cognitive development in the modern era.

Piaget was by training a biologist, addressing questions of the origins and development of modern scientific ways of thought, in the Geneva of Calvin and Rousseau. Although Piaget's theory noted that the cognitive advances of the individual involve adaptations to the environment (including the social environment), his primary efforts were devoted to examining how the individual makes sense of an unexamined "generic" world, common to the species as a whole. When Piaget's theory attracted interest in the United States, it was Piaget's characterization of stages of individual cognitive development that became the focus of extensive study. Americans first devoted themselves to verifying the phenomena that Piaget described (i.e., that 5-year-olds believe that the quantity of water changes when it is poured into a container of a different shape). When the phenomena were substantiated, many American researchers then tried to challenge Piaget's theory by demonstrating that children can advance beyond preoperational thinking at earlier ages. (Piaget jokingly referred to such efforts to rush individual development as "the American question," as Piaget himself was not concerned with particular ages, but with the sequence in advancement of thinking across a broad set of problems.)

Although Piaget was not easily understood by American researchers and was mistakenly assumed to consider *only* the individual at the expense of the environment, it was indeed the case that Piaget's primary focus was on the individual rather than on the aspects of the world that the child struggles to understand or on how the social world contributes to individual development. Piaget assumed that children's cognitive activities are general across problems, requiring no consideration of the specifics of a problem. It was troublesome for his theory that particular children do not use uniform reasoning on problems that are logically similar. There have been many demonstrations that the form of problems affects how children reason about them (see especially Donaldson, 1978, who argues that when Piagetian problems make "human sense," they are clear to younger children).

An example is provided by Valerie, at age 5½ years, who could explain the principles of class inclusion (i.e., that subclasses have a hierarchical relation to superordinate classes) in a problem involving her classmates, but could not solve Piaget's class-inclusion problem using wooden beads:

> Valerie asked her mother if she loved her more, or all the kids in her kindergarten. Her mother hesitated, since Valerie's brother was also in the kindergarten, and answered that she loved Valerie and David more than the kids at the kindergarten. Valerie looked at her mother with a "Silly Mom" kind of look, and explained, "David and I are *some* of all the kids at the kindergarten—so if you said you loved the kids at the kindergarten you'd be saying you love us too, and you wouldn't have to leave anybody out!"
>
> The next day, Valerie's curious mother tried Piaget's traditional class-inclusion problem with Valerie, using about 12 red and 6 green wooden beads. When asked to indicate all the wooden beads, Valerie pointed to all the beads. But when asked whether there were more red beads or more wooden beads or the same amount, Valerie claimed that there were more red beads.

When Piaget was faced with differences in children's reasoning about problems that logically should be resolved in the same stage, he labeled the problem *décalage* and suggested that such differences might have to do with varying amounts of "friction" in the specifics of the problem. But this is hardly a satisfying way to characterize the involvement of the environment in cognitive development.

Furthermore, Piagetian research devoted little attention to the role of the social world in providing structure to reality or in helping the child to make sense of it. Instead, in the main line of Piagetian research, the child was seen as inventing operations to understand a physical reality that was defined in broad logical terms rather than in terms of specific features of problems. Although Piaget speculated about the role of social factors and especially of peer interaction in middle childhood, the bulk of his research did not examine how the reality that children investigated has social structure or how children's interaction with companions contributed to cognitive development. And the version of Piaget's theory that came to ascendence in the United States, appropriated by readers seeking connections with American work of the time, focused on the solitary child.

A focus on the solitary child, learning general skills and strategies spontaneously, characterized research in the eclectic U.S. cognitive development tradition until recently. Debates centered around whether children have or do not have sophisticated skills that were assumed to be of general utility. For example, research investigated questions of the age at which children can rehearse material to be remembered, the number of generic things children can remember at specific ages, and the age at which children begin to plan, perceive depth, understand concepts, classify along two dimensions, and so on. There was little concern with what was being remembered or classified or perceived, for what purpose, in what human circumstances.

In the past decade or so, however, there has been widespread recognition that cognitive processes may differ according to the domain of thinking and the specifics of the task context. Cognitive development is now considered to involve advances in skills and knowledge in particular domains, rather than increases in general capacity (Feldman, 1980; Fischer, 1980; Rogoff, 1982b; Siegler, 1981). Hence research in cognitive development has become much more grounded in the specific problem definitions and goal structures of the skill being developed, and has grown to include topics such as language, reading, writing, and mathematical development, which had been considered separate from "basic" cognitive processes, such as memory and attention. Careful analyses of task requirements and elegant descriptions of the transformations in thinking that characterize the learning of particular skills have occurred in cognitive science traditions, largely taking the place of studies that overlooked the specifics of the task.

To this extent, the study of cognitive development has become much more tied to the specifics of the cognitive performance. Rather than assuming that the skills and problems of thinking are generic, their specific nature is being studied. These changes place context in a much more central position, with cognitive developmental sequences defined in terms of both the efforts of the child and the domain of the problem.

These approaches make appreciable advances in our views of cognitive development, but they limit consideration of context to the structure or features of the task or to the domain of knowledge. A broader view of cognition and context requires that task characteristics and cognitive performance be considered in the light of the goal of the activity and its interpersonal and sociocultural context. The purpose of thinking is to act effectively; activities are goal directed (tacitly or explicitly), with social and cultural definition of goals and means of handling problems.

The structure of problems that humans attempt to solve, the knowledge base that provides resources, and the strategies for solution that are considered more or less effective or sophisticated are situated in a social matrix of purposes and values. The problems that are posed, the tools that are available to solve them, and the tactics that are favored build on the sociocultural definitions and available technologies with which an individual functions. Further, the solution to problems often occurs in social situations that define the problems and provide opportunities for learning from social transactions.

Figure 1.1   Guided participation. This child of 2½ years is learning to use a tool; notice the boy's hand on his father's arm as they saw the sapling together. (United States)

   This book considers children as apprentices in thinking, active in their efforts to learn from observing and participating with peers and more skilled members of their society, developing skills to handle culturally defined problems with available tools, and building from these givens to construct new solutions within the context of sociocultural activity.

   I present this framework for conceptualizing the development of mind in sociocultural context, building on the guidance provided by others (especially Vygotsky, Leont'ev, Bruner, Piaget, Cole, Whiting, Wertsch, and Trevarthen), through elaboration from discussing these perspectives with colleagues and students of like and different perspectives.

   My view fits the general perspective that children's cognitive development is embedded in the context of social relationships and sociocultural tools and practices. The specific framework that I offer stresses

1. Children's active role in making use of social guidance
2. The importance of tacit and routine arrangements of children's activities and their participation in skilled cultural activities that are not conceived as instructional
3. Cultural variation in both the goals of development and the means by which children achieve a shared understanding with those who serve as their guides and companions through explanation, discussion, provision of expert models, joint participation, active observation, and arrangement of children's roles

I develop the concept of *guided participation* to suggest that both guidance and participation in culturally valued activities are essential to children's apprenticeship in thinking. Guidance may be tacit or explicit, and participation may vary in the extent to which children or caregivers are responsible for its arrangement.

Guided participation involves children and their caregivers and companions in the collaborative processes of (1) building bridges from children's present understanding and skills to reach new understanding and skills, and (2) arranging and structuring children's participation in activities, with dynamic shifts over development in children's responsibilities. Children use social resources for guidance—both support and challenge—in assuming increasingly skilled roles in the activities of their community.

Underlying the processes of guided participation is *intersubjectivity:* a sharing of focus and purpose between children and their more skilled partners and their challenging and exploring peers. From guided participation involving shared understanding and problem solving, children appropriate an increasingly advanced understanding of and skill in managing the intellectual problems of their community.

Assumptions About Thinking and Development

The approach taken in this book focuses on thinking as functional effort to solve problems and on development as progress in skill, understanding, and perspective regarding problems and their appropriate solution, as defined by the local culture. These assumptions warrant some attention.

Assumptions Regarding the Nature of Thinking

For the purposes of this book, cognition and thinking are defined broadly as problem solving. I assume that thinking is functional, active, and grounded in goal-directed action. Problem solving involves interpersonal and practical goals, addressed deliberately (not necessarily consciously or rationally). It is purposeful, involving flexible improvisation toward goals as diverse as planning a meal, writing an essay, convincing or entertaining others, exploring the properties of an idea or unfamiliar terrain or objects, or remembering or inferring the location of one's keys.

Problem solving emphasizes the active nature of thinking, rather than focusing on cognition as the passive possession of mental objects such as cognitions and percepts. People explore, solve problems, and remember. rather than simply acquire memories, percepts, and skills. The purpose of cognition is not to produce thoughts but to guide intelligent interpersonal and practical action. A problem-solving approach places primacy on people's attempts to negotiate the stream of life, to work around or to transform problems that emerge on the route to attaining the diverse goals of life.

The view of thinking as problem solving examines the integrated mental processes that have in some approaches been dissected and treated as separate. It includes remembering, planning, and categorizing as aspects of problem solving. It also includes cognitive processes that have been studied as skills in using technologies (such as writing and calculating) and problems that involve figuring out how to reach interpersonal goals (such as using other people instrumentally to reach goals, constructing narratives, and communicating successfully).

The traditional distinction among cognitive, affective, and social processes becomes blurred once we focus on thinking as the attempt to determine intelligent means to reach goals. Human goals involve other people and carry feelings with them. Thinking, feeling, and acting are integrated in the problem-solving approach that I use in this book. As Vygotsky (1987) stated,

> Thought . . . is not born of other thoughts. Thought has its origins in the motivating sphere of consciousness, a sphere that includes our inclinations and needs, our interests and impulses, and our affect and emotion. The affective and volitional tendency stands behind thought. Only here do we find the answer to the final "why" in the analysis of thinking. (p. 282)

The concept of intersubjectivity between people—stressed in this book as sharing of purpose and focus among individuals—is itself a process involving cognitive, social, and emotional interchange.

The research reported in the book focuses on problem solving and developing skill, emphasizing processes rather than products of development and problem solving. While the research falls largely within the traditional field of cognitive development, it also involves social and emotional processes. The traditional fields of social and emotional development (like the field of cognitive development) vary in their pursuit of processes versus products of development. What is of greatest interest to me is research that addresses processes of intelligent adaptation to interpersonal and practical problems. Hence work on social or emotional status or traits (e.g, aggressiveness, nurturance, independence, security) is not as relevant to this approach as are attempts to examine social or emotional processes in action (e.g., emotional communication, social problem solving).

Although this book does not focus specifically on the development of social and emotional skills, the approach that it takes to cognitive development could fruitfully be applied to topics that traditionally fall within the domains of social and emotional development. Gender roles and other interpersonal relations develop along with other skills and understanding and can be addressed by a close examination of guided participation in learning to manage these social roles and skills.

For example, parental treatment of daughters and sons in daily interaction reveals communication of expected roles, relations, and skills. It may be most clearly seen in the unexpected practices and communication of others, as we are likely to be blind to our own practices and tacit communication. An example of communication of gender and age roles in training for work is available from LeVine and LeVine's (1956) field observations:

> A Nyansongo [Kenyan] mother works in the garden with her 6-year-old son. She keeps him involved in the task of hoeing and praises him for his performance. Challenging fellow workers to competition is typical of Nyansongo adult work groups, and thus, by engaging her son in friendly competition, the mother treats him like an older individual (that is, a circumcised boy).
>
> Aloyse, hoeing a field beside his mother, stops working.
> *Mother:* "Finish that part quickly."
> *Aloyse:* "I am looking for some nails that I lost here."
> *Mother:* "Are you after nails, or digging?"
> Aloyse resumes hoeing. He comments, "Why is the soil so tough? Uh! Uh!"
> *Mother:* "You fool, why do you leave some places not properly dug?"
> *Aloyse:* "No. I do it properly. I want to work hard, finish this portion, then go into the shade."
> *Mother:* "Here or at home?"
> *Aloyse* (indicating nearby trees): "Here . . . You've gotten so close to me here, I must work hard."
> *Mother:* "I'm not so close. You're defeating me by digging so quickly."
> *Aloyse* (resting): "Oh, you're almost overtaking me, I must work hard."
> *Mother:* "Who dug here so crudely? You, Aloyse?"
> *Aloyse:* "No . . . I'm afraid you are overtaking me."
> *Mother:* "No, you are an *omomura* [circumcised boy, or young man—not really true of Aloyse, of course]. I'm just a woman—I can't overtake you."
> *Aloyse:* "I'm almost reaching the end! You're going to pass me again, and finish before me. It's because I dig properly."
> Mother laughs. (quoted in Whiting & Edwards, 1988, pp. 95–96)

This example illustrates the communication of and participation in gender and status roles, as a child and mother work together in skilled subsistence activity, with its associated values and strategies. Although this book focuses on cognitive aspects of problem solving (such as reasoning, planning, remembering, communicating, or skillful hoeing), the development of interpersonal roles and relationships is not separate. Problem solving is not "cold" cognition, but inherently involves emotion, social relations, and social structure.

Assumptions Regarding the Nature of Development

The concept of development that is used in this book focuses on transitions of a qualitative (as well as quantitative) nature that allow a person to manage more effectively the problems of everyday life, relying on resources and constraints offered by companions and cultural practices to define and solve problems. Child development involves appropriation of the intellectual tools and skills of the surrounding cultural community. Hence it is essential to consider the role of the formal institutions of society and the informal interactions of its members as central to the process of cognitive development. (Of course, culture, in turn, develops as people transform the "given" institutions and practices to meet current needs, as one generation succeeds the next.)

The direction of development is channeled by the specific as well as the universal givens of the human physical and social endowment. That is, all humans share a great deal of universal activity because of the biological and cultural heritage that we have in common as a species (e.g., two legs, communication through language, helpless infancy, organization in groups, and capacity to invent tools), and at the same time, each of us varies because of differences in our physical and interpersonal circumstances (e.g., visual acuity, strength, family constellation, means of making a living, familiarity with specific languages). To understand development, it is essential to understand both the underlying cultural and biological similarities across individuals and groups, and the essential differences between them. As Shore (1988) puts it, "Each of us lives out our species nature only in a specific local manifestation, and . . . our cultural and historical peculiarity is an essential part of that nature" (p. 19).

Although this book focuses on infancy and childhood, development is assumed to proceed throughout the life span, with individuals' ways of thinking reorganizing with successive advances in reaching and contributing to the understanding, skills, and perspectives of their community. Examples of reorganization of thinking in adulthood include managing new roles, such as retirement or parenthood (consider parental hypothesis testing to handle a cranky baby); taking on new intellectual challenges, such as career changes or consuming hobbies, where transformation in levels of understanding can be seen; and achieving shifts in perspective where whole patterns of relationships fall into place, as in leaps of understanding of social institutions and interpersonal relationships.

In addition to considering transitions occurring across the years of an individual's life (ontogenetic development), I consider development as including transformations in thinking that occur with successive attempts to handle a problem, even in time spans of minutes (microgenetic development [see Wertsch, 1979a]). And I stress, with Vygotsky, that both ontogenetic and microgenetic development are embedded in the developmental processes involved in societal and phylogenetic change. Development within lives proceeds along with cultural and species development occurring over historical time (see Scribner, 1985).

I regard development as multidirectional, rather than aimed at a specified endpoint in a unique and unidirectional course of growth. Development proceeds in a variety of directions with some important commonalities as well as essential differences in the routes taken toward the goals that are sought in a particular community. Progress must be defined according to local goals, with development in specific domains specified by cultural as well as biological goals and problems. (For discussions of multidirectional versus unidirectional teleological models of development, see Chapman, 1988; Gollin, 1981; Scribner, 1985.)

The developmental endpoint that has traditionally anchored cognitive developmental theories—skill in academic activities such as formal operational reasoning and scientific, mathematical, and literate practices—is one valuable goal of development, but one that is tied to its contexts and culture, as is any other goal or endpoint of development valued by a community.

Each community's valued skills constitute the local goals of development. Societal practices that support children's development are tied to the values and skills considered important. In the final analysis, it is not possible to determine whether the goals or practices of one society are more adaptive than those of another, as judgments of adaptation cannot be separated from values. For middle-class American children, the skills of schooling may relate closely to the skills required for participation in many aspects of adult life, and many of the practices of middle-class American families and educators may be well adapted to support development of formal operational, scientific reasoning, literate communication, mathematical facility, and other skills that may be useful for children's eventual participation in the economic and political institutions of their society. In other communities (in the United States and elsewhere), other goals and practices take prominence.

The readers of this book are likely to share an emphasis on the skills promoted in academic settings and in literate, scientific activities, and to value these goals for their children. However, I feel that it would obscure our understanding of developmental process to assume that these are goals held by all communities for their children. Understanding the goals and skills valued in children's communities is essential for defining developmental endpoints as well as for examining children's cognitive skills and the specific practices of guided participation used by children and their caregivers and companions.

Questions of the direction and goals of development are central to understanding the essence of developmental process. Although some scholars ask what makes children develop, in my view, development, change, and activity are inherent to human existence. Rather than having to explain the fact that development occurs, it is necessary to determine the circumstances in which development takes one course rather than another. In studying physical motion, Newton long ago pointed out that matter does not remain motionless when there is no outside influence; rather, it continues going in the direction in which it has been going unless something deflects it. A still object stays still, yes, but a moving object keeps moving along its trajectory unless something intervenes (friction or impact with another object, for instance). In living organisms, change is inherent. Humans (and other organisms) are more than physical matter; life itself involves rhythms and goals that provide motion and direction beyond those of the uniform course of physical matter. Shotter (1978), commenting on Susan Langer's discussion of how rhythms of the organic world result in acts motivating other acts, states, "Only if one holds in the back of one's mind the idea that all motions are essentially mechanical ones, does one find it necessary to postulate a special external "motive force" to account for changes in activity" (p. 61). Development is built on the transformations and rhythms intrinsic to life; what needs explanation is the direction of change and the patterns of life that organize change in specific directions.

A Conceptual Framework for the Sociocultural Context of the Developing Mind

Perspectives that emphasize the societal context of individuals' cognitive development derive from the sociohistorical theory of Vygotsky, Leont'ev, and Luria, the cultural practice theory of Cole and Scribner, and the writings of Wertsch, as well as research on human variation across cultures and across historical periods. Leont'ev (1981) provides a summary of Vygotsky's views of the relation between the tools for thinking provided by culture and the development of individual thought processes:

> Vygotsky identified two main, interconnected features [of human productive activity] that are necessarily fundamental for psychology: its tool-like ["instrumental"] structure, and its inclusion in a system of interrelations with other people. It is these features that define the nature of human psychological processes. The tool mediates activity and thus connects humans not only with the world of objects but also with other people. Because of this, humans' activity *assimilates the experience of humankind*. This means that humans' mental processes (their "higher psychological functions") acquire a structure necessarily tied to the sociohistorically formed means and methods transmitted to them by others in the process of cooperative labor and social interaction. But it is impossible to transmit the means and methods needed to carry out a process in any way other than in external form—in the form of an action or external speech. In other words, higher psychological processes unique to humans can be acquired only through interaction with others, that is, through *interpsychological* processes that only later will begin to be carried out independently by the individual. (pp. 55–56)

Sociohistorical theory offers a unique seamlessness of individual, social, and historical (or cultural) processes. G. H. Mead's theory is related, in its emphasis on mind as developing from interpersonal activity, although it does not share the sociohistorical school's emphasis on societal history as the context of the development of mind.

> We must regard mind . . . as arising and developing within the social process, within the empirical matrix of social interactions. We must, that is,

get an inner individual experience from the standpoint of social acts which include the experiences of separate individuals in a social context wherein those individuals interact. The processes of experience which the human brain makes possible are made possible only for a group of interacting individuals: only for individual organisms which are members of a society; not for the individual organism in isolation from other individual organisms. (Mead, 1934, p. 133)

The appeal of the sociohistorical theory offered by Vygotsky, Leont'ev, Luria, and others who have followed lies in the primacy it places on Mind *in* Society (Vygotsky, 1978) and the associated examination of cognitive development in sociocultural activity. From the sociohistorical perspective, the basic unit of analysis is no longer the (properties of the) individual, but the (processes of the) sociocultural activity, involving active participation of people in socially constituted practices. I explain these ideas in greater detail in Chapter 2 and build on them throughout the book.

My work, like that of anyone else, involves the appropriation of concepts that I have found useful in the work of others. The use that I make of their ideas undoubtedly involves some transformation from the ideas they offered. This is in the nature of dialogue. The transformation is liable to be greater the more distinct the backgrounds of the speaker and the listener, or the author and the reader. The refraction of Vygotsky's ideas, like those of Piaget, through a foreign lens—through differences in time and place, language and intellectual climate—contributes to the listener's making something new of the speaker's words, for better or for worse. My purpose in this book is not to explain Vygotsky or Piaget or others, but to build from what I make of them.

Central to Vygotsky's theory is the idea that children's participation in cultural activities with the guidance of more skilled partners allows children to internalize the tools for thinking and for taking more mature approaches to problem solving that children have practiced in social context. Cultural inventions channel the skills of each generation, with individual development mediated by interaction with people who are more skilled in the use of the culture's tools.

Vygotsky provided the concept of the "zone of proximal development," in which child development proceeds through children's participation in activities slightly beyond their competence (in their "zone of proximal develment") with the assistance of adults or more skilled children (Vygotsky, 1978; Wertsch, 1979a). Vygotsky proposed that cognitive processes occur first on the social plane; these shared processes are internalized, transformed, to form the individual plane. Thus the zone of proximal development is a dynamic region of sensitivity to learning the skills of culture, in which children develop through participation in problem solving with more experienced members of the culture (Laboratory of Comparative Human Cognition, 1983; Rogoff, 1982b; Rogoff, Gauvain, & Ellis, 1984; Vygotsky, 1978).

Cole (1985) suggests that in the zone of proximal development, culture and cognition create each other. Children and their partners appropriate from their interactions with each other a derived understanding based on their

Figure 1.2 Developing expertise. This 9-year-old, already expert in following recipes, calculating amounts, and using cooking utensils, has asked her grandmother to check the whipped cream to see if it is the right consistency. (United States)

efforts to apply the tools of culture, with which each partner is likely to vary in skill. Culture itself is not static but is formed from the efforts of people working together, using and adapting tools provided by predecessors and in the process creating new ones. Interactions in the zone of proximal development are the crucible of development *and* of culture, in that they allow children to participate in activities that would be impossible for them alone, using cultural tools that themselves must be adapted to the specific practical activities at hand, and thus both passed on to and transformed by new members of the culture.

I extend the concept of the zone of proximal development by stressing the interrelatedness of the roles of children and their caregivers and other companions and the importance of tacit and distal as well as explicit face-to-face social interaction in guided participation. The thesis is that the rapid development of young children into skilled participants in society is accomplished through children's routine, and often tacit, guided participation in ongoing cultural activities as they observe and participate with others in culturally organized practices.

The elaboration presented in this book, while consistent with the Vygotskian approach, provides more focus on the role of children as active participants in their own development. Children seek, structure, and even demand the assistance of those around them in learning how to solve problems of all kinds. They actively observe social activities, participating as they can. I stress the complementary roles of children and caregivers in fostering children's development.

In addition, I emphasize tacit forms of communication in the verbal and nonverbal exchanges of daily life and the distal arrangements for childhood involved in the regulation of children's activities, material goods, and companions. This contrasts with the more usual focus on explicit and even didactic dialogue that has characterized Vygotskian theory as well as American views of socialization. Vygotsky, of course, emphasized language as the most important tool of thought and stressed higher cognitive functions such as those promoted in school. Vygotsky's emphasis may have derived from the agenda of his nation at the time he was writing, to establish a new Soviet nation with widespread literacy; it may also reflect the values of Vygotsky's own upbringing and early career, as a Jewish intellectual and literary critic. (Vygotsky was born in 1896, the same year as Piaget, and died in 1934. For a discussion of schooling and intellectual emphases in traditional East European Jewish culture and child rearing, see Zborowski, 1955.)

I agree that language provides humans with a powerful tool for both thinking and communicating, but I prefer to view communication more broadly to include nonverbal as well as verbal dialogue rather than to focus so exclusively on words. This, I believe, allows us to examine development in the early years, when words are not the primary currency of communication, and to address cognitive development in realms that may be less dependent on the analytic use of language than are didactic schooling and cultures emphasizing talk and analysis. In this more inclusive approach, I think it is possible to encompass more of the daily activities in which children participate that are not explicitly designed to instruct, and to speak reasonably of the cultural differences in arrangements for children's learning.

For example, broadening the view of communication allows consideration of the shared meaning developed between caregivers and infants in routine interaction, such as the following:

> While Valerie and David (9½-month-old twins) were eating dry Cheerios in their highchairs, their mother popped a couple of Cheerios in her mouth and ate them. Both babies thought it was hilarious for their mother to eat their food (she wasn't usually tempted by it!), and laughed enthusiastically over the next 5 minutes each time their mother snatched a Cheerio for herself.
>
> Then their mother put a Cheerio in Valerie's fingers, and opened her mouth, bending close to Valerie. Valerie began putting the Cheerio in her own mouth reflexively but stopped abruptly when her mother opened her mouth. Valerie looked at her mother's open mouth and began laughing hilariously with her hand poised in midair.

Such passing moments of shared activity, which may or may not have explicit lessons for children, are, I believe, the material for development. The notion of guided participation is intended to stress shared activity with communication that includes words as well as actions, and to encompass the routine, tacit activities and arrangements of children and their companions.

Children and their parents are adapted to their mutual roles and involvement. Young children appear to come equipped with ways of ensuring proximity to and involvement with more experienced members of society, and of becoming involved with their physical and cultural surroundings. The infants' strategies (if one ignores connotations of intentionality) appear similar to those appropriate for anyone learning in an unfamiliar culture: stay near a trusted guide, watch the guide's activities and get involved in the activities when possible, and attend to any instruction the guide provides.

Infants' strategies are complemented by features of caregiver–child relationships that encourage the gradual involvement of children in the skilled and valued activities of the society. Caregivers arrange the occurrence of children's activities and facilitate learning by regulating the difficulty of the tasks and by modeling mature performance during joint participation in activities. While caregivers may rarely regard themselves as explicitly teaching infants or young children, they routinely adjust their interaction and structure children's environments and activities in ways consistent with providing support for their learning.

It is worth commenting on intentionality in communication, given that I asked you to ignore it in the previous paragraphs. It is easy to assume that interactions between caregivers and children must be intentional or self-conscious. Although this may sometimes be the case with the didactic instruction in some middle-class American homes, it is unlikely to characterize what goes on for the rest of the day in those homes or for most of the day in many cultures where social interaction and children's activities are not designed explicitly for the future edification of the children. Although parents everywhere likely consider the future for their children, most of children's lives involve interactions and social arrangements that are organized to accomplish the task of the moment. Caregivers may be deliberate in their actions, and their actions may carry tacit lessons for alert children, without being explicitly or intentionally focused on communication or instruction.

My point is that through children's everyday involvement in social life, "lessons" regarding skilled and valued (or at least necessary) cultural activities are available to them. It is part of the nature of communication, perhaps especially the communication between children and caregivers (whether adult or child), that these cultural lessons are somewhat tailored to the particular child. It is part of the nature of children to seek the meaning—the purpose and connotation—of what goes on around them, and to involve themselves in ongoing activity.

Guided participation involves adults or children challenging, constraining, and supporting children in the process of posing and solving problems— through material arrangements of children's activities and responsibilities as well as through interpersonal communication, with children observing and participating at a comfortable but slightly challenging level. The processes of communication and shared participation in activities inherently engage children and their caregivers and companions in stretching children's understanding and skill to apply to new problems. Practical considerations of culturally organized activities (such as avoiding damage or waste), along with young children's eagerness to be involved, lead to structuring of children's participation so that they handle manageable but comfortably challenging subgoals of the activity that increase in complexity with children's developing skill and understanding.

The Book's Structure and Main Points

Part I of this book (Chapters 2 and 3) extends the introduction to discuss the sociocultural context of human activity and examines assumptions underlying the notion of interrelatedness of the roles of the individual child and of other people in their sociocultural context.

To consider the roles of individual, social partners, and cultural context, Chapter 2 discusses conceptions of mutuality. The individual and the social are not analytically separate influences on the course of development. Neither is the relation an interaction, because that still implies separability of individuals and the social context. Instead, I view the individual child, social partners, and the cultural milieu as inseparable contributors to the ongoing activities in which child development takes place. The concept of guided participation attempts to keep the roles of the individual and the sociocultural context in focus. Instead of working as separate or interacting forces, individual efforts, social interaction, and the cultural context are inherently bound together in the overall development of children into skilled participants in society. This chapter deals with the classic problem of seeing the forest *and* the trees. By analogy, investigation of cognitive development has focused on the individual young tree, ignoring the role of the surrounding individual trees and having difficulty keeping in mind the fact that the trees are members of a larger organization of forest. I use the analogy of apprenticeship to focus on how the development of skill involves active learners observing and participating in organized cultural activity with the guidance and challenge of other people.

Chapter 3 examines how cognitive functioning is embedded in cultural practices that focus individuals on particular problems, provide tools and technologies for their solution, and channel problem-solving efforts toward valued means of solution. The sociocultural context of individual thinking includes cultural institutions, tools and technologies for handling problems, and valued goals and means of reaching them. A central example is the Euro-american institution of schooling, with its technologies of literacy, memory for unrelated bits of information, and solution of self-contained logical problems, along with value judgments about appropriate solutions and means for reaching them.

Part II (Chapters 4, 5, and 6) explores the processes of guided participation in the arrangements and interactions between caregivers and children to suggest how caregivers facilitate child development and how children channel their own development and use of social support. Two chapters describe processes of guided participation and examine research primarily on middle-class families, and the third addresses cultural similarities and variations in the goals and means of guided participation.

The process of building bridges from current skills and understanding to those needed in novel situations, based on research with middle-class families, is the focus of Chapter 4. Caregivers help children find connections between old and new situations by providing emotional cues about the nature of the situation, models of how to behave, interpretations of children's behavior and the meaning of events, and labels for objects and events that provide information about similarities across situations. Simultaneously, children attempt to pick up information about the nature of situations and their caregiver's interpretation of the situation and how to handle it.

Communication involves bridging between two views of a situation with some modifications in the perspectives of each participant. In the middle-class populations that have been studied, the bridge between adults' and children's points of view is often built from children's starting point, with adults building on children's perspectives by focusing on children's direction of attention and by adjusting adult concepts to reach children's understanding.

Chapter 5 focuses on how middle-class adults and children adjust the structure of situations in which children are involved through both their distal arrangements and their explicit interaction. Assignments of and opportunities for children's activities, as well as structuring of children's level of participation and choosing the tools and companions available, are forms of management of social activity. Both adults and children are responsible for deciding children's activities and their role in them, often through tacit and pragmatic determination of children's skills and interests, as well as through more explicit arrangements for children's growing participation in the activities of their culture.

During adult–child communication, participants collaborate in structuring children's roles through division of responsibility for the activity. Interaction with adults may support and extend children's growing skills so that children can achieve more in collaboration than they can independently. Children's roles in structuring an activity in social interaction may involve central responsibility for managing the situation—even when adults are more skilled—and for adjusting their own level of participation.

The collaborative arrangement of children's learning includes transfer of responsibility to children as they become more capable of handling problems. Transfer of responsibility for managing situations may involve close engagement of adults and children to ensure a challenging but comfortable level of participation for children. Adults often evaluate children's current skill level in the task and use a tacit task analysis to guide their efforts to support children's developing skill. Even when interaction with children is not the adults' focus, there is often adjustment of children's participation through social interaction in the middle-class American and European families that have been the focus of research. Children are active in adapting their involvement to take on more or less responsibility in a joint activity. Children also enlist adult involvement in their activities and observe or force their way into adult activities according to their interests.

Chapter 6 examines evidence for cultural similarities and variations in guided participation. Although most of the research on social interaction has been done in North America and Europe, ethnographic observations of other cultural groups support the idea that guided participation is a widespread process of development.

Differences across cultures include the skills and values that are promoted, which vary as a function of the tools and means of subsistence of the community. In addition to variations in the goals of development, there appear to be differences in the means of communication used between caregivers and children: the explicitness or subtlety of messages, the intensity of and relative balance in the use of verbal and nonverbal communication, and the extent to which adults simplify communication for young children or children have the responsibility and opportunity to make sense of the adult world themselves. Underlying some of these differences may be cultural variations in the interactive role that children are expected to play. In some communities, children are clearly subordinate to adults and should be seen and not heard. In others, children may frequently relate with their parents as peers, initiating conversations and making demands.

Children in cultures that do not strictly segregate them from adult activities may develop largely in the context of observing and participating in adult activities, with children being responsible for learning through active observation, sometimes with little adult–child reciprocal conversation. In cultures that restrict children's access to adult activities, through age segregation and compartmentalization of roles, it may be necessary for adults to present children with a watered-down version of adult activities and to work to motivate children to learn these activities out of the context of actual contribution. Hence a major cultural difference may be the extent to which adults adjust activities to children or children are responsible for adjusting to the adult world.

It is important to keep these cultural differences in mind, as most research has been conducted in cultures and research settings in which the prototype of socialization is explicit instruction from parents. This has undoubtedly influenced how researchers have conceptualized the social context of cognitive development, overlooking the tacit and routine arrangements between children and caregivers and the active role of children in arranging for their development through observation as well as interaction and participation with other children and adults.

Part III (Chapters 7, 8, and 9) reviews research and theory on the consequences of social interaction for individual development, grappling with the questions of the sorts of communication that foster individual development, and the processes by which individuals gain from engagement with others.

The perspectives of Vygotsky and Piaget regarding the mechanisms by which social interaction may influence individual development—expertise and cognitive conflict between equals—are examined in Chapter 7. This leads to a consideration of the relative value of interaction with adults and with peers. In Vygotsky's view, expertise in the use of cultural tools is central to the role of social interaction, and interaction with expert peers can be similar to that with adults in guiding young children's cognitive development. In Piaget's view, interaction with peers promotes children's cognitive development through exploration of cognitive conflict (i.e., discrepancy) when children become able to consider another's perspective in middle childhood. Both theorists stress the importance of shared understanding, but the means by which it contributes to development differs in the two views.

Chapters 8 and 9 consider research and speculations on the importance of interaction with adults and peers, respectively, in fostering children's cognitive development, to address the question of the consequences for children's independent skills resulting from having participated in shared problem solving. Since development involves skills closely tied to the technology (e.g., books, number system, language, logic) of the culture that children learn to master with the assistance of others, it would be difficult to believe that there is *not* a relationship between sociocultural contexts and individual development. As children develop, they are constantly involved with people and social conventions that channel development. Thus the impact of social interaction and of the cultural context may be a logical necessity inadequately addressed by research attempting to separate social interaction and individual learning.

The available research investigating the influence of social interaction (discussed in Chapter 8) nonetheless suggests how and under what circumstances social interaction facilitates individual development, although it is limited by ignoring the societal context of communication, cultural variation in cognitive and communicative goals and skills, and children's initiative in recruiting or making use of the assistance of adults and in engaging on their own terms with peers in situations that are not controlled by adults.

The chapter reviews research on the role of guided participation between adults and children in children's language and conceptual development, exploration and construction of objects, and memory and planning. The research points to the importance of the partner's skill in the task as well as to the processes of guidance with participation in shared thinking.

The role of peer interaction is the subject of Chapter 9. Peer interaction may be especially important in its encouragement of children's exploration without immediate goals (as in play or curious fooling around), its motivating nature that channels children's choice of activities, and its availability. Adults may be less involved in creative playfulness that has no goal beyond exploration and enjoyment.

The concluding chapter (Chapter 10) summarizes central points of the book and suggests that the skills and understanding involved in shared thinking become part of individual children's repertoires through their appropriation of social activity as they participate in the activities of their culture. I address the role of guided participation in creativity and the role of challenge and sensitivity in guided participation with familiar and less familiar partners. I consider asymmetries in children's and their partners' responsibilities in shared thinking, and the role of children's active observation as a social activity. I propose that we regard children's relationships with other people in sociocultural activities as interdependent rather than as involving the meeting of independent individuals. Instead of viewing children as separate entities that become capable of social involvement, we may consider children as being inherently engaged in the social world from before birth, advancing throughout development in their skill in independently carrying out and organizing the activities of their culture.

PART I

THE INDIVIDUAL AND
THE SOCIOCULTURAL CONTEXT

2

Conceiving the Relationship of
the Social World and the Individual

Humans are born with a self-regulating strategy for getting knowledge by human negotiation and co-operative action. (Trevarthen, "Universal Co-operative Motives")

Developmental and social processes constrain the nature of skills themselves. We should say that the evolution of skill, of human anatomy, of the brain, and of social systems all must have proceeded hand in hand. (Kaye, "The Development of Skills")

The child is *not* a self-contained homunculus, radiating outward in development from some fixed configuration of traits, dispositions, or preformed potencies; and . . . the world, in turn, is not some eternal and objective network of causal factors converging on the neonate to shape an unresisting, passive blob to its external, pregiven structures. To put this positively: the child is an agent in its own *and* the world's construction, but one whose agency develops in the context of an ineluctably social and historical praxis, which includes both the constraints and potentialities of nature and the actions of other agents. Nurture, in short, is both given *and* taken; and so is Nature. (Wartofsky, "The Child's Construction of the World and the World's Construction of the Child")

It is important to be clear about the relationship between the efforts and development of the individual and the arrangements and history of the sociocultural world. This chapter argues that individual effort and sociocultural activity are mutually embedded, as are the forest and the trees, and that it is essential to understand how they constitute each other.

Rather than according primacy to the role of sociocultural activity or of the individual, the aim is to recognize the essential and inseparable roles of societal heritage, social engagement, and individual efforts. For example, to understand the development of skill in reading, it is important to attend to the limitations and resources in the individual's genetic makeup and pattern of interests, in the examples and instruction provided by caregivers and teachers, and in technology structured over social history to involve specific alphabets, syllabaries, and conventions of written representation. Reading would not be possible without human efforts and human genes, without models provided by other people who read and assist in learning to read, or without a literate society in which there is material and reason to read and a system to organize written communication.

Even Sequoyah, who invented a system of writing for the Cherokee people at the beginning of the nineteenth century, did not produce his monumental work in a cultural vacuum. He is reported to have been impressed with the message-sending facility provided by the "talking leaf" used by whites, and he set himself the task of devising an alphabet for his people. His alphabet of 85 letters was used for years for correspondence and for producing newspapers. Sequoyah's feat is notable for his personal genius, for the interpersonal context of the introduction of the idea, and for building on a borrowed technological history (Carpenter, 1976).

Rather than viewing individuals, their social partners, and the sociocultural context as independent "influences" or factors of development, I argue that they represent differing angles of analysis of an integrated process. Although researchers and scholars find it convenient to focus their investigation on a specific angle, looking at the complex process of development through a particularly interesting window, the different angles or windows may artificially divide a unified, whole developmental process. For convenience of study or discussion, we may focus on one or another, but we must remember the integrated nature of the developmental process.

The relationship between context and human behavior is not a new concern; there have been varying attempts to conceive of their combination or integration (Barker, 1978; Bowers, 1973; Ekehammar, 1974; Goffman, 1964; Keller-Cohen, 1978; Mischel, 1979; Murray, 1938; Ochs, 1979; Van Valin, 1980).

Several approaches focus on levels of analysis of the environment (Lerner, 1978; LeVine, 1989). Bronfenbrenner (1979) characterizes the ecological environment as "a set of nested structures, each inside the next, like a set of Russian dolls" (p. 3). At the innermost level is the immediate setting in which the individual is involved. Surrounding this are the relations between such immediate settings, and then a level of settings in which the person is not present (such as conditions of parental employment). Finally, enveloping this whole package is a more abstract level of cultural "blueprints" for the organization of the more immediate settings.

White and Siegel (1984) propose that cognitive development consists of the broadening of contexts in which children navigate. Children begin with involvement and skills supported in the close home environment. Gradually, they become able to navigate broader familiar settings. Eventually, they become capable of active involvement in complex community activities and even activities that require communication and action with people distant in time and place (in books or over electronic mail), whom they have never met.

Mutuality of Individuals and Context

The literature stressing the role of context contains varying concepts of the relation between the individual and the environment. My stance is that the individual's efforts and sociocultural arrangements and involvement are inseparable, mutually embedded focuses of interest. Rather than examining context as an influence on human behavior, I regard context as inseparable from human actions in cognitive events or activities. I regard all human activity as embedded in context; there are neither context-free situations nor decontextualized skills. In a 1982 paper, I argued for the importance of a "contextual event" approach:

> In the contextual perspective, meaning and context are not elements that can be handled separately or derived from adding elements together. Context is not so much a set of stimuli that impinge upon a person as it is a web of relations interwoven to form the fabric of meaning. (Rogoff, 1982b, p. 149)

It has been common in developmental psychology to attend to either the individual or the environment—for example, examining how adults teach children or how children construct reality. The focus has been on the individual as the basic unit of analysis, either as recipient of environmental stimuli or as constructor of reality. To understand child development, however, it is necessary to consider the mutual involvement of children and the social world.

Such mutual involvement can be understood in different ways, which have parallels with the age-old question of nature and nurture that has long interested scholars. The history of psychology has long pitted nature against nurture, with questions of how much of development should be credited to nature (seen variously as genes or as the characteristics of the individual) and how much to nurture (seen as the influence of the environment or of the individual's experiences). This traditional view places nature and nurture in opposition. Most developmentalists, as one reads in early chapters of introductory texts, are no longer trying to figure out if development is "more nature" or "more nurture." Instead, they view nature and nurture as interacting to produce development, arguing that development does not occur solely through individual effort or preprogramming, nor does it occur entirely under the direction of the environment.

However, the notion of interaction often involves an assumption that the interacting entities are separable. In the nature–nurture debate, nature and nurture are regarded as independent influences—definable in terms not involving each other—that happen to co-occur. In much of psychology, the roles of the individual and of the social world are treated as separable. In such an interactional perspective, researchers assume that if the elements (nature and nurture, or the individual and the social world) are well enough studied, it will be possible to put them together to examine the "dynamic" process of interaction and interdependence (Endler & Edwards, 1978). But this approach, if used exclusively, would lead to consideration of high-order interactions that would lead us to "a hall of mirrors that extends to infinity" (Cronbach, 1975, p. 119).

Aside from pointing out such technical impracticalities in an interactional attempt to produce the whole picture, authors espousing a transactional or contextual event approach argue that the whole does *not* equal the sum of the parts; the whole has an essential character and process that must be studied for itself. Human activity involves the roles of both the individual and the social world, inseparably involved in the meaningful and purposeful events of life (Altman & Rogoff, 1987; Angyal, 1941; Dewey & Bentley, 1949; Kantor, 1946; Lerner & Kauffman, 1985; Meacham, 1977; Mead, 1934; Overton & Reese, 1973; Rogoff, 1982b; Valsiner, 1987).

Dewey and Bentley (1949) warn against reducing events to the interaction of separate elements. If the integral nature of the whole event is overlooked, the relations between elements are conceived of as merely another element. That is, if human behavior and the context are conceived of as separate elements, a mediating element is required to relate them.

Bates (1976) provides an example of a transformation from an interactional to a contextual approach in describing how the efforts of psycholinguists to formalize semantics led to the necessity of considering context in the study of pragmatics:

> At first, it seemed that pragmatic information was ancillary to the rest of semantics, something that could be added on or studied separately. It is now far less clear that this is the case. Pragmatics is perhaps best defined as rules governing the use of language in context. As such, it does not define a separate kind of linguistic structure or "object." Rather, all of language is pragmatic to begin with. We choose our meanings to fit contexts and build our meanings onto those contexts in such a way that the two are inseparable, in the same way the "figure" is definable only in terms of "ground." (p. 420)

This book is built on the premise that the child and the social world are mutually involved to an extent that precludes regarding them as independently definable. Even when we focus attention separately on the roles of the individual and of the social milieu, these roles are defined in terms that take each other into account (Rogoff & Gauvain, 1986). For example, when we focus on the actions of the child or of the caregiver at different moments, we define each person's actions with respect to the context provided by the other's actions, goals, and circumstances.

In the perspective offered in this book, development involves individual effort or tendencies as well as the sociocultural context in which the individual is embedded and has been since before conception. Biology and culture are not alternative influences but inseparable aspects of a system within which individuals develop.

This approach is consistent with Pepper's (1942) contextualist world hypothesis, which denies that the parts making up the whole are separable elements, or that the whole "is a sort of added part like a clamp that holds together a number of blocks" (p. 238). Pepper identified the *event* as the "root metaphor" of the contextualist view.

Pepper analyzes the structure of an event in terms of its *quality* and *texture*. Its quality is the total meaning and character; its texture is the details and relations among details that make up the wholeness and quality. Quality and texture are not separable (they are "fused"), although one or the other may be more prominent in a particular analysis. For example, we may attend at one time to the meaning of a sentence (the quality), and at another time to its words (the texture). Quality and texture are nested such that words are texture when one attends to the sentence, but words are quality when they are the focus of attention. Then letters become the texture.

Using event or activity as the unit of analysis, rather than focusing on the interaction of individual and environment, involves a shift in perspectives on the process of understanding cognitive development (see Rogoff, 1982b). Some examples of events or activities of interest in human development include remembering the location of an object, planning how to solve an interpersonal problem or how to navigate from one place to another, and understanding an unfamiliar text. Viewing these as events or activities involves the following shifts:

1. Instead of studying a person's possession of a capacity or an idea, the focus is on the active changes involved in an unfolding event or activity in which people participate. Events or activities are inherently dynamic, rather than consisting of static conditions with time added to them as a separate element. Change or development, rather than static characteristics, is assumed to be basic. Understanding processes becomes essential.

2. Events and activities are organized according to goals. For example, remembering serves the function of being able to retrieve something wanted, and planning serves the function of being able to achieve something desired. It is only when the purposes of the participants in events or activities are understood that their actions make sense.

3. Meaning and purpose are central to the definition of all aspects of events or activities and cannot be separated or derived from summing the features of the individual and features of the context.

4. Mental processes such as remembering or planning or calculating or narrating a story occur in the service of accomplishing something, and cannot be dissected apart from the goal to be accomplished and the practical and interpersonal actions used. Cognitive processes serve the function of guiding intelligent, purposeful action and interaction.

5. Specifics of the circumstances of an event or activity are essential to understanding how people act in the attempt to reach their goals. For example, a child attempting to find his mother's office telephone number will take different courses of action, depending on whether he can ask someone else present, can find and read a list containing the number, or can with some certainty remember the number, perhaps with some mnemonics used previously to fit pieces of the telephone number together. All these strategies require

thinking and action tailored to the circumstances to reach the goal. Thinking cannot be meaningfully separated from the actions, the circumstances, and the goal.

6. Human goals, actions, circumstances, and thought are a function of both cultural and biological inheritance, with individuals actively and purposefully handling problems (defined culturally and biologically) according to means (built culturally and biologically).

7. The inherent variability of particular historical and present circumstances, along with structured variation in cultural and biological resources and constraints, produce inherent variation in human events and activities. Variability is central to the process of development. Rather than assuming that development proceeds toward a single universal endpoint or ideal state, multiple courses and directions of development are to be expected across groups. The particulars of development are built into the process of development, not options added on to a generic course of development. The inherent variations in development that occur with different groups and circumstances are ordered in their own terms, with progress toward developmental goals over the course of life. The idea of a single universal goal of development is discarded; instead, developmental work examines the internal coherence of developmental progress in any group according to the combined local and species structure of goals and processes.

Several psychological theories use activity or event as the unit of analysis, and stress the mutuality of the individual and the environment. The next section focuses on two theories of cognitive development—Piaget's and Vygotsky's—that deal with the interdependence of organism and environment.

Gibsonian ecological theory also stresses the mutuality of the organism and the context. While some colleagues have questioned the applicability of Gibson's work to issues of the relationship between the individual and the social world, I find the Gibsonian philosophical stance to be very useful. Of course, interpretation of Gibson—like interpretation of Piaget or Vygotsky—varies with the reader. What I find most useful in my reading of Gibsonian work is the emphasis on events as the unit of analysis; on the active role of the organism in perceiving, understanding, and remembering; and on animal–environment mutuality in which the characteristics of animal and environment are defined and develop in relation to one another (Johnston & Turvey, 1980; Reed & Jones, 1977; Shaw & Bransford, 1977). As pointed out by Michaels and Carello (1981), the features of animals and environments each fit with the characteristics of the other:

> An animal's wings, gills, snout, or hands describe that animal's environment. Likewise, a complete description of a niche describes the animal that occupies it. For example, if we specify in detail the niche of a fish (its medium, its predators and prey, its nest, etc.), we have in a way described the fish. Thus, just as the structure and functioning of an animal implies the environment, the particulars of the niche imply the structure and activities of its animal. (p. 14)

The mutuality of animal and environment is expressed by J. Gibson (1979) and is elaborated by Turvey and Shaw (1979) and E. Gibson (1982) in terms of the *affordance* of the environment and the *effectivity* of the animal. Affordance is what the environment offers or means to an animal; effectivity is the purposive potentials of the animal. The two terms are complementary. For example, a particular object has the potential to be grasped by a particular animal; the animal has the potential to grasp that object (Prindle, Carello, & Turvey, 1980).

The mutuality of animal and environment is also seen in the active role the animal plays in determining the information available by investigating the environment. In this perspective, cognitive processes are considered to be actions (e.g., remembering, thinking, perceiving) rather than objects possessed by a thinker (e.g., memories, cognitions, perceptions) (Bransford, McCarrell, Franks, & Nitsch, 1977; Gibson, 1979; Johnston & Turvey, 1980; Michaels & Carello, 1981; Pick, 1979). The thinking organism is active in participating in an event, exploring a situation, directing attention, attempting solutions. The individual is not merely a receptacle for interacting mental entities that are themselves responsible for selecting information, adding interpretations, and embellishing stimuli according to the biases of memory. Thinking is an event in which the animal seeks information relevant to functioning effectively in the environment and transforms itself to better fit its niche.

Developmental Theories Involving Mutuality: Piaget and Vygotsky

Piaget

Piaget (1952) describes relativity between organism and environment in his discussion of assimilation and accommodation: "The organism and the environment form an indissoluble entity, that is to say . . . there are adaptational variations simultaneously involving a structuring of the organism and an action of the environment, the two being inseparable from each other" (p. 16). Contrary to the initial assimilation of Piaget's theory in American psychology, the theory does not stress the importance of inborn features. Rather, the individual's development in Piagetian theory is based on the species-typical genetic background *and* the species-typical environment, which together form the basis of the individual's effort to construct an understanding of reality (Furth, 1974; see also Voneche, 1984).

In an essay dealing specifically with the relation between the individual and society, Piaget (1977) claimed that neither can be removed from the other; the individual and society are bound together through the social relations between individuals living and past: "What is primary is not . . . the individual, nor the collection of individuals, but the relation between individuals, a relation that endlessly modifies the individual consciousnesses themselves" (p. 146).

Kitchener (1985) summarizes the attributes of Piaget's relational perspective: neither the parts nor the whole is primary; rather, the relations between parts are primary. Both the structure and the parts are secondary and derived.

The structure simply consists of all the relations between the parts, which are Piaget's composition laws, to which the whole is reducible. Parts have no separate existence and no intrinsic boundaries, as the boundaries change over time.

Vygotsky

Vygotsky's approach to the mutuality of individual and environment involves the study of four embedded levels of development (Scribner, 1985; Wertsch, 1985). The level with which developmental psychologists traditionally deal is ontogenetic development—changes in thinking and behavior arising in the history of individuals, such as across childhood. But this is merely a grain of analysis differing from the other three developmental levels. Phylogenetic development is the slowly changing species history that leaves a legacy for the individual in the form of genes. Sociocultural development is the changing cultural history that leaves a legacy for the individual in the form of technologies such as literacy, number systems, and computers, as well as value systems and scripts and norms for the handling of situations met by the individual. Microgenetic development is the moment-to-moment learning by individuals in particular problem contexts, built on the individual's genetic and sociocultural background. In this system, the roles of the individual and the social world are seen as interrelated in the levels of analysis reflecting learning, ontogenetic development, phylogenetic development, and sociohistorical development, all of which continue to transform in their respective time frames.

Leont'ev (1981) has elaborated Vygotsky's concept of activity, a molar unit of analysis that mediates between the individual and the social context in a "process of reciprocal transformations between subject and object poles." An activity is not

> an aggregate of reactions, but a system with its own structure, its own internal transformations, and its own development. . . . If we removed human activity from the system of social relationships and social life, it would not exist and would have no structure. With all its varied forms, the human individual's activity is a system in the system of social relations. (pp. 46–47)

Leont'ev (1981) distinguishes activities, goal-directed actions, and operations as levels of analysis in activity theory. However, these are not independent elements that form activity; they themselves make up the structure of activity. Transformations that occur over the development of activity are set within this system of relations.

Vygotsky was concerned with using a unit of analysis that preserved the inner workings of larger events of interest, rather than separating an event into elements that no longer function as does the larger living unit. One of his important contributions was his search for a unit that

> designates a product of analysis that possesses *all the basic characteristics of the whole*. The unit is a vital and irreducible part of the whole. The key

to the explanation of the characteristics of water lies not in the investigation of its chemical formula but in the investigation of its molecule and its molecular movements. In precisely the same sense, the living cell is the real unit of biological analysis because it preserves the basic characteristics of life that are inherent in the living organism. (Vygotsky, 1987, p. 46)

Vygotsky attempted to determine the psychological analogue of the living cell and focused on the unit of word meaning, as it condenses all the senses of meaning associated with it in its contexts of use. Although other scholars in the sociohistorical tradition have questioned this particular unit of analysis or emphasized others—such as practical activity, use of intellectual tools, propositions, or dialogue—the basic concept of using a unit of activity that maintains the functions of the larger system is Vygotsky's contribution (Bakhtin, 1981; Cole, 1985; Leont'ev, 1981; Wertsch, 1985; Zinchenko, 1985).

Building on Vygotsky's and Leont'ev's activity theory to specify a unit of analysis that preserves meaning, the cultural practice theory of the Laboratory of Comparative Human Cognition (1983) focuses on "socially assembled situations" as the unit of analysis. "Socially assembled situations" are cultural contexts for action that are constructed by people in interaction with one another. Cultural practices are learned systems of activity in which knowledge consists of standing rules for behavior appropriate to a particular socially assembled situation, embodied in the cooperation of individual members of a culture.

Differences in the Social World in the Theories of Piaget and Vygotsky

Despite the emphasis of both Vygotsky and Piaget on the idea that the individual and the environment are inseparable for understanding intellectual development, they differed in both the centrality of the role of the social world in their theories of development, and the way in which they conceived of the role of the social world and the individual.

Piaget

Although many have considered Piaget to have overlooked the role of social interaction in cognitive development, in some of his writing Piaget focused directly on the social context of cognitive development. He argued that the development of the child is an adaptation as much to the social as to the physical milieu: "Social life is a necessary condition for the development of logic. We thus believe that social life transforms the individual's very nature" (Piaget, 1928/1977, p. 239). Piaget's theory touches only occasionally on social factors, however, and he did not direct the work of his laboratory to investigate social influences (see Doise, 1985; Forman & Kraker, 1985). The question of social context appears to have been an issue that forced itself on him, rather than a central tenet of his theory. In a 1927 speech, he admitted that "one cannot speak of the child without asking whether logic is a social thing and in what sense. I have been bothered by this question; I have sought to put it aside; it has always returned" (Piaget, 1977, p. 204).

In his early writings, Piaget provided cogent speculation that individual development is facilitated by cooperation between peers in resolving cognitive conflicts provided by their differing perspectives. Some of Piaget's (1928/ 1977) statements about the mechanisms of social influence have parallels in Vygotsky's theory. For example, "one might suppose that it is the individual that holds the truth up against society, but individual independence is a social fact, a product of civilisation" (p. 220). Piaget's statements to the effect that reflection is internalized dialogue resemble Vygotsky's chief principle that higher mental functions are internalized from social interaction: "Reflection is an internal discussion. . . . In social conflict is born discussion, first simple dispute, then discussion terminating in a conclusion. It is this last action which, internalized and applied to oneself, becomes reflection" (Piaget, 1928/ 1977, p. 219).

Despite the lucidity of Piaget's comments on collective activity, it was not a central tenet for him, as it was for Vygotsky, and it did not become a major focus of his theory or research. Instead, Piaget's interests focused on the active involvement of the child *as an individual* working with objects and making sense of the world through that activity.

Piaget's followers, notably Doise and Perret-Clermont, have extended Piaget's discussion to include the effects of peer interaction on children's development of a variety of Piagetian concepts. Chapter 7 examines Piaget's speculations regarding cognitive conflict between peers of equal status, and Chapter 9 discusses peer research in the Piagetian tradition. Some of this work begins to consider the sociocultural context in addition to the interpersonal context, developing the seed of Piaget's ideas about the social world beyond the work of Piaget himself.

The sociocultural context received relatively little attention in the bulk of Piaget's work. His speculations on the social world were largely limited to the interpersonal context providing for cognitive conflict, without substantial consideration of the sociocultural context of the intellectual problems and solutions of cognitive development. While Piaget acknowledged that the logical operations of adolescents are themselves of social origin, this was as close as he came to considering the societal context of thinking.

A critique of Piaget's model of development is expressed by Newman, Riel, and Martin (1983), who point out that while Piaget noted a close relation between individual and social action, the relation is conceived of as isomorphic only at an abstract, general level, free of content. In contrast, they refer to El'konin in arguing that when content is not removed from cognitive activity, all activities and objects involve culturally specific, socially determined function and meaning.

Newman et al. extend Piaget's metaphor for equilibration, which compares the biological system of digestion and cognitive processes. Piaget's metaphor uses the process of digestion to discuss the processes of assimilation and accommodation, which are central to his theory. Newman et al. (1983) describe Piaget's metaphor:

> The digestive system of an organism dictates which of the range of possible nutrients it can and cannot accommodate. The assimilation of acceptable nutrients will lead to slow changes in the system, which will alter the selection of future nutrients. Similarly, the intellectual system dictates which of a range of possible intellectual experiences it can and cannot assimilate. The assimilation of acceptable experiences will lead to slow changes in the system, altering future ability to assimilate.

And they extend it to involve the social world:

> The availability of biological nourishment and intellectual experience, however, [is] not determined solely by the efforts of individuals. Foods that are made available to children are carefully selected, processed and prepared for children by their parents and by their culture. Just as parents carefully prepare food for children, so, too, parents (and others in the child's environment) prepare and constrain the type of intellectual experiences to which the child will be exposed. By analogy to the prepared baby-food or food-processing devices available to parents, the social distribution of knowledge in any society provides normative guides for the preparation and distribution of "baby experiences" that will lead to the intellectual growth valued by the culture. It is in these ways and in terms of these cultural practices that all reality can be said to be a social reality. (pp. 149–150)

Vygotsky

Vygotsky's theory was built on the premise that individual intellectual development cannot be understood without reference to the social milieu in which the child is embedded. For Vygotsky, children's cognitive development must be understood not only as taking place with social support in interaction with others, but also as involving the development of skill with sociohistorically developed tools that mediate intellectual activity. Thus individual development of higher mental processes cannot be understood without considering the social roots of both the tools for thinking that children are learning to use and the social interactions that guide children in their use.

Vygotsky (1978) suggested that rather than deriving explanations of psychological activity from the individual's characteristics plus secondary social influences, scholars should focus on the social unit of activity and regard individual higher cognitive processing as derived from that (Wertsch, 1985). In reference to Piagetian theory, Vygotsky (1987) stated,

> The child is not seen as a part of the social whole, as a subject of social relationships. He is not seen as a being who participates in the societal life of the social whole to which he belongs from the outset. The social is viewed as something standing outside the child. (p. 83)

The sociohistorical context is considered by Vygotsky to become accessible to the individual through interaction with other members of the society who are more conversant with the society's intellectual skills and tools. Social interaction of children with more competent members of their society is essential to cognitive development. Vygotsky (1978, 1987) emphasized that cognitive development occurs in situations where the child's problem solving is guided by an adult who structures and models the appropriate solution to the problem (in the "zone of proximal development," the region of sensitivity to social guidance where the child is not quite able to manage the problem independently). In Vygotsky's view, the child's individual mental functioning develops through experience with cultural tools in joint problem solving with more skilled partners working in the zone of proximal development.

In a fascinating essay on the philosophical basis of activity theory as proposed by Vygotsky and argued philosophically by Ilyenkov, Bakhurst (1988) maintains that the tenets of activity theory require a radical shift in world view from the predominant Cartesian philosophy, which stresses the individual. The shift makes individual thinking a function of social activity in which the individual internalizes the ways of thinking and acting that have developed in sociocultural history; mind is "in society":

> The idealisation of nature by human practice transforms the natural world into an object of thought, and by participating in those practices, the human individual is brought into contact with reality as an object of thought. Each child enters the world with the forms of movement constitutive of thought embodied in the environment surrounding him or her, and as he or she is led to reproduce those practices so he or she becomes a thinking being, a person. (Bakhurst, 1988, p. 37)

> For Ilyenkov, thought *necessarily* exists in the form of its expression, that expression *necessarily* presupposes a socially-constructed culture (i.e., an idealised environment), and entrance into the culture is a *necessary* condition of consciousness. And it follows from this that the study of mind, of culture, and of language (in all its diversity) are internally related: that is, it will be *impossible* to render any one of these domains intelligible without essential reference to the others. (Bakhurst, 1988, p. 39)

Vygotsky (1987) stressed that children play an active role in their development. However, his theory has been criticized for overlooking the role of "natural" factors in development, those assumed to be available to human infants through phylogenetic development (Wertsch, 1985). Vygotsky's greatest interest was in understanding "higher" mental processes—those that make use of cultural mediators to extend human thinking beyond the "natural" level characteristic of other animals or of involuntary mental processes in humans. Since these higher mental processes, such as voluntary attention and voluntary memory, rely on the use of cultural tools, it makes sense to emphasize the social context of the origin of these tools and their transmission to children. Vygotsky (1981) simply assumed the availability of natural development as a substrate on which cultural development (the development of "higher" mental processes) is built. Although the distinction between "natural" and "higher" mental processes poses problems of its own, understanding Vygotsky's interest in higher mental processes helps explain his emphasis on cultural mediation.

In sum, while it is fair to say that both Piaget and Vygotsky considered both social and natural processes in development, Piaget focused on the individual, sometimes interacting with others on logical problems with social origin, and Vygotsky focused on children participating with other people in a social order.

Focusing on Both Individual and Sociocultural Contributions

While emphasis on either the social or the individual can be profitable as a research strategy to focus centers of interest, my goal is to stress the mutual roles of the efforts of the individual and of social partners in sociocultural activities. Cognitive development occurs in socioculturally organized activities in which children are active in learning and in managing their social partners, and their partners are active in structuring situations that provide children with access to observe and participate in culturally valued skills and perspectives. Collective activity, in turn, constitutes and transforms cultural practices with each successive generation. The integration of individual and social activity is necessary for a balanced consideration of the role of individuals and their social partners, with the individuals actively participating in socioculturally structured collective activity.

Children are active participants in understanding their world, building on both genetic and sociocultural constraints and resources. Babies enter the world as active organisms, equipped both with patterns of action from their genes and prenatal experience, and with caregivers who structure the biological and social worlds of these dependent organisms in ways deriving from their own and their ancestors' phylogenetic and cultural history.

From birth (and probably before), children's development occurs in a biologically given social matrix characteristic of our species. The availability of intellectual tools and practices deriving from sociocultural history is also a feature of the human species. Different human communities produce variations in the specific genetic and social resources of new individual members, and these variations are as essential to understanding human development as are the genetic and social resources that humans have in common. (At the same time, of course, the active role of new generations transforms cultural institutions and practices, and contributes to biological evolution.)

My attempt to keep the roles of both the individual and the social environment in focus, to acknowledge that they build integrally on each other, is consistent with other work on socialization in the early years (Brazelton, 1982; Condon, 1977; Fogel & Thelen, 1987; Halliday, 1979; Lancaster, Altmann, Rossi, & Sherrod, 1987; Lerner, 1978; Papousek, Papousek, & Bornstein, 1985; Rheingold, 1969; Richards, 1978; Schaffer, 1984; Shotter, 1978; Trevarthen, 1988; Tronick, Als, & Adamson, 1979; Valsiner, 1987; Wells, 1979).

As Als (1979) states, the human newborn is biologically a social organism. Papousek and Papousek (1983) suggest that the intuitive didactic interactions of parents and infants are biologically determined by the endowments of adults as well as infants:

> The infant is intrinsically motivated to learn, recognize, and acquire knowledge and skills, in short, to integrate experience as well as to communicate about the outcome of such integration. . . . The parent is intrinsically motivated to share his knowledge, particularly with his progeny, and has a biologically determined capacity to modify the form of conveying knowledge to the infant in accordance with the developmental state and momentary course of the infant's integrative capacity. (p. 226)

West and King (1985) propose the term "ontogenetic niche" to signify that organisms inherit parents, peers, and the places they inhabit, in addition to inheriting parents' genes. Some investigators of early socialization focus on the mutuality of children and their social partners, and some place such mutuality in sociohistorical context as well, as is my aim.

When individual and social contributions are seen as inseparable aspects of whole events in which children develop, the biological heritage of the human species and the cultural inventions of the human species become aspects of each other as well. Instead of working as distinct or interacting forces, nature and nurture (and individual and social world) are related historical transformations in the overall functioning of humans.

In an insightful essay on language development, John-Steiner and Tatter (1983) argue for the unity of biological and cultural aspects of development: "The full development of symbolic language is possible only for humans who are essentially intact biological organisms within essentially intact social environments" (p. 84).

The specific instantiations of the unity of biology and culture occur in the concrete situations of socialization, where children and those around them collaborate to construct meaning and to further children's growth and participation in more mature forms of action. As John-Steiner and Tatter (1983) put it,

> The prolonged dependence of young children on their caretakers is a basic condition of human life. The adult–child interactions during this period of dependency form the primary social sources for the development of linguistic and cognitive processes. The subsequent mastery of language, extending the meaning and scope of these early reciprocal exchanges, enables growing children to internalize the cultural knowledge of their communities and to reflect on their experiences. There is both receptivity to others and self-initiated exploration in the behavioral repertoire of very young children. The tension between these two highly adaptive tendencies contributes to the processes of individuation and enculturation. (p. 86)

As is apparent from these quotations, scholars working in a variety of domains have emphasized the mutuality of nature and culture, and of the individual and the social world. A metaphor that has appealed to many is that of apprenticeship—in which active novices advance their skills and understanding through participation with more skilled partners in culturally organized activities.

Development as Apprenticeship

The notion of apprenticeship as a model for children's cognitive development is appealing because it focuses our attention on the active role of children in organizing development, the active support and use of other people in social interaction and arrangements of tasks and activities, and the socioculturally ordered nature of the institutional contexts, technologies, and goals of cognitive activities. Although young children clearly differ from older novices in the extent to which they can control their attention and communication and in their general knowledge, there is a useful parallel between the roles of young children and the roles of novices in general in apprenticeship. (Although my focus is on cognitive development in infancy and childhood, apprenticeship and guided participation are also visible as adults develop their skills and understanding.)

Novices actively attempt to make sense of new situations and may even be primarily responsible for putting themselves in the position to learn. At the same time, their partners who have relatively greater skill and understanding can often more easily find effective ways to achieve shared thinking that stretch the less skilled partner's understanding. Skilled partners may also help novices with difficult problems by structuring subgoals of problem solving to focus the novice on a manageable aspect of the problem.

Shared problem solving—with an active learner participating in culturally organized activity with a more skilled partner—is central to the process of learning in apprenticeship. So are other features of guided participation that I emphasize: the importance of routine activities, tacit as well as explicit communication, supportive structuring of novices' efforts, and transfer of responsibility for handling skills to novices.

Furthermore, the apprenticeship model has the value of including more people than a single expert and a single novice; the apprenticeship system often involves a group of novices (peers) who serve as resources for one another in exploring the new domain and aiding and challenging one another. Among themselves, the novices are likely to differ usefully in expertise as well. The "master," or expert, is relatively more skilled than the novices, with a broader vision of the important features of the culturally valued activity. However, the expert too is still developing breadth and depth of skill and understanding in the process of carrying out the activity and guiding others in it. Hence the model provided by apprenticeship is one of active learners in a community of people who support, challenge, and guide novices as they increasingly participate in skilled, valued sociocultural activity.

Lave (1988) suggests that "apprentices learn to think, argue, act, and interact in increasingly knowledgeable ways with people who do something well, by doing it with them as legitimate, peripheral participants" (p. 2). Ap-

Figure 2.1   The beginning of apprenticeship in a skilled cultural activity. This 22-month-old has put aside the bell she was given when lifted onto the chair, and intently watches the violinist practice. She reaches for the bow with his encouragement. (United States) (Photograph © B. Rogoff)

prenticeship has been used as a metaphor in language development (Adams & Bullock, 1986; Bruner, 1983; Miller, 1977; Moerk, 1985; Wells, 1979), and has been studied with youth and adults in skill training, academic learning, and career preparation of scientists and artists (Collins, Brown, & Newman, in press; Greenfield & Lave, 1982; John-Steiner, 1985). (Others, such as Kaye, 1982, have used the term in a slightly different way—for instance, portraying young children and apprentices more passively than in the model presented here.)

In a study of the career development of prominent and creative thinkers, John-Steiner (1985) argued that development of a specific language of thought is fostered more by interacting with a knowledgeable person than by studying books or attending classes and exhibits. Apprenticeships provide the beginner with access to both the overt aspects of the skill and the more hidden inner processes of thought. "It is only through close collaborations that the novice is likely to learn what the mentor may not even know: how he or she formulates a question or starts a new project" (p. 200).

The apprenticeship model threads through this book, beginning with consideration in Chapter 3 of the structured fashion in which individual cognitive skills relate to cultural institutions, technologies, and intellectual traditions provided by previous generations. The remainder of this book explores the processes that may function in apprenticeship in cognitive development, broadly conceived, to unite the efforts of children and those around them to advance the children's knowledge and skills through guided participation in skilled cultural activity.

3

The Cultural Context of Cognitive Activity

The young child is often thought of as a little scientist exploring the world and discovering the principles of its operation. We often forget that while the scientist is working on the border of human knowledge and is finding out things that nobody yet knows, the child is finding out precisely what everybody already knows. (Newman, "Perspective-taking versus Content in Understanding Lies")

Writing, the art of communicating thoughts to the mind through the eye, is the great invention of the world . . . enabling us to converse with the dead, the absent, and the unborn, at all distances of time and space. (Abraham Lincoln, 1860 [quoted by Freedman, "Newbery Medal Acceptance"])

Reply of the Indians of the Five Nations to an invitation in 1744 by the commissioners from Virginia to send boys to William and Mary College: "You who are wise must know, that different nations have different conceptions of things; and you will therefore not take it amiss, if our ideas of this kind of education happen not to be the same with yours. We have had some experience of it: several of our young people were formerly brought up at the colleges of the northern provinces; they were instructed in all your sciences; but when they came back to us . . . [they were] ignorant of every means of living in the woods . . . neither fit for hunters, warriors, or counsellors; they were totally good for nothing. We are, however, not the less obliged by your kind offer . . . and to show our grateful sense of it, if the gentlemen of Virginia will send us a dozen of their sons, we will take great care of their education, instruct them in all we know, and make *men* of them." (Drake, *Biography and History of the Indians of North America*)

It is essential to view the cognitive activities of individuals within the cultural context in which their thinking is embedded. The human heritage is notable for the cultural legacy of values and skills, which each new individual inherits from near and distant ancestors and practices with the assistance of caregivers and the companionship of peers.

This chapter focuses on the heritage of cultural institutions, technologies, and traditions built by previous generations. Cultural practices are influential in setting the problems that need solving, providing technologies and tools for their solution, and channeling problem-solving efforts in ways that are valued by local standards.

Examination of cognitive processes in different cultures or historical periods brings to light the sociocultural channeling of individual thinking, as with the fish that is unaware of water until it is out of it. Smedslund (1984) argues that psychology is not an exploration of the unknown but an explication of the well-known. People have a propensity to assume that the perspective on reality provided by their own community is the only proper or sensible one (Berger & Luckmann, 1966; Campbell & LeVine, 1961) and to view the practices of others as barbaric. Riegel (1973) argued that the ancient Greeks facilitated their own cultural identity by downgrading people with different languages, customs, and conceptions of human nature. Indeed, the word *barbarous* derives from the Greek term for "foreign," "rude," and "ignorant" (Skeat, 1974), applied to neighboring tribes who spoke languages unintelligible to the Greeks (who heard only "bar-bar" when they spoke).

Researchers and scholars are as prone to such assumptions as are others. For example, Neisser (1976) points out that self-centered definitions of intelligence form the basis of intelligence tests:

> Academic people are among the stoutest defenders of the notion of intelligence . . . the tests seem so obviously valid to us who are members of the academic community. . . . There is no doubt that Academic Intelligence is really important for the kind of work that we do. We readily slip into believing that it is important for *every* kind of significant work. . . . Thus, academic people are in the position of having focused their professional activities around a particular personal quality, as instantiated in a certain set of skills. We have then gone on to *define* the quality in terms of this skill set, and ended by asserting that persons who lack these special skills are unintelligent altogether. (p. 138)

However, we may attempt to examine our system of assumptions. Careful studies of varying communities or of previous historical periods provide the opportunity to test our assumptions against arrangements that vary in structured and valued fashions. Such research has provided evidence for the importance in individual problem solving of societal institutions, technologies and tools, and values regarding important problems and sophisticated means of solution.

The Institutions of Culture

Among the many societal structures that contribute to the organization of activities of individuals are subsistence and economic institutions, religious systems, political systems, medical systems, and instructional systems such as schools, apprenticeships, and media. Each of these has received some attention in social and historical analyses (Kessel & Siegel, 1985; Kessen, 1979;

Kohn & Schooler, 1973; Newson & Newson, 1974; Riegel, 1972; Wertsch & Youniss, 1987).

All these institutions are related to one another in important ways. For example, models of education may reflect the skills of the work place of adult members of society and social class (Smollett, 1975). Economic, political, and religious values tie to such issues as the importance of individual achievement in schooling, the marketplace, and salvation; the appropriateness of competition as motivation for individuals to study and to work; and the centrality of literacy as a tool for personal advancement, for the achievement of an informed citizenry, and for knowing the Word of God. Each of these issues is worthy of extended discussion; the point here is that there are many such relationships that tie to the specific cognitive skills that researchers have studied.

An example of the relation between individual thinking and political systems involves moral development. Edwards (1981) suggests that Kohlberg's hierarchy of moral development can be related to the political system of a society, with the bureaucratic systems' perspective (Stage Four) fitting a political frame of reference in a large industrialized society, but inappropriate for people in small traditional tribal societies: "The two types of social systems are very different (though of course both are valid working types of systems), and thus everyday social life in them calls forth different modes of moral problem solving whose adequacy must be judged relative to their particular contexts" (p. 274). The political institutions of a society may channel individual moral reasoning by providing standards for the resolution of moral problems.

Another example links societal models of economic exchange with individual thinking. Light and Perret-Clermont (1989) argue that Piagetian logical concepts of amount, number, area, volume, and weight derive from practical purposes associated with sharing and distributing commodities: "The various conservations are *embodied* in these concepts, since they refer precisely to those properties which are conserved across particular kinds of transformation" (p. 109). Light and Perret-Clermont propose that conservation concepts are not transcendent logical entities, but are historically elaborated products of practical and social purposes: "Thus the child's task in mastering conservation concepts is arguably only possible to the extent that he or she is able to share in the purposes and practices to which these concepts relate" (p. 109). Their argument is supported by evidence that children who are asked conservation questions in contexts that stress the need to equate quantities for fair distribution are more likely to answer correctly:

> In place of a Piagetian focus on cognitive development as a sequence of emerging logical competences, pragmatic, intersubjective agreements-in-meaning are seen as lying at the heart of the developmental process. Such agreements (established in and through the child's day-to-day interpersonal behaviour) are envisaged as both the source and the substance of conservation itself. (p. 110)

Figure 3.1 Number concepts as economic activity. Children carefully determine the fair distribution of Easter candy. (United States) (Photograph © B. Rogoff)

The institutions of culture include not only bureaucratic or hardened institutions, such as schools and economic and political systems, but also informal systems of practices in which people participate. Berger and Luckmann (1966) speculate that habitual relations between people become institutionalized as expected and accepted rules and approaches that humans come to regard as external to their functioning. Shotter (1978) effectively describes such institutional settings:

> For the structure of human exchanges, there are precise foundations to be discovered in the *institutions* we establish between ourselves and others; institutions which implicate us in one another's activity in such a way that, what we have done together in the past, *commits* us to going on in a certain way in the future. . . . The members of an institution need not necessarily have been its originators; they may be second, third, fourth, etc. generation members, having "inherited" the institution from their forebears. And this is a most important point, for although there may be an intentional structure to institutional activities, practitioners of institutional forms need have no awareness at all of the reason for its structure—for them, it is just "the-way-things-are-done". The reasons for the institution having one form rather than another are buried in its *history*. (p. 70)

The Cultural Institution of Schooling

The institution that has received the greatest attention in channeling cognitive development has been formal schooling. Although all societies have ways of ensuring that the young become prepared to take on the mature skills of the culture, the means of enculturation or instruction vary from close participation in the contexts of practice, to formal apprenticeships, specialized inculcation rites at periods of transition, and various forms of schooling (Greenfield & Lave, 1982; Scribner & Cole, 1973).

The institution of formal schooling, universal in industrial nations, has been exported to many less industrialized nations but is not yet universal. Thus research comparing individuals with and without schooling provides the opportunity to examine how cognitive skills vary as a function of experience with this institution. (Although it should be recognized that schooling has many forms, it has been treated as rather uniform in such research. The form of schooling that has been exported to many "developing" nations generally follows the old style of lecture and response between teacher and pupils, with little in the way of manipulative materials or visual aids.)

In a review of research on cognitive skills of schooled versus nonschooled individuals, I concluded that schooled individuals gain a variety of cognitive skills that bear a relationship to the activities of schooling (Rogoff, 1981b): schooling fosters perceptual skills in the use of graphic conventions to represent depth in two-dimensional stimuli and in analysis of two-dimensional patterns. Schooled people are skilled in deliberately remembering disconnected bits of information, and are more likely than nonschooled individuals to spontaneously engage in strategies that organize the unrelated items to be remembered. Schooled individuals are more likely to organize test objects on a taxonomic basis, putting categorically similar objects together, whereas nonschooled people often employ functional arrangements of objects that are used together. Schooled people show greater facility in shifting to alternative dimensions of classification and in explaining the basis of their organization. Schooling appears not to relate to rule learning or to logical thought *as long as* the individual has understood the problem in the way the experimenter intended. Nonschooled subjects seem to prefer, however, to come to conclusions on the basis of experience rather than by relying on the information in the problem alone. Schooling may be necessary for the solution of Piagetian formal operational problems.

I concluded that the data do not support a notion of general cognitive skills or of a general effect of schooling on cognitive performance. Rather, there appear to be local relationships between school practices and specific cognitive activities (see also Wagner & Spratt, 1987).

Scribner and Cole (1981) similarly conclude from their extensive research with Vai (Liberian) men who varied in experience with schooling that although performance on many tasks showed a relation to schooling, the relation was not a general one. The tasks that showed most consistent effects of schooling were those requiring expository talk in contrived situations, an observation consistent with the conclusions of Rogoff (1981b) and Scribner and Cole (1973).

The relation between schooling and cognitive skills may appear widespread in part because of the historical relationship between tests of intellectual ability and schooling. As Cole, Sharp, and Lave (1976) point out, Binet's original tests of intelligence were based on school tasks, as his goal was to predict performance in school. So it is not an accident that our measures of intelligence relate to schooling. This relationship may also derive from the fact, as Neisser (1976) points out, that the skills of those who devise the tests (academics) are chosen to define intelligence.

To illustrate the specific relations between school practices and test skills, I will focus on two cognitive skills that have received research attention and that appear to tie to skills practiced in school: memory for disconnected bits of information, and logical problem solving in syllogism word problems.

MEMORY FOR DISCONNECTED BITS OF INFORMATION

In many memory tests, subjects are presented with lists of unrelated pieces of information (such as words) that may be more fully remembered if the subjects apply a strategy (such as rehearsing, categorizing, or elaborating connections between items) to coordinate the items. Nonschooled people have difficulty with such memory tasks and often do not spontaneously employ strategies to organize such lists (Cole & Scribner, 1977; Rogoff & Mistry, 1985). (Young children and older adults in the United States show similar difficulty, which may also relate to their schooling [Flavell, Beach, & Chinsky, 1966; Mueller, Rankin, & Carlomusto, 1979; Perlmutter, 1979; Pressley, Heisel, McCormick, & Nakamura, 1982].)

The use of memory tasks employing unrelated bits of information has a long history in psychology, since Ebbinghaus introduced the nonsense syllable. The presentation of discrete bits of information was regarded as simplifying the units of information to be recalled and limiting the role of previous experience brought to the particular associations to be remembered. This simplicity is likely to be an illusion, however, as Bartlett (1932) pointed out in his critique of the nonsense syllable:

> Uniformity and simplicity of structure of stimuli are no guarantee whatever of uniformity and simplicity of structure in organic response . . . isolation [of response] is not to be secured by simplifying situations or stimuli and leaving as complex an organism as ever to make the response. What we do then is simply to force this organism to mobilise all its resources and make up, or discover, a new complex reaction on the spot. (pp. 3–6)

Literate young adults in industrial societies have special demands and opportunities to develop the use of memory aids appropriate for remembering lists of isolated pieces of information. Facility with tests involving lists of unrelated words may stem from familiarity with lists and the classification systems (e.g., alphabetic, categorical) that lists—products of literacy—promote (Goody, 1977). Furthermore, remembering lists of items unorganized by meaningful schemas may be an unusual experience except in school, where pupils frequently have to use strategies to ensure recall of material they have not understood. In fact, elementary-school teachers provide instruction in the use of such mnemonic strategies (Hart, Leal, Burney, & Santulli, 1985).

While less-schooled individuals may have less practice in organizing isolated bits of information, people from all backgrounds may have similar needs to remember information that is embedded in a structured context and to use strategies that incorporate the existing organization, using meaningful relationships among items as an aid to recall. Subjects in American research use their knowledge of usual relationships among objects and events to organize their memory for items appearing in a meaningful context (Friedman, 1979; Mandler, 1979).

With contextually organized materials, there may be fewer cultural and developmental differences in memory performance, since the majority of memory problems for any individual involve material that is organized in a complex and meaningful fashion (think of the nonlinear organization of the top of your desk), rather than lists of items that have been stripped of organization. Indeed, few cultural differences appear in studies of memory for spatial arrangements or for organized prose (Cole & Scribner, 1977; Dube, 1982; Kearins, 1981; Mandler, Scribner, Cole, & DeForest, 1980; Neisser, 1982; Ross & Millsom, 1970).

Rogoff and Waddell (1982), for example, found similar performance by Guatemalan Mayan and U.S. 9-year-olds on the reconstruction of contextually organized three-dimensional scenes. Each child watched as a local experimenter placed 20 familiar miniature objects—such as cars, animals, furniture, people, and household items—into a panorama model of a town that contained familiar props, such as a mountain, a lake, a road, houses, and trees (the panorama and objects were designed for cultural appropriateness). The 20 objects were removed from the panorama and reintegrated into the pool of 80 objects from which they had been drawn, and after a brief delay, the child reconstructed the scene. The Mayan children performed slightly *better* than U.S. children. The skill shown by the Mayan children in remembering contextually organized information in this task contrasts sharply with the striking decrements in list-memory performance (compared with U.S. children) that they displayed in a previous study (Kagan, Klein, Finley, Rogoff, & Nolan, 1979).

The slight advantage of the Mayan children seemed to be due to the attempts by about one-third of the U.S. children to apply a strategy useful for remembering unorganized lists—rehearsing the names of the objects in the panorama as they studied them. This strategy for remembering lists of unrelated items immediately after presentation may be inappropriate for remembering contextually organized material. Rehearsal of object names may help only minimally in reconstruction, since the objects are present in the pool at the time of the delayed test, and the major task is remembering their locations.

Successful reconstruction of spatial arrays may rely on deliberately re-

Figure 3.2   Mayan 9-year-old and tester in the scene-reconstruction task. On the left is the panorama, with its houses, volcano, lake, and other scenic elements, along with the objects to be remembered. At the bottom of the photograph is the pool of objects from which those to be remembered are drawn. (Guatemala) (Photograph © B. Rogoff)

membering the "look" of the arrangement or using spatial relationships to organize memory, rather than on employing verbal strategies, as in list-memory tasks (Kearins, 1981; Rogoff & Waddell, 1982; Waddell & Rogoff, 1987). As U.S. schoolchildren learn to master mnemonic strategies useful for remembering lists, they may overgeneralize their application to tasks that might better be approached by attention to meaningful relationships between features of the array (Skeen & Rogoff, 1987).

LOGICAL PROBLEM SOLVING IN SYLLOGISM WORD PROBLEMS

In work done during the 1930s, Luria (1976) presented verbal syllogisms such as the one quoted below to probe the use of logical "devices" that allow deduction and inference without reliance on direct experience. He found that Central Asian subjects did not treat syllogisms as though the premises constituted a logical relation but handled them as unrelated judgments. The task demands differ from the usual demands involved in asking an opinion.

When asked to make inferences on the basis of the premises of syllogisms, the literate subjects solved the problems in the desired manner, but many nonliterate subjects refused, not accepting that the major premise is a "given" and protesting that they "could only judge what they had seen" or "didn't want to lie."

> [Syllogism] In the Far North, where there is snow, all bears are white. Novaya Zemlya is in the Far North and there is always snow there. What color are the bears there?
>
> . . . "We always speak only of what we see; we don't talk about what we haven't seen."
>
> [E:] But what do my words imply? [The syllogism is repeated.]
>
> "Well, it's like this: our tsar isn't like yours, and yours isn't like ours. Your words can be answered only by someone who was there, and if a person wasn't there he can't say anything on the basis of your words."
>
> [E:] . . . But on the basis of my words—in the North, where there is always snow, the bears are white, can you gather what kind of bears there are in Novaya Zemlya?
>
> "If a man was sixty or eighty and had seen a white bear and had told about it, he could be believed, but I've never seen one and hence I can't say. That's my last word. Those who saw can tell, and those who didn't see can't say anything!" (At this point a young Uzbek volunteered, "From your words it means that bears there are white.")
>
> [E:] Well, which of you is right?
>
> "What the cock knows how to do, he does. What I know, I say, and nothing beyond that!" (pp. 108–109)

The subject and the experimenter seemed to disagree about the kind of evidence that one should accept as truth. The subject insisted that truth should be based on first-hand knowledge, or perhaps on the word of a reliable, experienced person, while the experimenter attempted to induce the subject to play a game involving examination of the truth value of the words alone.

Given differing criteria for determining truth, the peasant's treatment of the syllogism cannot be taken as evidence of his logical functioning. Luria notes that the nonliterate subjects' reasoning and deduction followed the rules when dealing with immediate practical experience, making excellent judgments and drawing all the implied conclusions. However, in a system of "theoretical thinking," they showed several differences from the literate subjects: they refused to accept the premise as a point of departure for subsequent reasoning; they treated the premise as a message about some particular phenomenon rather than as a "universal" given; and they handled the syllogism as a collection of independent statements rather than as a unified logical problem. (Luria's findings have been replicated by Cole, Gay, Glick, & Sharp, 1971; Scribner, 1975, 1977; Fobih, 1979; and Sharp, Cole, & Lave, 1979.)

When nonliterate individuals treat a problem as a self-contained logical unit, they show the same logicality as literate individuals. When Cole et al. (1981) changed the problem format so that subjects simply evaluated the truth of conclusions stated by the experimenter on the basis of the premises, nonschooled subjects had much less difficulty than when they had to state conclusions on the basis of the premises. This supports the argument that the nonliterate subjects were uncomfortable having to answer questions for which they could not verify the premises. When conclusions were provided by the experimenter, the subjects were willing to consider whether the hypothetical premises and the conclusion fit logically.

Scribner (1975, 1977) argues that nonliterate peoples' unwillingness to treat syllogisms as logical problems should not be confused with failure to think hypothetically. She quotes a subject using the hypothetical mode to explain his reason for not being able to answer the question: "If you know a person, if a question comes up about him, you are able to answer." He reasoned hypothetically about the practical situation in denying the possibility of reasoning hypothetically about information of which he had no experience.

Verbal syllogisms represent a specialized language genre that is recognizably different from other genres and that becomes easier to handle with practice and with understanding of the specialized form of this kind of problem (Scribner, 1977). In school, people may become familiar with the genre through experience with story problems and other verbal problems in which the answer must be derived from the relationships presented in the problem.

These examples—memory for unconnected bits of information and logical solution of syllogisms—illustrate the connection between the performance of individuals on cognitive tasks and their experience with particular problem structures or genres through schooling. The examples tie the institutional level of culture to processes of individual problem solving. They also lead us into the next aspect of culture to be discussed—the tools and technologies provided by culture—because the structure of problems and genres for thinking can be regarded as technologies for organizing thought processes that are utilized in individuals' problem solving and practiced in institutional activities such as schooling.

Tools and Technologies for Individual Problem Solving

Each generation of individuals in any society inherits, in addition to their genes, the products of cultural history, including technologies developed to support problem solving. Some of the technologies that have received attention as inherited tools for handling information include language systems that organize categories of reality and structure ways of approaching situations, literate practices to record information and transform it through written exercises, mathematical systems that handle numerical and spatial problems, and mnemonic devices to preserve information in memory over time. Some of these technologies have material supports, such as pencil and paper, word-processing programs, alphabets, calculators, abacus and slide rule, notches on sticks, and knots in ropes. All the technologies have systems for handling information that are passed from one generation to the next.

The specifics of each technology are inseparable from the cognitive processes of the users of the systems. Different technologies require varying skills for their use and promote specific approaches that can nevertheless be exported to other problems as people generalize familiar approaches to handle new problems that appear related to known ones. Cognitive activities and technologies are specific in their range of applicability; they may be used outside the context of their practice but yield skills tied to the activity rather than general abilities.

Japanese abacus experts, for example, evidence specific but powerful consequences of their skill in the use of the abacus as a tool for mathematical operations. They use interiorized representations of the abacus that allow them to mentally calculate without an abacus as accurately as with an abacus, and often faster (Hatano, 1982; Stigler, Barclay, & Aiello, 1982). Their mental abacus is of extended size and can represent numbers of many digits. This mental version of the tool facilitates a memory skill related to abacus use: abacus experts can recall a series of 15 digits either forward or backward. However, their memory span for the Roman alphabet and for fruit names is not different from the usual 7 plus or minus 2 units found for most adults in memory-span tasks. The processes involved in their impressive mental-abacus operations are tailored to the activities in which they were practiced and applied specifically to related activities.

Similarly, children experienced with the mathematical conventions provided by schooling and those experienced with the mathematical practices involved in selling candy on the streets in Brazil manage to apply the specific tools with which they are skilled to solve novel arithmetic problems (e.g., use of mathematical notation from school math or of regrouping of the terms of a problem, as in currency-based arithmetic operations [Saxe, 1988; see also Carraher, Carraher, & Schliemann, 1985]).

These examples demonstrate how mathematical tools are an essential aspect of numerical thinking, and how individuals' skills are specific to the tools they have used. A cultural tool of widespread importance in thinking is language, which has engendered general agreement about its importance as a cognitive tool and debate about the role of specific language systems for specific intellectual approaches (Lucy & Wertsch, 1987). The next section describes research focusing on the role of literacy, an intellectual tool that varies in its availability as well as its structure in different cultural traditions.

Literacy

Literate activities have received a great deal of attention as cultural practices that channel individual thinking. The invention of literacy has been suggested to have had profound historical cognitive effects. With the availability of written records, the importance of memory for preserving chronicles in the form of narrative diminished. At the same time, the concept of remembering information word for word (rather than for gist) may also have arisen with the possibility of checking recall against written records (Cole & Scribner, 1977).

In his account of the uses and historical development of literacy, Goody

Figure 3.3 A cultural setting that emphasizes literacy and the analytic use of language. Teacher and young students examining a Jewish text. (Zborowski, 1955)

(1977) argues that writing "is a tool, an amplifier, a facilitating device . . . which encourages reflection upon and the organisation of information" (p. 109). Using illustrations from early written records, Goody suggests that making lists is dependent on writing, and that comparison, classification, and hierarchical organization of items are greatly facilitated by spatial arrangement of items in a list. He proposes that classifying information by category and remembering lists of items are skills that derive from literacy.

Olson (1976) suggests that human intellect cannot be separated from the technologies (e.g., writing, speech, numerical systems) invented to extend cognitive processes. He argues against the notion of general abilities, since it is only with specific technologies (writing, navigational systems, and so on) that cognitive processes operate. Luria (1971) argued similarly that intellectual processes do not exist outside the sociohistorical (material) conditions in which they operate. Literacy is instrumental in the construction of a particular form of knowledge relevant to culturally valued activities.

Literacy, it has been argued, fosters the examination of propositions for their internal logic (Goody & Watt, 1968; Olson, 1976), as written statements may be examined for consistency, and in the case of essayist prose, statements can be treated as though meaning were contained in the text itself, independent of the social context of the writer and reader. In oral language, the context and the interaction between speaker and listener help to establish the meaning, which can be "negotiated" in the interaction.

Olson (1976) argues that people who are literate become practiced in examining statements in isolation for logical meaning (as in logical syllogisms). He suggests that literacy encourages the formulation of general statements and generalizations, and that the cognitive changes observed near the onset of schooling (White, 1965) derive from the familiarity with literacy developing at 5 to 7 years of age. Gellatly (1987) argues that the concept of logical necessity, so essential to Piaget's theory and to the solution of logical syllogisms, derives from literacy.

The work of Scribner and Cole (1981) carefully examines the relation between cognitive skills and literacy of varying types. These authors point out that most speculations about literacy focus on the genre of essayist text (expository writing). They studied individuals who differed in the type of literacy practiced, with a sample of Vai people from Liberia. The Vai have independently developed a phonetic writing system, widely available throughout the society, consisting of a syllabary of 200 characters with a common core of 20 to 40. Vai script is used for the majority of personal and public needs (such as letter writing) in the villages and is transmitted informally by nonprofessional literates who teach friends and relatives over a period of up to 2 months. In addition, some Vai individuals are literate in Arabic from their study of religious texts in traditional Qur'anic schools, which emphasize memorizing or reading aloud, often without understanding the language. And some Vai are literate in English from their study in Western-style official schools.

The Vai script has many important uses, but it does not involve learning new knowledge or writing essays to examine ideas. Hence Scribner and Cole (1981) predicted that Vai literacy would not have the intellectual consequences that have been suggested to result from high levels of school-based literacy. Indeed, they found little difference between individuals literate and not literate in Vai on logical and classification tasks.

In subsequent tasks, Scribner and Cole carefully related specific cognitive skills to particular aspects of the different systems of literacy. For example, in communication tasks requiring the description of a board game in its absence, Vai literates excelled, compared with nonliterates and with Arabic literates. Scribner and Cole expected this relationship, since Vai literates frequently write letters—a practice requiring communication to be carried in the text, unsupported by other aspects of context. Vai literates were also more skilled in comprehending sentences presented syllable-by-syllable at a slow rate; this resembles the necessity in Vai literacy to integrate syllables into meaningful linguistic units (e.g., words), since Vai script is written without word division. Arabic literacy was associated with skill in remembering a string of words in order, with one word added to the list on each trial. This test resembles the method for learning the Qur'an by the Arabic literates.

Scribner and Cole's (1981) results suggest that literacy relates to cognitive skills through specific practices involved in the use of literacy, with different forms of written script (e.g., alphabetic, phonemic, with or without word divisions) and literate genres (e.g., essayist prose, letters, story problems, lists, chants) promoting different cognitive skills.

Literacy is an excellent example of the levels of relationship between the cognitive skills of the individual, the cultural technologies employed, and the societal institutions in which skill with technologies is practiced and developed. Variations in the purposes and practices of literacy appear to be closely related to the skills that individuals using a technology gain from its use; such variations are embedded in societal arrangements of human activities.

An example of the variation in societal uses of literacy is available in recent history. Historical changes in Western Europe and the United States brought shifts in the definition of functional literacy, from being able to sign one's name, to decoding without comprehension, to reading for new information (Resnick & Resnick, 1977). Wolf (1988) describes how the definition of literacy has evolved in U.S. history:

> Colonists were literate enough if they could sign their name, or even an X, on loans and deeds. When immigrants arrived in large numbers in the 1800s, educators urged schools to deliver "recitation literacy" to the foreign children who filled the schoolrooms. That literacy was the ability to hold a book and reel off memorized portions of basic American texts such as the opening paragraph of the Declaration of Independence, a part of the Gettysburg address, or some Bryant or Longfellow. With the coming of World War I, and the prospect of large numbers of men handling new equipment in foreign countries, Army testers redefined reading. Suddenly, to the dismay of men used to reading familiar passages, passing the army reading test meant being able to make sense, on the spot, of never-before-seen text. Currently, that kind of "extraction literacy," so revolutionary in 1914, looks meager. Finding out who, what, when, where, or even how simply does not yield the inferences, questions, or ideas we now think of as defining full or "higher" literacy.
>
> But, in all of this, we are not inventing new forms of literacy; we have always offered writing rather than X's or questioning rather than recitation to the gifted and the privileged. What is unprecedented is the notion that this kind of literacy should be common. The idea of a classroom where young women, poor and minority students, and learning disabled students *all* read (not recite) and write about (not copy) Shakespeare or Steinbeck is a radical and hopeful departure from the long-running conception of literacy as serviceable skills for the many and generative, reflective reading and writing for the few. (p. 1)

This account of historical shifts in the use of a cultural technology underscores the relation between individual cognitive practices and the specific institutions, technologies, and goals of society. It brings us to consider the next aspect of culture that relates to individual cognitive activity: cultural values that define what goals are important and what means to reach them are sophisticated.

Valued Goals and Means in Societal Traditions

Assumptions about the appropriate ways to solve problems and the relative sophistication of different sorts of solutions are nested within the practices of the institutions and technologies of a society. Choice of a particular technology—such as a language to explain events or tools to use on a specific problem—reflects societal consensus favoring certain approaches in accord with cultural value systems and goals (Berger & Luckmann, 1966; Wertsch, 1987; Wertsch & Youniss, 1987).

An example of goals and values associated with social institutions is provided by Wertsch, Minick, and Arns (1984), who argue that the goals of school-oriented instruction contrast with those of teaching and learning in household economic activity, such as food production: school emphasizes learning, even through errors, in order to encourage independent functioning, whereas the successful operation of the household economic system may require error-free performance of consolidated skills. In household economic activity such as food or textile production, errors are costly; children may participate in tasks in which they have become proficient, so that parents can be certain that they will not waste materials by making mistakes. Thus the value of learning through errors may vary as a function of the cost of errors, which differ between schooling and household learning.

Goodnow (1980) points out that values are involved in judgments of the outcomes or endpoints of development, methods of facilitating development, and assessments of progress toward an endpoint. Concerns about assumptions of unique developmental endpoints have become an issue in recent historical and cross-cultural analyses in which the goals of development may not match the naïve or explicit theories of current researchers (Buck-Morss, 1975). Piaget's theory has been criticized for assuming that the ideal endpoint of development resembles becoming a Swiss scientist; evidence of cultural variation encouraged Piaget (1972) to acknowledge that such an endpoint might not be universal.

Many other theories focus on an ideal endpoint for development, and few theorists have escaped putting their own valued characteristics at the pinnacle (e.g., Werner). Although Vygotsky's theory stresses the contextual specificity of intellectual functioning, it focuses on the development of higher mental processes that are connected with formal instructional contexts (Wertsch & Youniss, 1987) and the use of language in an analytic form that is valued by some cultural groups and not by others. These values are consistent with Vygotsky's own cultural milieu and upbringing as a Jewish intellectual. Vygotsky's work with Luria was inconsistent with the contextual tenet, in its apparent conclusion that there is a general change in the complexity of thought accompanying the socioeconomic transformation from agricultural to industrial modes of production (Cole, 1985, 1988; Scribner, 1985).

A contextual approach to understanding active thinking and development assumes multiple directions of development rather than accepting the premise of a unique ideal endpoint. Depending on the circumstances, both immediate and societal, as well as the individual characteristics of the person, appropriate development may take many courses. This is not to say that development is aimless. Although chance plays an important role in characteristics of the circumstances and of the person, the activity of individuals and their social partners has purpose. Development involves progress toward local goals and valued skills. The issue is to open our view to multiple value systems and appropriate goals, and to define the purposes of development in a fashion that is sensitive to "local" circumstances and aspirations.

Evidence of Sociocultural Values Involved in Cognitive Skills

The institutions of society carry with them prescriptions for skilled performance, and the use of particular technologies channels problem-solving choices to favor certain means of solution. For example, the value assigned by researchers to taxonomic classification (rather than functional classification) as more mature or sophisticated classification may relate to schooling's and literacy's emphasis on defining, organizing, and classifying, and on learning concepts from general definitions rather than from exemplars. The taxonomic categories valued in school may not be valued by nonschooled people, as illustrated by Glick's (1975) report of Kpelle subjects' treatment of a classification problem. Kpelle farmers sorted 20 objects into functional groups (e.g., knife with orange, potato with hoe) rather than into categorical groups that the researcher considered more appropriate. When questioned, the subjects often volunteered that that was the way a wise man would do things. "When an exasperated experimenter asked finally, 'How would a fool do it', he was given back sorts of the type that were initially expected—four neat piles with food in one, tools in another, and so on" (p. 636).

The academic emphasis on logic and paper problems may appear to those outside the ivory tower as an exercise in triviality, lacking insight into what really matters (Neisser, 1976). Goodnow (1980, citing an unpublished paper by Tamigawa & Willis, 1977) provides a telling example of an outsider's view of academic pursuits: an elderly lady who was asked to complete Raven's Progressive Matrices scolded, "A Professor, and still playing with puzzles!"

Similarly, judgments about the characteristics of a good narrative vary across cultures. Abstract story grammars differ in format across cultures, and these differences lead to distortions in recall of stories that do not fit the ideal; American groups, by contrast, distort stories to avoid ending a story on a negative note or with unresolved problems (Matsuyama, 1983; Rice, 1980).

Other skills show similar links with approaches that are valued by the local culture. The skills of observation and fine discrimination and the ability to ignore unimportant information in order to focus on essential demands of a task are highly valued among members of a nomadic tribe of magicians and performers, the Qalandar of Pakistan (Berland, 1982). Such skills are vital in their nomadic life and for their magic performances, in which the magician must mislead others by focusing their attention on nonessential features of perceptual displays. This sensitivity to distinctions between perceived and actual properties of stimuli also appeared in performance by the Qalandar (compared with sedentary groups) on tests of perceptual embedding.

The motor skills of infants relate to the value the culture ascribes to different abilities. Parents in some African groups actively encourage their infants to learn to sit and to walk by propping them in a sitting position or exercising their legs from an early age, and they discourage the infants from crawling. They arrange explicit learning situations for the valued skills, and their infants show precocious development in these, but not in the less valued skills (Kilbride, 1980; Super, 1981).

Goodnow (1976) proposed that many differences among cultural groups in performance of common cognitive tasks may be due largely to varying interpretation of what problem is being solved in the task and different values defining "proper" methods of solution (e.g., speed, reaching a solution with the minimum moves or redundancy, physically handling the materials versus "mental shuffling," original solution versus deference to authority). To perform a skill before it is consolidated (as in a test) may be considered an important part of the learning process in some cultures, but regarded as inappropriate in others (Cazden & John, 1971).

Indigenous Definitions of Intelligence

Indigenous concepts of intelligence vary widely, with some behaviors valued at opposite extremes. For example, Chinese students regard memory for facts as important, whereas Australian students see memory skills as trivial (Chen, Braithwaite, & Huang, 1982). Ugandan villagers associate intelligence with adjectives such as *slow, careful,* and *active,* whereas Ugandan teachers and Westernized groups associate intelligence with the word *speed* (Wober, 1972).

Popular conceptions of intelligence held by middle-class groups in the United States differ from those of some other groups in valuing the separation of form from content (in abstract formalisms) and in favoring technical intelligence as distinct from social and emotional skills (Lutz & LeVine, 1982). This middle-class American view contrasts with judgments of adults from some African groups in regard to children's intelligence, which stress both capability in specific situations and social responsibility, such as co-operativeness and obedience (Serpell, 1977, 1982). Kipsigis (Kenyan) parents interpret intelligence as including responsible participation in family and social life (Super & Harkness, 1983), and Malay students and the Baoulé of the Ivory Coast similarly regard intelligence as involving social and cognitive attributes (Dasen, 1984; Gill & Keats, 1980). The Ugandan view casts intelligence as both knowing how to do and *doing* the socially appropriate thing. The Ifaluk of the western Pacific similarly regard intelligence as not only having knowledge of good social behavior, but also performing it (Lutz & LeVine, 1982).

Thus cultural variation appears in value judgments about the desirability of speed, abstraction, and memory skills, and the separability of social from cognitive skills and knowledge from action. The indigenous concepts of intelligence that stress appropriate behavior with others are consistent with my claim in the next section that performance in cognitive tasks is inseparable from values about appropriate social relationships in such situations.

Social Relationships in Cognitive Tasks

As with indigenous concepts of intelligence that consider social features of problem solving, evidence suggests that researchers' observations of cognitive skills (and thinking outside research settings) are intrinsically tied to social aspects of problem-solving situations. Such social aspects may carry different values with different groups of people, resulting in varying approaches to the problem.

People's reliance on others in cognitive problem-solving and problem-setting situations varies according to societal traditions and values. In schools, for example, reliance on a companion for help may be considered cheating, whereas in everyday situations in many cultural settings, not to employ a companion's assistance may be regarded as folly or egoism.

In addition, interpretation of the meaning of a cognitive task depends on how the individual conceives the importance of focusing on the task as a self-contained intellectual puzzle independent of the social context (Goodnow, 1976). Cultural groups differ in experience with puzzles, as discussed in the section on syllogisms and schooling. They also differ in the primacy accorded to building and maintaining appropriate social relations. For example, schooled people are familiar with an interview or a testing situation in which a high-status adult, who already knows the answer to a question, requests information from a lower-status person, such as a child. In some cultural settings, however, the appropriate behavior may be to show respect to the questioner or to avoid being made a fool of by giving the obvious answer to a question that must be a trick question whose answer is not the obvious one (otherwise why would a knowledgeable person be asking it?).

In her discussion of poor performance by Wolof people on Piagetian conservation tasks in Greenfield's (1966) study, Irvine (1978) suggested that the subjects' interpretation of the experimenter's purpose may have conflicted with their giving straightforward answers to the questions. Irvine reports that it is uncommon, except in schoolroom interrogation, for Wolof people to ask one another questions to which they already know the answers: "Where this kind of questioning does occur it suggests an aggressive challenge, or a riddle with a trick answer" (p. 549). When Irvine modified the form of investigation by presenting the task in an informal context of language-learning questions about the meaning of quantity terms like *more* and *the same,* using water and beakers for illustration, her informants elaborated responses that reflected understanding of conservation of quantity.

Values about social relationships may also influence people's response to cognitive questions that would require them to overstep their roles. For example, in contrast to the encouragement of mainstream U.S. children to perform and compete as individuals, children in some cultures learn to avoid calling attention to themselves by egotistically volunteering an answer and thereby distinguishing themselves from the group (Philips, 1972; Whiting & Whiting, 1975). Similarly, prescribed relationships between children and adults may conflict with children's treating a cognitive puzzle as a self-contained problem. In many societies, for instance, the role of children may be to observe and to carry out directives, but not to initiate conversation or talk back to a person of higher status (Blount, 1972; Harkness & Super, 1977; Ward, 1971).

An example of social values that conflict with the purpose of a cognitive test appears in my study of Mayan children recalling a story to an adult. This social situation conflicted with local values in a Mayan community where children are taught to avoid challenging an adult with a display of greater knowledge by telling them something, especially if they have not directly observed what they recount (Rogoff & Waddell, reported in Rogoff & Mistry, 1985). Although several studies find that individuals from nonindustrial societies may be very skilled in prose recall (Dube, 1982; Mandler et al., 1980), the story recall of the Mayan children was characterized by great hesitation, need for prompts, disjointed accounts, and frequent use of the word *cha* ("so I have been told"), which is used by children when passing messages to adults. In contrast, U.S. children recalled fluently, with connected narrative and little need for prompts. Social values regarding the roles of children who transmit hearsay accounts to adults entered centrally into the memory performance of these children.

Young children may answer a question in terms of what the tester seems to intend, focusing on social aspects of the situation rather than on the question as asked. Several studies have found improved performance when social cues that conflict with the experimental procedure are adjusted. McGarrigle and Donaldson (1975) and Light, Buckingham, and Robbins (1979) found greater conservation responses by young children when the transformation of materials appeared to be accidental (carried out by a "naughty teddy bear" or incidental to a game with a peer) rather than a clearly deliberate act of the tester.

Light and Perret-Clermont (1989) point out that young children's confusions in a Piagetian task may be "not so much conservational as conversational" (p. 103). They review studies suggesting that children have difficulty with the experimenter's conservation question of whether the amounts of material have changed or remained the same, since the question is unlikely to be a straightforward request for information because the adult has all the information that the child has. The experimenter is not really interested in the information about quantity, but in what the child knows about quantity—a type of examination question that may be uncommon for young children and for most people in some cultures.

Indeed, when a naïve experimenter took the place of the one who had carried out the transformations, the conservation question became much easier for young children to handle as a straightforward request for information. Light, Gorsuch, and Newman (1987) had pairs of 5- and 6-year-old children divide a heap of dried peas into two equal piles. The experimenter put the piles into two differently shaped containers, and asked the children whether there was the same amount of peas in each. Less than 20% of the children responded correctly. But another sample of children, who were asked the question by another experimenter (who called the original experimenter to the phone and then took over the task), gave over 50% correct answers.

These results support the theme of this chapter: that cognitive activities occur in socially structured situations that involve values about the interpretation and management of social relationships. Individuals' attempts to solve problems are intrinsically related to social and societal values and goals, tools, and institutions in the definition of the problems and the practice of their solution.

PART II

PROCESSES OF
GUIDED PARTICIPATION

4

Providing Bridges
from Known to New

Valerie, age 15 months, crawled under her changing table as though she wanted to get something, stayed for a moment, and then backed out of the small space, crying. Her mother asked, "What do you want?" and looked under the table but, not seeing anything, stopped looking. Valerie continued to fret, and her mother asked, "What's the matter?" Valerie looked at her mother thoughtfully for a moment, and then bent over and pointed up under the back of the table. So Valerie's mother looked there and saw Valerie's favorite book stuck behind the table. When she extracted it, Valerie smiled contentedly and held the book.

It is the way in which the mother replies [to her infant's acts] in terms of her *interpretation* that is crucial. Only by replying in socially proper terms to his responses is he presented with an opportunity to learn the proper social use to which his activity may be put. If, for instance, everytime he made a pointing-like movement he was given a reward, a sweet, say, or anything, other than his mother attending to the object he was looking at (or in some contexts giving him it), then one may indeed increase the frequency of his pointing-like movements. But the infant could never possibly learn that such movements were something that could be used, not for getting sweet rewards, but for the social purpose of directing someone else's attention. (Shotter, "The Cultural Context of Communication Studies")

Part II discusses processes of guided participation in which caregivers and children collaborate in arrangements and interactions that support children in learning to manage the skills and values of mature members of their society. Guided participation is presented as a process in which caregivers' and children's roles are entwined, with tacit as well as explicit learning opportunities in the routine arrangements and interactions between caregivers and children. (See also Papousek & Papousek, 1983, on intuitive parenting.)

In Chapters 5 and 6, focusing on processes of bridging from known to new and structuring of children's activities, observations are based on the limited cultural context of North American and European research—largely middle class and English speaking. There are, however, important differences among cultural communities in arrangements for and communication with children, discussed in Chapter 6, where I present them as variants of guided participation in which adults and older children facilitate children's development of culturally valued skills, whether by design or by the nature of human give-and-take. The cultural variation draws attention to the importance of community goals and practices in the arrangements of children's activities and their engagements with others, to asymmetries in the responsibility of children for learning from the activities in which they participate and observe, and to the tacit and routine nature of children's guided participation in the shared activities of daily life. These facets of guided participation, noticeable in the practices of other cultures, are also important to middle-class children and their families, but are less visible to researchers who share the culture of middle-class families and are therefore often less aware of their cultural context of development.

This chapter discusses how guided participation provides bridges between familiar skills or information and those needed to solve new problems. In the context of communication, caregivers and children make connections between what the children already know and what they must learn to handle a new situation (D'Andrade, 1981; Erickson, 1982; Pearson & Gallagher, 1983; Wertsch, 1979b). Examples of middle-class adults' efforts to bridge from known to new within classrooms occur in Petitto's (1983) observation of a fourth-grade teacher who introduced long division by tying the procedure to multiplication and simple division, which the children already knew, and Schallert and Kleiman's (1979) observation of teachers who explained the dimensions of sequoia trees by comparing the trees with large objects with which the students were familiar.

Adults helping children make connections may specify how the new situation resembles the old. For example, in a picture-classification task, most mothers provided links between the laboratory task and a more familiar context to assist children in stretching their knowledge to encompass the new situation (Rogoff & Gardner, 1984). Some mothers made comments such as "You need to put the things together that go together, just like on 'Sesame Street' when they say 'three of these things belong together.' " And in a laboratory classification task that involved sorting groceries onto shelves, mothers often drew parallels with their kitchen at home to guide 6-year-olds' transfer of relevant information about classification to the laboratory task. One mother explained, "We're going to organize things by categories. You know, just like we don't put the spoons in the pan drawer and all that stuff."

Caregivers build bridges that aid children in understanding how to act in new situations by providing emotional cues about the nature of the situations, nonverbal models of how to behave, verbal and nonverbal interpretations of behavior and events, and verbal labels that classify objects and events.

All these activities by caregivers are coupled with children's efforts (intentional or not) to pick up information—through such means as social referencing and nonverbal and verbal cues—about the nature of situations and about caregivers' interpretations of situations as well as appropriate ways to handle them. Everyday communication between caregivers and children bridges two views of a situation, building from the child's starting point, with modifications in the perspectives of each participant. Such communication is used throughout life, but this chapter focuses on infancy and early childhood to stress the availability of such bridging from the earliest years.

The mutual understanding that is achieved between people in communication has been termed *intersubjectivity,* emphasizing that understanding happens *between* people; it cannot be attributed to one person or the other in communication. The concept of intersubjectivity, and questions about its origins and development in infancy, will be discussed after we examine evidence of how middle-class adults and young children use emotional and nonverbal communication as well as words as bridges that extend children's understanding to new points.

Emotional and Nonverbal Communication

Young children are so skilled at obtaining information from adults' glances, winces, and mood that one of the greatest challenges of testing preschoolers is to avoid nonverbal actions that may be construed as cues. Children press for and use such cues even when given standardized intelligence tests (Mehan, 1976).

From the first year of life, children look to adults to interpret situations that are ambiguous from the children's point of view, in a process termed *social referencing* (Feinman, 1982; Gunnar & Stone, 1984). Interpretations offered by adults inform infants about the appropriate approach to take to a new situation. For example, if a toddler is crawling toward its mother and reaches what appears to be a drop-off, the child searches the mother's face for cues regarding the situation. If the mother's emotional expression indicates fear, the child does not proceed, but if the mother has an encouraging expression, the child carefully crawls across clear glass suspended a foot above what appears to be the floor (Sorce, Emde, Campos, & Klinnert, 1985).

Social referencing is facilitated by the ability that appears by 8 to 12 months of age to obtain information from the direction in which caregivers point and gaze (Bruner, 1983; Butterworth & Cochran, 1980; Churcher & Scaife, 1982). At age 2 to 4 months, infants begin to adjust their gaze when adult partners change the direction in which they are looking, although they are not accurate until 12 months of age in determining the location of the target of the adults' attention within their visual field solely on the basis of direction of the partners' gaze (Bruner, 1987; Butterworth, 1987; Scaife & Bruner, 1975). Throughout the first year, however, infants are able to use contextual clues, such as a change in what is happening nearby, to augment the information from the direction of adult gaze and thereby frequently achieve joint attention. By the end of the first year, infants look for something happening in the line of their partners' gaze, and if they find no target, they look back at their partners to recheck their gaze direction.

The development of skill in following another's attention is supported by the efforts of caregivers to regulate joint attention during children's first year. If infants appear not to understand a pointing gesture, mothers facilitate babies' comprehension by touching the indicated object (Lempers, 1979). With infants as young as 3 months, mothers attempt to achieve joint reference by introducing an object between themselves and their babies as a target for joint attention, using a characteristic intonation and shaking the object (Bruner, 1983).

Of course, caregivers are also active in maintaining joint attention by following their infants' direction of gaze (Schaffer, 1984). Bakeman and Adamson (1984) suggest that mothers socialize reference to objects, "embedding it within the interpersonal sphere well before infants can structure this integration by themselves" (p. 1288). Indeed, infants are more than four times as likely to engage in joint attention when interacting with their mothers as when interacting with peers (Bakeman & Adamson, 1984). It appears that with adult support, infants' use of social referencing may provide increasingly advanced means of gathering information about their caregivers' interpretation of new situations.

Caregivers may at times intentionally attempt to communicate a particular understanding of a new situation through managing their emotional and nonverbal communication. At a doctor's office, for example, a mother may try to mask her apprehension when her baby is receiving a shot, in order to minimize the baby's reaction. Or parental management of cues may enter into instruction in potentially frightening situations, as suggested in the following advice to parents on teaching 3-week-old babies to swim in the bathtub:

> Your attitude toward water is important. An infant who sees her mother wince in terror every time she floats in deep water is not going to have a very confident picture of the strange situation. Since panic is the single most deadly factor in water, parents should be acutely aware of their responsibility in teaching their child a healthy respect for water. . . . If you show enjoyment of the water, she will imitate your excitement and pleasure. . . . Lift your baby into the water, and rest her on your bent knees, facing you. Dip your hands into the water, and pat your baby's body to help her adjust to the water temperature. Talk and smile constantly throughout the entire session. Gradually lower your knees until the baby is completely submerged in the water, head resting comfortably on your knees, body on your thighs. Take this part slowly, allowing enough time for your baby to become acquainted with the water. (Poe, 1982, pp. 12, 20)

Such intentional communication of how to interpret a situation may be rare. But in a less self-conscious fashion, middle-class adults handling babies as young as 6 weeks of age seem almost inevitably to provide interpretation for the infants' actions, their own actions, and events in the environment

(Harding, 1982; Packer, 1983; Shotter, 1978; Shotter & Newson, 1982; Snow, 1984). For example, a mother may respond to a baby's attempt to push an approaching spoon away with a running commentary such as "You getting full? . . . Oh, you're not done with that bite yet? . . ." Kruper and Uzgiris (1985) found that 12% of parents' utterances to 3-month-olds were interpretations of the babies' actions in terms of feelings, needs, or wishes.

While young infants are unlikely to understand the words addressed to them, they may well interpret the "tune" carrying the message, using intonation contours and timing and emotional tone of an adult's commentary to understand the gist. Preliminary data suggest that infants of 4 or 5 months are attuned to the emotional content of speech intonation; they respond with knit brows and downcast expressions to an overheard voice expressing a warning to another infant, and with coy smiles to an overheard voice praising an infant, even in unfamiliar languages (Fernald, 1988).

Adults sometimes find it difficult not to provide "intuitive" nonverbal cues to help babies interpret a situation. For babies learning to eat from a spoon, adults frequently give supplementary cues about the appropriate action to be taken by the children: they open their own mouths wide at the time babies are to do the same (Valsiner, 1984) and may not be aware that they are doing so. To ensure a happy response to a potentially startling event, adults may make an exaggerated face of surprise and enjoyment—for example, commenting "isn't that funny?" when concerned that a jack-in-the-box might startle a baby, even though the baby shows no sign of being startled (Rogoff, Malkin, & Gilbride, 1984). A caregiver's attempts to influence a child's emotional state may involve bridging from the child's current state and transforming to the desired state, as with mothers observed by Kaye (1979b) who responded to the beginnings of their children's cries by briefly mirroring the children's cry face and then immediately turning to a bright expression.

Such assistance in interpretation may be so habitual that it is difficult to suppress. In recent pilot work, Mosier and I attempted to get mothers to ignore a toy falling off their babies' highchair tray so that the infants would have to ask for their mothers' help to retrieve it. Unless mothers were already looking away before the toy fell, they found it impossible not to acknowledge the event to the infants, making an exaggerated surprise face to the babies before they remembered that they were not supposd to have noticed the toy falling.

This account stresses that in the process of everyday communication, partners share their focus of attention, providing a common ground from which to "comment" on events by means of emotional cues and interests as well as running interpretation of babies' actions and other events. Such joint focus and efforts to share interpretation are likely to be woven into the fabric of interpersonal relations, and seldom to be the focus of explicit attention. In other words, we may skillfully share events with our social partners without having to be aware of these efforts or intending them to be instructional. The ubiquity of sharing of experiences is likely to aid infants in interpreting new events in ways that stretch their understanding and channel it to the viewpoint of those around them.

Words as a Cultural System for Bridging

Beyond the information carried in the emotional tone of communication, the use of specific words in a language system provides children with the meanings and distinctions important in their culture. As Vygotsky (1987) put it, "The word is the most direct manifestation of the historical nature of human consciousness" (p. 285).

Labels categorize objects and events in ways specific to the language of the child's culture. Or they inform babies of the nature of an event and the appropriate reaction, as with a mother who commented when her baby smiled at a visitor's sneeze, "That was funny, wasn't it? Sneezing" (Snow, 1984, p. 77).

Roger Brown (1958) pointed out this function of language learning in his comments about the Original Word Game, in which a child and a mature language user refer to objects, with the child forming hypotheses about the category of objects to which a label refers, and the partner helping the child to improve the fit between the child's hypotheses and the cultural designations of categories encoded by labels: "In learning referents and names the player of the Original Word Game prepares himself to receive the science, the rules of thumb, the prejudices, the total expectancies of his society" (p. 228).

Word learning is an important aspect of children's learning of connections between individual objects, as demonstrated by research showing that provision of a novel label induces 3-year-olds to classify items (Waxman & Gelman, 1986). Of course, language provides far more structure for understanding than simply the labels for classifying objects; the propositions and means of expression used in language structure the user's attention to and understanding of events.

Language development requires social involvement as well as the child's natural propensity to learn language. In this view, the Language Acquisition Device, posited by Chomsky to account for the complexity and speed of young children's understanding of grammar, requires the cooperation of Bruner's Language Acquisition Support System, which frames or structures the input of language and interaction to the child's Language Acquisition Device in a manner to "make the system function" (Bruner, 1983, p. 19). Consistent with this view, Lock (1978) refers to language development as a process of guided reinvention.

Evidence of parental simplification and framing of language is used to support the view that language acquisition rests on social supports (Bruner, 1981, 1983; Edwards, 1978; Hoff-Ginsberg & Shatz, 1982). For example, in the earliest months, the restrictions of parental baby talk to a small number of melodic contours may enable infants to abstract vocal prototypes (Papousek, Papousek, & Bornstein, 1985). The mother of Roger Brown's subject Eve used rich and frequent input, with semantic and linguistic redundancy and contingent instructional relationships between her utterances and those of her child, framing Eve's language development (Moerk, 1983).

Similarly, maternal labeling of objects and explanation of categories may assist children in understanding category hierarchies and learning appropriate labels (Callanan, 1985). Mothers use child-basic level labels for objects (such as referring to a round bank as a ball) in keeping with their infants' usage; then with slightly older children, mothers demonstrate critical distinguishing features of an object as they introduce adult-basic level labels (e.g., by putting a penny in the slot of the round bank and labeling it "bank" [Mervis, 1984]). Such fine-tuning and explanation of labels appear well designed to foster children's conceptual development:

> Children are told that bats are mammals, penguins are birds, and New-foundlands are dogs. In addition, they are *taught* features that can help them avoid assimilating these exemplars to more or equally compelling categories (bats to *bird,* penguins to *sea mammal,* Newfoundlands to *bear*), or features that provide evidence of family membership (e.g., Newfound-lands bark, just like other dogs). But it may be years before children are introduced to the language-game of tracing evolutionary lineages—and it is only then that the distinctions drawn earlier become grounded by primary functional considerations (the scientific need to accurately map the ramifying evolutionary tree). In such cases, the child's early convergence with adult concept/usage must be understood on the model of guided reinvention rather than as autonomous reinvention because data critical for the latter will not be at hand until years after the initial convergence in usage. (Adams & Bullock, 1986, p. 161)

The question of the impact of communication on children's growth in understanding will be taken up in Chapter 8, where we consider research on the relation between guided participation and children's language and conceptual development, as well as skills in object exploration and construction, memory, and planning.

Intersubjectivity

The process of communication, whether verbal or nonverbal, is a social activity that can be regarded as the bridge between one understanding of a situation and another. By its nature, communication presumes intersubjectivity (Newson & Newson, 1975; Riegel, 1979; Rommetveit, 1985; Wertsch, 1979b)—that is, shared understanding based on a common focus of attention and some shared presuppositions that form the ground for communication. Trevarthen (1980) defines intersubjectivity as "both recognition and control of cooperative intentions and joint patterns of awareness" (p. 530). Lomov (1978) argues that the first stage in communication is

> the *determination of common "coordinates"* of joint activity (reference points, reference models). These serve as a basis that, in a certain sense, guides the construction of the entire process of communication and the distribution and coordination of the operations carried out by each member

> of the communicating group. . . . The process of communication produces
> a *common program* and *common strategy* for joint activity. (p. 20)

My earlier references to the bridging between the known and the new in communication presume intersubjectivity. As Vygotsky (1987) points out, intersubjectivity provides the grounds for communication and at the same time supports the extension of children's understanding to new information and activities, as communication of an experience or idea requires relating it to a known class of phenomena, thereby generalizing the phenomenon in order to communicate.

Some modifications in the perspectives of each participant are necessary in order to reach understanding of the other person's perspective. If we focus on the modifications of a novice's perspective, they can be seen as the basis for development; as the novice adjusts to better understand and communicate, the new perspective amounts to greater understanding itself and is the basis for further growth (Isaacs & Clark, 1987; Wertsch, 1984). As such, bridging from the known to the new necessarily involves both initial differences in perspective and attempts to reach a common ground for communication.

An example is provided by a baby of 12½ months who adjusts to take another person's perspective in an effort to share an experience. Perspective taking is central to many accounts of development, especially that of Piaget. Its necessity derives from social interaction, which further promotes it.

> David was enjoying a pacifier he had recently discovered, trying it himself
> and one day offering it to his mother. But he offered it to her backward,
> holding the ring side rather than the nipple toward her mouth. Then he
> turned it around to the correct orientation so the pacifier would go in his
> mother's mouth. After that, he turned it to the correct orientation when-
> ever he offered it to her.

In adult–child communication, middle-class adults often search for common reference points, translating the adult understanding of the situation into a form that is within children's grasp (Rogoff, 1986; Wertsch, 1984). Some of the simplifications provided by adults in interaction with young children may serve to focus children's attention on the crucial aspect of a situation. For example, in directing children to look at an interesting event for common reference, parents may shield children's vision from alternatives by using their hands as blinders beside the children's eyes.

Similarly, middle-class adults may simplify their presentation of an idea even to the extent that the less complex version would not be considered accurate among adults. This simplification may be necessary for communication and may provide children with a familiar enough anchor from which to develop a new idea. Such adjustment of the adult's perspective in the service of communication is apparent in the way adults occasionally misclassify an atypical exemplar of a category in order to avoid confusing toddlers about the basic nature of the category. For example, adults may state that a whale is a fish or that an electric outlet is "hot." Bruner (1983) suggests that the fact that a physicist mother and her 4-year-old are unlikely to have an identical concept of "electricity" does not matter as long as their shared meaning is sufficient to allow their conversation about shocks to continue.

Similarly, in introducing labels for animals, mothers focus on immediate communicative concerns rather than on technical accuracy. Mothers ignore unusual cases until a baseline of shared reference has been established (Adams & Bullock, 1986). To maintain understanding of the message, mothers label penguins "penguins" rather than "birds" until children have established the bird prototype, at which time mothers begin remarking that "penguins are birds." They appear to protect the process of forming prototypes by not distinguishing the specific exemplar birds until children have a well-established set of prototypes and have labels for atypical birds. While these maternal adjustments may be useful for children's concept acquisition, they also reflect adherence to principles of communication (e.g., Clark & Haviland, 1977): that a speaker be sensitive to the perspective and knowledge of the listener, and that conversation focus on what is deserving of comment from the joint perspective of speaker and listener.

This effort to communicate draws the child into a more mature understanding that is linked to what the child already knows. In the process of communicating, adults tie new situations to more familiar ones, drawing connections from the familiar to the novel through their verbal and nonverbal interpretation. When working with toddlers on puzzles, for example, mothers often began by ensuring that their children perceived the overall puzzle in the same way they did (as a truck), by asking the children to identify the overall array and its pieces (Wertsch, 1979b). This establishment of intersubjectivity enabled the mothers to refer to the pieces with terms such as *wheels* and *headlights* that both partners understood and that tied the pieces to the whole.

Just as adults may modify their presentation to allow children to grasp an idea, children are tuned to pick up the interpretation and viewpoint of others. Partners in communication adapt to each other, with their mutual adjustments facilitating interpersonal understanding for the purpose of communication and changing the nature of the understanding that they may bring to other situations.

The work of communication is likely to be asymmetrical between adults and young children. When adults are interested in communicating with children, they may have an easier time than children in knowing how to adjust their communication to meet children's understanding. However, with regard to the changes in understanding embodied in children's cognitive development over the first years of life, the changes in children's understanding appear more impressive than those of adults. Adults may make less crucial changes in their view of a situation as a function of communication with a child; their understanding is usually more sophisticated to begin with, so their adjustments are practical, momentary adaptations to the needs of communication and, sometimes, shifts in understanding the topic or the child. In contrast, shifts in understanding characterize the children's role over the first years of life. Less able to adjust to ensure communication, but more in need of developing understanding (and more willing to change), children stretch to understand the interpretation available in interaction with their caregivers and companions.

How can young children share meaning with others? Questions of the origins and developmental course of intersubjectivity are important to the definition of intersubjectivity and to views of young children's roles in guided participation.

Origins of Intersubjectivity

There is general agreement among those who study the development of mutual adjustment and meaning-making between parents and children that early childhood involves transformations in the nature of the sharing of meaning between partners. But there is disagreement about the origins of intersubjectivity—whether infants are born equipped to share meaning with social partners or whether meaning is initially provided by parents' interpretation of infants' random or independent rhythmic actions and this parental structuring is responsible for organizing infants' later communication (Schaffer, 1977b).

Some scholars argue that intersubjectivity between human infants and others is innate, that from the earliest interactions infants are involved socially in the sharing of meaning (Brazelton, 1983; Luria, 1987; Newson, 1977; Trevarthen, Hubley, & Sheeran, 1975). In this view, the infant's contribution changes with development, as does the nature of the shared meaning, but the infant is a social being from the start.

Other scholars suggest instead that adults act *as if* human infants were achieving some form of communication (e.g., Kaye, 1982). They argue that adults ascribe meaning to infants' facial expressions, hand movements, and gaze patterns, and insert social meaning into the autonomous patterning of infant behavior. Such social interpretation and action by caregivers are presumed to assist babies in adding meaning to their initially random or nonsocial actions. Kaye and Charney (1980) state, "The infant's rhythms provide a structure to which parents can respond—indeed, cannot help responding—and in so responding the parents create a semblance of a dialogue involving the infant at a level well beyond his actual capabilities for intentional discourse" (p. 228).

Kaye (1979b) proposes that dialogue begins with the mother trying to fit in to the infant's more or less autonomous patterns of behavior—as in mothers' conversational turns fitting the timing of bursts and pauses in neonatal nursing sequences—and only later moves to mutual contingency in interactional "games," such as peekaboo, and face-to-face interaction. Kaye proposes that development proceeds in cycles involving a search for regularity (initially from mothers fitting their moves to infants' autonomous rhythms), then mutual contingency, and then on to variation leading to new irregularities—continuing to elevate the dialogue to more sophisticated levels with each advance from the initial adult-structured turn taking to contingent games and beyond.

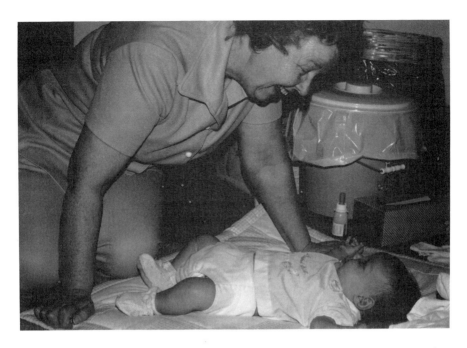

Figure 4.1　Grandmother and 12-week-old baby "chatting" during face-to-face interaction. (United States) (Photograph © B. Rogoff)

In contrast, scholars arguing for innate intersubjectivity assert that from birth infants engage with their social partners with mutual contingency. Trevarthen presents evidence from an ingenious study that examined the effect of uncoupling the communication between mothers and their 6- to 12-week-old infants, who interacted over a double video setup with cameras trained on each partner and monitors presenting each to the other (Murray & Trevarthen, 1985). When the babies were in live interaction with their mothers over the video equipment, they appeared responsive, making eye contact, moving their mouths, and gesturing as in normal interaction. But when the "exchange" was really a replay of the mothers' role in the former mother–infant interaction, the babies turned away from their mothers' image and more frequently showed signs of distress. Even when they looked at the image, they seldom showed communicative effort; they appeared detached, puzzled, and confused at the absence of synchrony. Murray and Trevarthen (1985) interpret these results as showing that infants as young as 6 to 12 weeks are able to detect features of their partner's behavior involved with interactional synchrony, and respond with "coordinated structures of interpersonal and emotional value . . . [regulating] their own expressions in appropriate, complementary response patterns that can be perceived by the mother as particular emotions. This close coordination of behavior between mother and infant requires a circle of emotional communication" (p. 192).

Other observations also suggest that face-to-face interaction between mothers and infants is structured in turns that resemble the give-and-take of adult dialogue in some respects, with contributions to the structure by both partners even in the first months of the baby's life (Beebe, Jaffe, Feldstein, Mays, & Alson, 1985; Tronick, 1982). Consistent with these observations are suggestions that newborns (like adults) move in synchrony with the speech of others (Condon, 1977) more than with sounds from inanimate sources, with a responsive sensitivity to the human voice.

What is at issue is whether babies' actions and their turns in interchanges are truly social. Underlying this question are different definitions of "truly social." Does a person's turn have to be intentional, with some awareness of its impact on the partner, in order to consider it social? Must an organism demonstrate reflective subjectivity in order to participate in intersubjectivity? Clearly, a person's turn cannot be social if the person has the same pattern of moves when in isolation. But if children are involved with their partners in interchanges that facilitate shared meaning, it may be unnecessary to require the little tykes to have planned it all out in advance or to reflect on it.

Although Kaye and Charney (1980) see the baby as a participant in ongoing discourse, on topics often chosen according to the baby's interests, they distinguish this early participation from being a social agent with understanding: "His meanings are interpreted, expressed, and expatiated upon before he even knows what meaning is" (p. 228).

How can we determine understanding of meaning? I argue that participation in flexible interaction with a variety of structured strategies to fit a situation is evidence at least of participating in meaning. We should not require babies to be able to explain themselves reflectively in order to credit them with participating in meaningful exchanges, for that confounds reflection and action.

Babies' repertoires of action are complex and structured, with active efforts to seek and interpret information and with organized movements that resemble the gestures and emotions of more mature people, as demonstrated in extensive research on infants in the past two decades. Infants' caregivers find information—cues to guide their caregiving and interaction—in the timing and nature of babies' vocalizations, varying cries, postural and gaze cues, facial expressions, hand and foot movements, and body tension. Do babies *mean* to communicate with these cues?

(For that matter, when adults communicate, are they invariably *intending* their communication? We may be limited here by an assumption that adult communication is conscious, intentional, planned; but for the most part, adult communication may also take place in a deliberate fashion that is neither accidental nor at the top of consciousness.)

A baby in a particular situation may not arch her back purposefully to tell an intrusive adult to leave her alone, although she is likely to have escalated to this cue from more subtle ones, such as avoiding eye contact and knitting her brow, with some flexibility in choice of next move. A baby of 4 months may not ask himself, "Wonder what mama's looking at," when he turns to follow a change in the direction of her gaze. But as a class, babies may be well equipped with a variety of cues that are used flexibly in interaction to achieve meaningful exchanges in the service of social goals.

Rheingold (1969) argues that even the youngest babies direct adults to fulfill their goals, socializing their caregivers and teaching them—through the power of the cry and the rewards of smiles and vocalization—what the infants need to have them do: "From his behavior they learn what he wants and what he will accept, what produces in him a state of well-being and good nature, and what will keep him from whining" (p. 786).

With skilled partners—people experienced with babies and, especially, with the individual baby—babies' cues work effectively. Infants seem to use whatever means are at their disposal to communicate their needs, as do adults to figure out what babies need and to communicate. The misreading of infants' cues by people unfamiliar with babies requires babies to work harder to "make their point," changing strategies until either communication occurs or things fall apart and more experienced people intervene on the babies' behalf.

The assumption that babies do *not* mean what they do is as big an inference as the assumption that babies are prepared to engage in meaningful exchanges with social partners. If we assume that babies start out without meaning what they do, and hence without involvement in shared meaning— which they attain only later, through interaction with others—we have to explain how the little ones go from the absence of some form of communication to its presence. This is a more difficult transition to explain than the alternative: that infants are prepared to seek and share meaning in a rudimentary and nonreflective fashion that transforms over development to more sophisticated forms.

The idea that young babies are ready to interact with and attend to others seems less surprising when we remember that many other newborn mammals are able to establish what seems to be intersubjectivity (in terms of eye contact and mutual involvement) within a much shorter time after birth than are humans. Harlow (1963) notes that from the first days of life, baby monkeys are alert to and follow their mothers, looking in the same direction she looks if she looks at an object, moving to where she moves, manipulating objects after she does, and attempting to eat the same type of food she eats.

Perhaps what needs explaining is why human newborns are *less* skilled in social exchange than the newborns of many other species, rather than the fact that they make rudimentary social moves. One would suppose that the developmental immaturity of humans may serve the eventual extension of human abilities—especially the capacity to communicate through complex and flexible forms of language—beyond those of other animals. The immaturity may relate to the flexibility of the human neonate to learn the language and accompanying forms of communication, as well as other human practices, of any community in which it is raised.

If we assume that humans come equipped with the propensity and skills to establish some form of intersubjectivity, we need not explain the development of something from nothing. However, we still must distinguish the transformations of intersubjectivity across development. Clearly, the intersubjectivity between newborn and parent is of quite a different nature from that between the same partners just 2 years later.

Developmental Changes in Intersubjectivity

Developmental changes in intersubjectivity have to do with the topic on which meaning is shared, ranging from shared emotional state to sophisticated discourse. Intersubjectivity in early infancy involves shared emotions and mutual engagement; reference to events and objects separate from the interacting partners appears in later infancy.

Trevarthen has distinguished primary and secondary intersubjectivity in infancy on the basis of whether infants and caregivers establish a joint focus of attention that includes only the people involved (primary intersubjectivity, occurring in the first months of infancy) or incorporate other events or objects in the shared focus of the people involved (secondary intersubjectivity, appearing at about 9 months). In secondary intersubjectivity, "a deliberately sought sharing of experience about events and things is achieved for the first time" (Trevarthen & Hubley, 1978, p. 184).

With the availability of formal language come possibilities for shared meaning in regard to events and objects that are not present, and with increases in children's knowledge and perspective come engagement that is less closely supported by their partners and more tuned to the skills and understandings of their society. It is an amazing transformation from the engagement of infants and their caregivers on topics of bodily comfort or interesting ongoing events to the engagement of 4-year-olds and their companions on topics of the origins of life or intentionality.

Across childhood, intersubjectivity may also shift in the symmetry with which each partner supports the other's choice of topic and comment for shared understanding, at least in cultures where adults seek interaction with babies at times. (Later discussion will stress that where adults are not actively attempting to communicate with young children, the children's role in attending to or participating in adult activities may be more apparent.)

Although both adults and infants can be active in seeking intersubjectivity, differences in communication skill and in general knowledge may make it easier for adults to adjust their attention to the interests and level of understanding of children to achieve mutual comprehension. Under conditions in which partners want to change one another's focus to match their own, it appears that adults have the advantage of strategies for inserting their own agenda into infants' current interests. But infants' cries and smiles are unequalled as forms of communication for recruiting adult attention and efforts to understand.

To get infants to attend to something—that is, to change infants' agenda to fit with their own—middle-class adults frequently build on children's perspectives by focusing on the events or objects to which children are attending. Adults insert their interaction into the ongoing activity of an infant, waiting for the infant to be in the appropriate state and providing verbal and nonverbal commentary on the object or event on which the baby is already focused (Kaye, 1982; Schaffer, 1984). Mothers fit their attempts to get toddlers to do specific tasks requested by an experimenter into the children's ongoing behavior (Schaffer, Hepburn, & Collis, 1983).

Hubley and Trevarthen (1979) noted that although mothers initiated most of the communicative sequences when teaching their 9- to 12-month-old daughters how to put an object together (usually by attracting the infants to the mothers' interests), after 10½ months babies chose new topics in one-third of the 15 to 30% of the interactions they started. In addition to increasing their role in initiating interaction, infants were primarily responsible for terminating interaction through their change of interests.

Some of these effects may be limited to the situation in which the infants were the center of attention for the researchers and mothers; when mothers are engaged in their own activities, it is likely that there is less joint attention and that infants may attend more to mothers' activities and focus of attention than the other way around. Toddlers who were observed in their natural activities at home spent approximately 55% of the time focusing attention on another person; the interaction noted during 44% of the observations was almost always initiated by the toddlers (Carew, 1980). These findings support the suggestion that the balance of children's versus adults' responsibility for focusing on another person's activity and engaging that person in interaction may differ in busy home situations from the experimental situations that researchers have studied.

Consistent with the speculation that children may play a greater role in managing the focus of joint attention when adults do not feel responsible for managing interaction, Bretherton and Bates (1979) found that mothers of 2- to 4-year-olds initiated topics in a joint drawing task, while the children initiated topics in a free play situation.

While adults bridge infants' understanding through recruiting the infants' attention and working from the infants' topic of attention, infants also attend actively to adults' focus of attention and recruit adults' attention to their own agendas when they are uncomfortable or bored or when they have something to communicate. An example of a young infant managing an adult's attention is provided by a 6-month-old who was sitting in a highchair, facing an adult who was inexperienced with babies but who had been asked to interact with the baby for the sake of a study I was doing:

> The adult began by trying to get the baby's attention, calling the baby's name in a loud and friendly manner as he shifted his face back and forth in front of the baby and leaned into the baby's line of gaze. The baby avoided the adult's line of gaze, and sat gazing fixedly into space to one side, where there was nothing obvious to attract his attention (Figure 4.2a). The adult stopped calling the baby's name and trying to move into the baby's line of gaze and, instead, looked over toward whatever the baby was looking at and asked softly, "What are you looking at?" (Figure 4.2b).

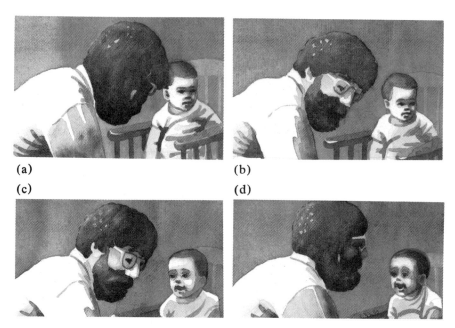

(a)   (b)

(c)   (d)

Figure 4.2 This sequence shows the episode described in the text involving a 6-month-old who is managing an unrelated adult's attention. (United States)

> Immediately after the adult's shift to share the baby's focus of attention, the baby sat up, looked directly at the adult, and smiled, ready to interact (Figure 4.2c). Then the adult turned back to meet the baby's inviting gaze, and the interaction continued with pleasure (Figure 4.2d).

In a study of developmental changes in intersubjectivity and guided participation, we observed 2 babies from 4 to 17 months of age as they interacted with 26 adults at approximately 2-week intervals (Rogoff et al., 1984). The adults were instructed to try to get the baby to talk and smile and play with toys as the baby sat in a highchair; we focused on their interactions around a jack-in-the-box.

When the babies were 4 to 6 months old, the interactions involved attempts to maintain the baby's attention to the adult and the ongoing activity through subtle negotiations. Both partners contributed to the management and focus of joint attention. The baby maintained eye contact, smiled, and cooperated with the adult as long as the adult meshed his or her agenda with the baby's interests and was sensitive to the baby's cues. If the adult missed the baby's cues, the baby escalated from listlessness to averting the gaze, to leaning away, and, finally, to turning the whole body away and hiding the face in the forearms. The adult's moves were contingent on the baby's involvement, with attempts to maintain joint attention through eye contact, verbal or nonverbal emphasis of events, and control of access to objects. This mutual adjustment was challenging, as noted by one adult regarding the difficulty of maintaining the baby's focus on the jack-in-the-box at this age: "You don't happen to look at the right time at the right thing, do you?"

When the babies were 6 to 7 months old, they and the adults slipped into joint attention to events with an ease that allowed the beginning of cooperative action with the jack-in-the-box, and when the babies were 9 months, the negotiations between partners focused on what game was being played according to what script, with the joint focus of attention taken for granted. The shift in focus from maintenance of joint attention to maintenance of joint involvement with the toy began at about 5½ months and became increasingly evident, as the partners negotiated the baby's involvement in winding the handle and closing the box. After 5½ months, the adult and baby jointly worked the jack-in-the-box during most interactions, but such sharing of activity with the toy never occurred before this age. By the time the babies were 12 months, the interactions were characterized by considerable meshing of details regarding how the partners would handle the toy, with scripts for each partner's role developing over the course of repeated episodes with the toy.

About the beginning of the second year, the focus of the interaction appeared to shift again. While interactions at 4 months focused on maintaining joint attention and those between 5½ months and 12 months focused on managing joint use of the toy, interactions early in the baby's second year began to emphasize the interpersonal involvement of the participants in their joint activity. The interactions showed an ease of communication that focused on managing the interaction as well as the manipulation of the toy. Before, the babies focused on the toy and used the adult as a tool in handling it. Now the adult collaborators became interesting in themselves, not just as tools.

This was most apparent in the advent of the babies' commentaries on the joint activity, with "discussion" of events through facial expression, gestures, and jabbering with meaningful intonation at points of interest. For example, as a 17-month-old and an adult coordinated turning the handle with ease and enjoyment, the baby looked up at the adult in anticipation of the popping of the jack-in-the-box, as though to see whether the adult was also anticipating this event; after the figure jumped up, the baby uttered joyful babbled phrases as though commenting on its emergence.

In addition, the newly developing skill in using symbolic means of communication (verbal and gestural), along with greater persistence, allowed for extended and focused exchanges between partners. An example of sophisticated and persistent communication occurred between an adult and a 14½-month-old who collaborated in an extensive series of clarifications in regard to which toy the baby wanted to handle:

> At the beginning of the session, the adult began looking for a toy in the toy box. When he touched the tower of rings, the baby exclaimed, "Aa!" The adult asked, "Aa?," picking up the tower. The baby continued looking at the tox box, ignoring the tower, so the adult showed the baby the tower and again asked, "Aa?" The baby pointed at something in the toy box, grunting, "Aa . . . aa. . . ." The adult reached toward the toy box again,

and the baby exclaimed, "Tue!" The adult exclaimed "Aa!" as he picked up the peekaboo cloth and showed it to the baby. But the baby ignored the cloth and pointed again at something in the toy box, then impatiently waved his arm. The adult exclaimed, "Aa!" and picked up the box of blocks. Offering it to the baby, the adult asked, "Aa?" But the baby pointed down to the side of the toy box. The adult discarded the blocks in the indicated spot. Then they repeated the cycle with another toy. The baby waved his arm impatiently, and the adult commented, "You show me!" and lifted the baby to his lap from the high chair. When the adult picked up the jack-in-the-box, asking "This?" the baby opened his hand toward the toy, and they began to play. (Rogoff et al., 1984, pp. 42–43)

During infancy, the basis for elaborating intersubjectivity may result from infants' maturing attentional and action skills and from adults' sensitivity in tailoring their contribution within the stream of events where it is most likely to fit infants' attention and understanding. Both partners are often active in building a shared focus of attention and acting within that focus, managing each other with whatever means they can muster. (In later chapters, I discuss individual and cultural variation in caregivers' support.) Increasingly, the infant's focus includes communication about objects and events separate from the dyad, and then appreciation for managing the communication itself.

The question of very young infants' intentions in social interaction—which some would hold as a criterion of being "truly social"—is not easily answered (nor is it simple for adult interactions, for that matter). To answer the question of intentionality would require a definition of intentionality and consciousness—a problem that has baffled philosophers and researchers for many years. But, I am arguing, it is not necessary for very young babies to *intend* to communicate in order for them to actually communicate.

Rather than determining the extent of infants' consciousness in their communication, I think it is more fruitful to examine their deliberateness or instrumentality, which can be inferred from flexible efforts to apply a variety of means to approach a goal. Such deliberateness need not be a criterion for active social engagement, or communication, but marks a level of persistent and flexible orientation toward a goal that provides an important advance over the more limited communication that precedes it.

Thus I see deliberateness as developing over infancy, one of the transformations of the intersubjectivity that exists from the start. In a study of the development of infants' instrumental interaction with adults, Rogoff, Mistry, Radziszewska, and Germond (in press) observed that the goal-directed, deliberate nature of two infants' attempts to use adults to assist them in reaching goals began at about 6 months and was more reliable by age 8 or 9 months.

Thus we have a picture of developmental change in intersubjectivity from early sharing of emotional states and mutual engagement to shared focus on external events and objects, accompanied by a shift in the deliberateness of infants' contributions. These shifts occur within the first year, with impressive potential for shared meaning already at this young age, even before the first words.

An example of how infants actively interpret and participate in the definition of a situation and in the direction an activity takes is provided by a 10-month-old who tested her understanding of an adult's intentions when he made some surprising moves, demonstrating her active involvement in a joke. The joke began after the adult invitingly tapped a ring halfway up a reclining tower of rings, suggesting to the baby to remove this ring, as she had removed two before:

> The baby looked up at the adult inquisitively as he sat quietly smiling and focusing on the tower of rings (Figure 4.3a). The baby looked again at the ring, then batted it toward the top of the tower. But the adult playfully tapped the third ring back *down* the tower. The baby hesitated, looking at her batting hand held against the ring (Figure 4.3b). Then she lifted her batting hand to strike, and the adult again tapped the ring back down the tower. The baby smiled, holding her batting hand against the third ring, keeping the ring from moving back down the tower (Figure 4.3c). The adult tapped the ring down several more times. The baby's smile broadened as she understood the joke.
>
> When the baby finally batted the ring off the end of the tower triumphantly, the adult immediately repeated the game, insistently tapping the next ring so that it bumped against the baby's resting batting hand. The baby absently moved her batting hand out of the way, but the adult continued tapping the ring against the baby's batting hand, gently but insistently. The baby looked at it, then inquisitively looked up at the adult, who was still smiling and focusing on the tower of rings. The baby lifted her previously inert batting hand and, with a broad smile, in one confident sweep pushed the ring off the tower.

The baby seemed to understand the adult's intentions and game script, actively examining multiple cues in the adult's gaze, expression, and timing. Neither the adult's foiling of her attempt to remove the ring nor his small focused smile made sense separately. But together, they allowed the communication of a joke, and subsequently the baby checked the adult's facial expression upon the slightest irregularity in his play to determine his intent (Figure 4.3d). Thus her sensitive interpretation and seeking cues made it possible for her to share in creating the subtle meaning of this interaction.

Significantly, the game ended on the baby's instigation. Instead of removing a ring from the tower as the adult offered it, the baby looked away and impatiently banged her hand against the tray:

> "Look at this one," insisted the adult, tapping a ring on the tower. The baby turned her head still further away. The adult understood the signal and put the other rings back on the tower, saying "too many, too many." As soon as he terminated the game, the baby raised her head again and watched him return the rings to the tower.

Thus it is clear that the baby was actively involved in the direction of the activity.

(a)

(b)

(c)

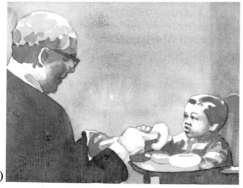

(d)

The idea that infants can enter into intersubjective engagement with others from the earliest months does not mean that they are equal partners, even in the middle-class families that have served as the focus of the research discussed in this chapter. Infants may hold the trump card, in that they are the ones who determine the direction of their attention and whether or not they cooperate, and they are able to disrupt their parents' activities in ways most parents would not consider using with another person. However, adults usually have advantages in adjusting their contributions to social interaction to ensure that information is presented in a way that secures the child's attention and fits the child's understanding.

Figure 4.3 This sequence shows the episode described in the text involving a 10-month-old who is interpreting and sharing a joke with an unrelated adult. (United States)

5

Structuring Situations
and Transferring Responsibility

> Watch a mother with her one-year-old sitting on her knee in front of a
> collection of toys: a large part of her time is devoted to such quietly
> facilitative and scene-setting activities as holding a toy that seems to re-
> quire three hands to manipulate, retrieving things that have been pushed
> out of range, clearing away those things that are not at present being used
> in order to provide the child with a sharper focus for this main activity,
> putting things next to each other that she knows the child will enjoy com-
> bining (such as nesting beakers), turning toys so that they become more
> easily grasped, demonstrating their less obvious properties, and all along
> moulding her body in such a way as to provide maximal physical support
> and access to the play material. (Schaffer, *Mothering*)

> A 4-year-old to her mother, working in the kitchen: "Can I help you with
> the can opener by holding onto your hand while you do it? . . . That's
> how I learn."

Caregivers and children arrange for socializing experiences through choice of
situations and arrangements for structuring them, at a distance as well as in
explicit social interaction. Both caregivers and children are responsible for
determining children's activities and roles, through tacit and pragmatic adjustment to children's skills and interests, as well as through more explicit
arrangements for children's growing participation in the activities of their
culture.

During explicit interaction, adults and children collaborate in structuring
children's roles by dividing the responsibility for activities, with caregivers
supporting and extending children's skills and subdividing tasks into manageable subgoals for children, and children guiding or even managing the caregivers' efforts. The structure to support children's learning and participation
evolves as children gain skills that allow them to assume increasing responsibility. This transfer of responsibility is jointly achieved by adults and children.

This chapter first discusses caregivers' and children's roles in the distal arrangement of children's activities—determining the activities in which children participate as well as the level of responsibility that children assume, outside of explicit interaction. Then the chapter turns to the structuring of caregivers' support and children's responsibility in face-to-face social interaction. Finally, we consider the processes by which caregivers and children transform the structure of support and transfer responsibility as children gain in skill and understanding.

Choosing and Structuring Children's Activities

Perhaps the greatest influence of the social world is the determination of which activities are available to children for observation and participation and who are their daily companions. Such choice of the scenario and cast of characters in children's lives constitutes a superordinate level of guided participation. The actual interactions between children and their caregivers and peers are nested within the constraints of the available activities and companions.

Societal structure and arrangements determine many aspects of the scenario and cast of characters, such as whether formal schooling is available or required, whether mothers' and fathers' work is distant from home or otherwise inaccessible to children, whether adult work requires strength or specialized knowledge unavailable to children, the extent to which gender roles prescribe separation of boys and girls, and whether and how infants are "cached" or carried.

Within such societal constraints on the activities and companions of children, caregivers have the power to determine children's activities and partners, assigning children tasks or restricting their mobility. At the same time, the children themselves play an active role in choosing the activities in which they are involved and with whom.

Although, for purposes of discussion, this chapter separates the roles of caregivers and of children in managing the arrangements of children's lives, the actual determination of the arrangements is mutual. A focus on either actor must be accompanied by the recognition that the other is also active and that the decisions and actions of each are made in the context of the other's decisions and actions. In the following discussion, as elsewhere in this book, we focus at different times on the roles of caregivers and the roles of children, not as separate influences but as actors whose roles *with regard to each other* are of interest.

Caregivers' Choice of Children's Activities and Roles

Caregivers frequently make arrangements for children, selecting activities and materials they consider appropriate for children of a particular age or interest level (Laboratory of Comparative Human Cognition, 1983; Valsiner, 1984). Such choices are frequently made without the intention of providing a specific learning experience, but at times may be designed explicitly for the socializa-

tion or education of the child. Whiting (1980) cogently points out the importance of parents and other caregivers in arranging children's learning environments:

> The power of parents and other agents of socialization is in their assign-
> ment of children to specific settings. Whether it is caring for an infant
> sibling, working around the house in the company of adult females, work-
> ing on the farm with adults and siblings, playing outside with neighbor-
> hood children, hunting with adult males, or attending school with age
> mates, the daily assignment of a child to one or another of these settings
> has important consequences on the development of habits of interpersonal
> behavior, consequences that may not be recognized by the socializers who
> make the assignments. (p. 111)

By making such choices and adjusting tasks and materials to children's
interests and skills, caregivers tacitly guide children's development. Parents
and other caregivers determine the activities in which children's participation
is allowed or discouraged, such as engaging in work, recreation, and sacred
activities of the community. They arrange the social environment to promote
or avoid certain relationships by assigning child care to a sibling or grandparent or baby sitter or day-care center and by encouraging or discouraging
particular playmates.

Parents' choices also determine what activities and materials are available
for children to observe. Children may or may not have opportunities to observe television, the birth of a sibling, or the death of a grandparent. Whether
children accompany parents in their work or are left in a specialized child-
care setting leads to very different opportunities for learning the skills of
adults. Whatever practices children observe their parents carrying out and
whatever goals children see their parents striving for have special significance
for children. Hence the common advice to parents concerned about how they
can help their children learn to read: if they see that you read, they will at-
tach importance to it, and that valuation will motivate their development as
readers. A telling example is available from Sartre's (1964) reminiscences:

> I began my life as I shall no doubt end it: amidst books. In my grand-
> father's study there were books everywhere. . . . Though I did not yet
> know how to read, I already revered those standing stones: upright or
> leaning over. I felt that our family's prosperity depended on them. . . . I
> disported myself in a tiny sanctuary, surrounded by ancient, heavy-set
> monuments which had seen me into the world, which would see me out of
> it, and whose permanence guaranteed me a future as calm as the past. I
> would touch them secretly to honor my hands with their dust, but I did not
> quite know what to do with them, and I was a daily witness of ceremonies
> whose meaning escaped me: my grandfather . . . handled those cultural
> objects with the dexterity of an officiant. (pp. 40–41)

It is interesting to consider how different Sartre's contributions might have
been if his family had been devoted to art or sport or music or politics instead
of literary activity!

(a)

(b)

Figure 5.1 These infants have been placed in devices that their parents believe encourage motor development. (a) The American baby is in a rolling walker propelled by her feet (sometimes down stairs). (b) The Mayan baby in Guatemala is in a walking pen made of cornstalks; his father offers a tidbit to encourage him to walk back and forth. (Photographs © B. Rogoff)

Beyond the models available to children observing their parents' activities, the role of parents includes arrangements of the material environment of children. They provide specialized objects that they believe assist children in achieving developmental milestones, such as the varying forms of baby walkers used around the world to help infants practice walking—ranging from wheeled vehicles to cornstalk railings to siblings assigned to "walk" the baby.

Parents designate some objects as appropriate for children, according to cultural lore and the recommendations of experts. Examples include baby-proofing houses and providing age-graded toys. Middle-class children of different ages are presented with books adjusted to their interests and skills: cardboard or plastic picture books for the smallest ones, who do not yet know how to respect the printed page; paper picture books with a few words for those whose language skills are not yet up to following a story; books with pictures and text for children whose budding comprehension of and interest in literacy needs pictorial support; and eventually books with pure text.

An analogous (although perhaps more deliberate) gradation of learning environments is apparent in ski coaches' arrangements for novice skiers. They adjust the length of the novices' skis and choose the type of terrain that will provide practice at an appropriate level—a hill with the optimal amount of slope, irregularity, and upturn at the bottom to help the novice stop (Burton, Brown, & Fischer, 1984).

Similarly, the "curriculum" of apprenticeship for Vai (Liberian) tailors involves steps for approaching the overall body of tailoring skill and knowledge: apprentice tailors begin by producing garments that are simple and informal, learning how to first sew and then cut each garment:

> Production steps are reversed [in learning processes], as apprentices begin by learning the finishing stages of producing a garment, go on to learn to sew it, and only later learn to cut it out. This pattern regularly subdivides the learning process for each new type of garment. Reversing production steps has the effect of focusing the apprentices' attention first on the broad outlines of garment construction as they handle garments while attaching buttons and hemming cuffs. Next, sewing turns their attention to the logic (order, orientation) by which different pieces are sewn together, which in turn explains why they are cut out as they are. Each step offers the unstated opportunity to consider how the previous step contributes to the present one. In addition, this ordering minimizes experiences of failure and especially of serious failure (errors in sewing may be reversed, those made while cutting out are more often irrevocable). . . . An apprentice watches masters and advanced apprentices until he thinks he understands how to sew (or cut out) a garment, until the shop is closed and the masters have gone home to try making it. (Lave, 1988, p. 4)

Hence the structuring of tasks in the relationship between master and apprentices provides the opportunity for the alert apprentice to observe the next step while participating in production steps already under control. Lave's account stresses the active role of the apprentice in learning in practice, participating as a peripheral and legitimate contributor to production. This account of adult apprenticeship is consistent with my emphasis on children's guided participation as apprenticeship in thinking—children's active learning in the context of sociocultural activity, with the guidance of more skilled partners.

Children's Choice of Activities and Roles

Children are very active in choosing their own activities and companions, directing themselves and their caregivers toward desirable and away from undesirable activities. Children refuse to engage in some activities and insist on others. If free to navigate in their own community, they often choose to be where the action is. An example is a child of 3 years from a Mayan community in Guatemala who was more interested in church than was the rest of her family; every evening, she put her shawl over her head and went to services at a church four blocks from her home, returning about 2 hours later.

Children's success in determining their own activities relies, of course, on the supportiveness or willingness of others to allow their choice of activities. But it is similarly the case that caregivers' choices of children's activities require some cooperation from the children. For the most part, children comply with the assignment of activities and the companions chosen by caregivers, and caregivers permit choice by children, within the limits of practical possibilities (e.g., economic, time, and comfort considerations). However, it is worth recognizing that not all parent–child relationships are characterized by such cooperation. Indeed, as I discuss later, hesitance and resistance by children and by caregivers play crucial roles in the adjustment of children's involvement, and there are important cultural and individual variations in who adapts to whom and in adults' support for children's learning.

Children's attempts to communicate desire for involvement in specific activities begin during the last half of the first year of life. Middle-class infants as young as 6 months, and more consistently by 9 months, attempt to influence adults to initiate or carry on activities or to provide access to specific objects (Bretherton, McNew, & Beeghly-Smith, 1981; Rogoff, Malkin, & Gilbride, 1984; Rogoff, Mistry, Radziszewska, & Germond, in press; Sugarman-Bell, 1978).

An example of a baby's insistence on her definition of a situation is provided by a 6½-month-old who used eye contact to attempt to maintain possession of a plastic "donut" ring (which she was mouthing contentedly [Figure 5.2a]) when an adult tried to institute a game of give-and-take:

> When the adult tried to take the ring, the baby firmly held onto it and looked away. When the adult forcibly removed the ring from the baby's grasp, the baby stared at him with a look of indignation, and then, with her eyes fixed on him, her face melted into a pout (Figure 5.2b). The adult immediately exclaimed, "Oh, don't cry, I'll give it back to you!" and extended the ring to the baby, who was by then shrieking.
>
> Despite repeated efforts by the adult to return the ring, the baby refused to attend to him or to take the ring. Some time later, after they played with other toys (but without the baby reinstating eye contact), the

(a)

(b)

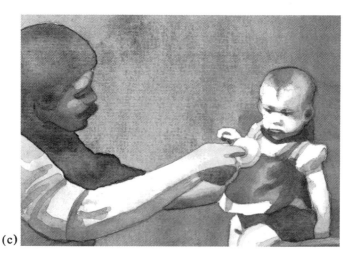

(c)

adult again offered the ring to the baby (Figure 5.2c). She pushed it away, but accepted it when the adult placed it in her hand. The adult tried four more times to play give-and-take, but each time he took the ring away and handed it back, the baby turned away or looked down, apparently displeased, but eventually grasped the ring when it came in contact with her hand. Finally, the baby pushed the adult's hand away from the ring, and the adult left the ring in the baby's possession. Throughout this interaction, the baby seemed to come to understand the adult's give-and-take game script, but to continue to show a distinct preference not to play it.

Structuring Responsibility in Joint Problem Solving

The previous section argued that a major influence on children's opportunities for learning is the distal arrangement of the scenario and cast of characters of the daily life that children observe and in which they participate. We now turn to the social interaction of children and their caregivers, as caregivers support children's efforts to participate in the cognitive activities of daily life, and children guide them in doing so as well as manage their interaction to get the assistance they need. The research has focused primarily on adult–child interaction in middle-class families; I consider the role of variation in caregivers' support shortly.

Adults' Support of Children's Learning

In addition to arranging and structuring learning activities by providing access to and regulating the difficulty of tasks, adults structure children's involvement in learning situations through joint participation. Adult involvement can motivate children toward a goal and focus their attention (Heckhausen, 1984).

In giving direct assistance, adults can handle difficult aspects of a task and organize children's involvement with features of the activity that are within their grasp. Wertsch (1978) points out that such joint problem solving is characterized by adults orienting children to the overall goal from the adult perspective and focusing the children's attention and actions on the steps required to handle subgoals of the problem. Adults thus take responsibility for managing and segmenting the problem-solving effort.

In engaging children in an appropriate handling of a task, adults create supported situations in which children can extend current skills and knowledge to a higher level of competence (Wood, in press; Wood & Middleton, 1975). Wood, Bruner, and Ross (1976) describe six functions of the tutor in such "scaffolding" of a child's performance:

Figure 5.2   This sequence shows the episode described in the text involving a 6½-month-old who is insisting on her definition of a situation in interaction with an unrelated adult. (United States)

1. Recruiting the child's interest in the task as it is defined by the tutor.
2. Reducing the number of steps required to solve a problem by simplifying the task, so that the learner can manage components of the process and recognize when a fit with task requirements is achieved.
3. Maintaining the pursuit of the goal, through motivation of the child and direction of the activity.
4. Marking critical features of discrepancies between what a child has produced and the ideal solution.
5. Controlling frustration and risk in problem solving.
6. Demonstrating an idealized version of the act to be performed.

Note that while the scaffold metaphor could imply a rigid structure or one that does not involve the child, most users of the term include notions of continual revisions of scaffolding to respond to children's advancements. Bruner (1983) characterizes scaffolding in language development as the adult acting on the motto "where before there was a spectator, let there now be a participant" (p. 60).

An example of adult support is the way adults structure children's developing narration skills by asking appropriate questions to organize the children's stories or accounts (Eisenberg, 1985; McNamee, 1980). If the child stops short or leaves out crucial information, the adult prompts, "What happened next?" or "Who else was there?" Such questions implicitly provide children with cues that may structure their developing narration skills. Adults' questions provide an outline for narratives. Mothers who rephrase and elaborate their memory questions to 2½-year-old children apparently provide more effective assistance than mothers who simply repeat a question that the child has not answered (Fivush & Fromhoff, 1988). Building on Bruner's perspective, McNamee suggests that "if story schemas exist for young children, they hover in the air between adults and children as they converse" (p. 6).

Such facilitation by adults provides structure as well as support. Adults may give children "metacognitive" support by structuring tasks in ways that are beyond children's skills: determining the problem to be solved, the goal, and the way the goal can be broken down into manageable subgoals. For example, the joint cleanup of a toddler's room may require the adult (even with a cooperative toddler) to define the goal of cleaning up the room; to divide the task into subgoals, such as picking up dirty clothes and putting toys in their proper places; and to determine the specifics of each subgoal (e.g., "can you find all the blocks and put them in the box?").

Structuring a problem in guided participation may involve caregivers providing children with the chance to participate in a meaningful subgoal of an activity that embodies the processes of the activity as a whole. Structuring does not focus on breaking a task into minutely ordered steps to be mastered in a lockstep fashion. Rather, effective structuring—in my view—maintains children's involvement with the purpose of the activity, integrating varying aspects of the task in a manageable chunk. Involvement in the overall process and purpose of the activity, in a manageable and supported form, gives children a chance to see how the steps fit together and to participate in aspects of the activity that reflect the overall goals, gaining both skill and a vision of how and why the activity works.

The adult's structuring of the problem may be tailored to the child's level of skill. With a novice, the adult may take responsibility for managing the subgoals as well as making sure the overall goal is met. A more experienced child may assume responsibility for achieving the subgoals and eventually for managing the whole task.

In addition to the executive role of adult–child interaction, structuring the goals and subgoals of an activity, adult–child interaction may provide children with routines that they can use as their contribution to more complex activities. That is, routines of adult–child interaction may provide ready-made pieces of meaningful actions on which children can build their further efforts. For example, infant games and routines may provide packaged words that are useful to infants outside the context of the games and routines. By filling in slots in social routines—such as saying "hello" or "excuse me"—and in social games—such as Peekaboo, All Gone, and Where Is It?—infants may learn chunks that they can later apply in conversation. They have used the chunks with understanding of their communicative function in the routines, although they do not as yet understand the chunks semantically (Snow, 1984). This role of games and routines with infants is supported by the fact that many of children's early words are those used in such routines and games.

Adults' assistance in children's activities is often not intended as instruction. It involves active attention and involvement for the sake of conversation or entertainment or achievement of immediate practical goals, but may not be regarded by the participants as a lesson. The support of children's activities by parents is often automatic. Indeed, parents often find it difficult *not* to support a child's activity, even when they are instructed to let the child handle the problem alone. For example, researchers find that when they evaluate a preschool child's skill, it is often necessary to arrange for the mother to be unavailable to the child so that the mother can resist assisting the child and the child cannot request assistance or feedback from the mother. Wood and Middleton (1975) noted that mothers knew that they were breaking the rules by intervening during their child's problem solving, but they found it difficult not to help when "needed."

One of the most difficult of parental tasks is to avoid helping children at points when they need the freedom to make their own decisions—and, often, their own errors. Many middle-class parents have trouble watching and keeping themselves from intervening as their child works on a project that could be improved with parental assistance, even when the parents feel strongly that the child will learn more by working with some independence. Effective structuring of children's activities requires monitoring children's need for assistance and need to work with greater independence, a topic that will be addressed in the discussion of the transfer of responsibility for managing problem solving. The point here is that parents' difficulties in avoiding taking over as their children stumble through a problem illustrate the automaticity of much parental support.

Variation in Caregivers' Support for Children's Learning

We have, for the most part, focused on middle-class dyads, engaged with each other exclusively. In Chapter 4, I referred to differences in interaction that I would expect when adults are busy with other activities, instead of engaging in exclusive interaction with children (as in the laboratory, when this is all they have to do). I expect that the "lessons" observed by researchers often occur naturally at home in middle-class families, but during a very small proportion of the day. Parents are busy with their own activities, not focused on preparing each of their children for his or her future occupation at each moment of the day. Middle-class mothers interacting with their children when they think they are not being observed are much less involved and less instructive than when they are aware of being observed (Graves & Glick, 1978).

There are important cultural differences in arrangements for and interactions with children. As I argue in Chapter 6, the face-to-face didactic interactions that characterize middle-class American parents in research settings are less prevalent and may be less necessary to reach local goals in some other cultures in which children have more opportunities for observing and participating in the actual skilled activities of mature members of the society.

Even in middle-class families, adults try to prevent rather than facilitate some learning. Some subjects are off-limits to children. Goodnow (1987) points out that adults protect or divert children from learning about many topics (e.g., sex, family income), and that children and caregivers are not always eager to participate in instructional situations across-the-board. Valsiner (1984, 1987) stresses that an important role of adults is to constrain children's exploration to safe activities—for example, refusing to let a 1-year-old too near a fire. Carew's (1980) observations of toddlers at home reveal that their activities were restricted during 8% of the observations, compared with being facilitated during 12%, engaged in with another person during 21%, and watched during 4% of the observations. These examples underline the importance of examining values in studying the information, skills, and activities promoted by the community and considered relevant for children.

A limitation of most research on parent–child interaction is that it focuses on dyads freed from the complexities of ordinary life, in which other people are likely to be competing for attention or serving as resources for either partner. The impact of people beyond the dyad is apparent in studies of twins, each of whom has fewer and shorter conversations and less joint attention with the mother than do singletons, and develop language skills more slowly (Tomasello, Mannle, & Kruger, 1986). The language development of later-born children is also routinely found to be slower than that of firstborns. Mothers of firstborns address more utterances to them during joint activities, and more time is spent in joint activities by mothers and their firstborn children than by mothers and their later-born children (Feinman & Lewis, 1983; Wells, 1975). Snow (1982a) found that in the presence of the older sibling, mothers' utterances to second-born 17-month-olds as well as vocalizations by the toddler were decreased by more than half, although the *proportion* of semantically related utterances by the mothers remained constant. Wellen (1985) found that when 8-year-old siblings were present, they answered more than half the questions that mothers addressed to preschool-age children, and mothers spoke less and provided fewer hints and expansions on their questions to the preschoolers. When both parents are with their newborn, mothers (and to some degree fathers) interact with the baby less than when each parent is alone with the newborn (Parke & O'Leary, 1976).

In addition to variations in parental support due to the presence of other people or competing activities, constraints due to danger or taboo, and cultural differences, there are many circumstances in which parents are not interested in interacting with young children, especially when they are exhausted or stressed to the extent that they focus on their own needs. There are times of day when most parents may try to keep from interacting with their children, or their interactions may be less patient and sensitive because they are distracted, tired, or have something else to accomplish.

For parents whose lives are constantly stressed, there may be few moments in which they focus on their child in a supportive and sensitive fashion, since their personal resources are depleted. For example, mothers suffering from depression are less sensitive in interactions with their infants, either avoiding involvement or interacting in an intrusive manner that does not adjust to the children's interests or pace (Tronick & Field, 1986). We are currently studying the sensitivity of guided participation of depressed and nondepressed mothers working with 5-year-olds to determine how the interaction varies as a function of the adult partner's mental resources (Fitz & Rogoff, in progress).

Children may find resources in other people (such as other relatives, peers, and teachers) when a parent is unavailable or having difficulties, and in many families, grandparents, siblings, and other relatives are central caregivers. The fact that research has focused on mother–child interaction in dyadic situations limits our understanding of the variety of social resources available to children and the probable richness and resilience of children's social lives.

In the concept of guided participation, I mean to include not just parent–child relationships, but also the other social relationships inherent to families and communities, such as those involving children and their siblings, grandparents, teachers, classmates, and neighbors, organized not as dyads but as rich configurations of mutual involvement. For reasons of convenience and bias, researchers focus on the individual child and dyadic relationships; however, this may distort our picture of children's social worlds. In guided participation, children are involved with multiple companions and caregivers in organized, flexible webs of relationships that focus on shared cultural activities, not exclusively on the needs of solitary individuals. Such variety of social relationships provides children with opportunities to participate in diverse roles important to development, and may buffer difficulties encountered by particular social partners.

Later chapters consider variations in guided particiaption according to partners' skills, relative status (e.g., adult versus peer), and familiarity to the child, as well as differences and similarities in guided participation across cultures. It is important to examine the circumstances involved in guided participation, as they are integral to the process of guided participation. Children come to share the world view of their community through the arrangements and interactions in which they are involved, whether or not such arrangements and interactions are intended to instruct them. Since children actively seek guidance and participation, the process marches on even when adults are focusing on other things or are engaged in activities in which they would prefer their children not to become involved.

Children's Management of Their Roles and Those of Adults

Children are very active in determining the level of their own involvement and the level of support provided by adults, according to studies of middle-class settings. At times, children are the partner responsible for structuring interactive situations. In a laboratory classification task in which mothers were to instruct children (Ellis & Rogoff, 1986; Rogoff & Gardner, 1984), we found that a few children took over management of the instruction, despite their mothers' assigned responsibility to prepare them for an upcoming test and their mothers' exclusive access to a cue sheet indicating the correct placement of the items shown in Figure 5.3.

> One 9-year-old took control when his mother indicated that she was totally confused about how to proceed and the items were in disarray. The child told her, politely but insistently, to look at the cue sheet. She followed the suggestion but was still confused, so the child led her through the process of checking the correct placement of items, picking up one item at a time and asking, "Is this one right? . . . Look at the sheet." The child structured the checking of each item to elicit the information about correct placement he needed from his mother to independently infer the category organization.

In situations in which the adult is not focused on teaching, the child is likely to take a large role in structuring interaction. As parents go about their own activities, not focusing on instruction, children may be more free to ask for help or to join the adult activity without worrying about overstepping the bounds of the teacher. In the example above, the boy certainly felt that he was stepping out of his appropriate role; he continually tried to mask the fact that he was telling his mother what to do. In explicit teaching situations, an important part of the learner's role is helping to preserve the greater status of the teacher by avoiding the impression of being "uppity."

In most of daily life, children may be relatively free to manage their own

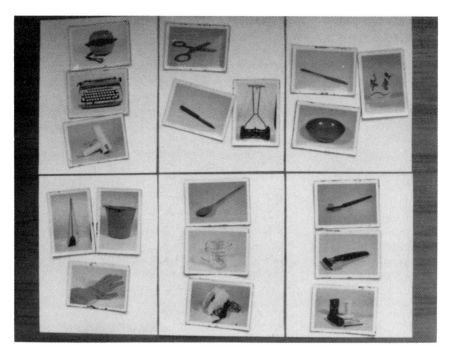

Figure 5.3   Photographs arranged in six categories (electrical appliances, cutting implements, eating implements, cleaning tools, cooking tools, and grooming items) used in the study of memory for a classification system by Ellis and Rogoff (1982, 1986) as well as in later studies described in subsequent sections. (Photograph © B. Rogoff)

learning. Wood (in press) argues that in noncontrived situations, children initiate their involvement with adults, and adults support children's learning through *leading by following,* fitting their assistance into children's interests and efforts. Consistent with this suggestion, Carew (1980) observed that 82% of toddlers' interactions at home were initiated by the toddlers.

In her proposal that children "bootstrap" their own language development, Shatz (1987) argues that young children are equipped with procedures for structuring and making use of language input—eliciting talk in relevant situations, and maintaining discourse and using overheard linguistic information even with only partial understanding. Children may further direct adults' assistance through their help seeking (Nelson-LeGall, 1985).

Even during the first year of life, infants actively interpret and participate in the definition of a situation and in the direction an activity takes. They attempt to direct others to help them achieve their own goals. An example of a baby directing an adult to assist him in a difficult task is provided by Rogoff et al.'s (1984) account of a 9-month-old who tried to get an adult to work a jack-in-the-box:

The baby began by pushing the box across the floor toward the adult, and patted the top of the box when the adult asked "What?" The adult responded to the baby's actions as a request, and asked "Should we make Jack come out?" The adult tried to get the baby to turn the handle (an action too difficult for this 9-month-old), and the baby responded with a series of frustrated yet determined moves—whining and fumbling with the box—that expressed his desire to have the box opened (as well as his inability to do it himself). Finally the adult began to turn the handle and the baby immediately relaxed. The adult asked sympathetically, "Is that what you wanted?" and the baby stared at the handle and let out a big sigh of relief.

The efforts of children to manage activities are influential in informing adults of the appropriate level for children's involvement as well as in directing the nature of the activity to more closely fit children's interests. Since children's skills develop in the context of ongoing activities, it is natural that the joint roles of adult and child should change over the course of an activity.

Transfer of Responsibility for Managing Activities

Children take on increasing responsibility for managing situations over the course of years as well as through the process of becoming familiar with a particular task. From the perspective of a caregiver, effective transfer of such responsibility is facilitated by sensitivity to children's competence in particular tasks so that responsibility is given according to their skills. Such caregiver sensitivity involves understanding (frequently tacit) of the skills and knowledge needed to independently handle the situation and of the course of the child's skill development in that particular situation.

Accompanying caregivers' adjustment of support according to children's skills are children's active efforts to arrange for participation at an appropriate level. Even when interaction with the child is not a caregiver's focus, there is adjustment of the child's participation through social interaction. Children enlist involvement of caregivers in their own activities and attempt to enter into caregivers' activities according to their interests. Such interaction is likely to fit the characteristics of guided participation for pragmatic reasons—the adult limits the amount of responsibility according to the child's skill, and the child insists on a role that is interesting and, hence, within the child's zone of proximal development. As in previous sections, the research largely involves middle-class adult–child relationships.

Adults' Adjustment of Support

In order to tailor their assistance, adults need a notion of both how the specific task could be accomplished and how the specific child is likely to approach it. Wood and Middleton (1975) point out that effective tutoring involves problem solving for the tutor, in terms of how to modify the approach on the basis of how the tutee responds to instruction. They liken instructional moves by the tutor to hypotheses about the most effective level for intervention. Depending on the tutee's response, the tutor modifies the hypothesis, providing a level of instruction sensitive to its effectiveness for the tutee. Wood and Middleton suggest that the "region of sensitivity to instruction" ideally involves one extra operation or decision beyond the level at which the child is currently performing.

Adults' initial models of how a particular problem can be approached and how a particular child is liable to handle it are likely to be based on preconceptions about both the task and the child. An example of how adults design their support on the basis of prejudgments of the difficulty of the task and the child's skill is provided by mothers who instructed 6- and 9-year-old children in classification tasks that resembled either a home situation (putting away groceries) or a school situation (sorting pictures of objects; Rogoff, Ellis, & Gardner, 1984). The mothers and children seemed to expect the school task to be more difficult and adopted a more formal stance, even though both tasks were arranged to be similar in difficulty. For the younger children—new to formal schooling—who were carrying out the school task, mothers provided more instruction than did mothers teaching older children in the school task or mothers teaching children of either age in the home task. Interestingly, this adjustment was accompanied by slightly better performance on the learning test by the younger children in the school task.

SENSITIVE ADJUSTMENT OF SUPPORT DURING INTERACTION

Evaluations of a partner's need for assistance are not only based on preliminary assessment of skill and task difficulty. Evaluation by a skilled adult or peer is an active process of adjustment to changes in skill and new evidence of readiness provided in the course of social interaction. Isaacs and Clark (1987) found that adults assess one another's level of expertise in a communication task almost immediately and adjust their contributions accordingly; the partners' collaborative adjustments in the process of making themselves understood quickly lead to novices coming to participate in the specialized understanding of the expert. With evidence of increasing skill and understanding, expert partners can revise their level of support to be at the edge of the novice's skill, where it is needed for both mutual understanding and the novice's progress.

Adults may obtain evidence of a child's skill through adjusting the amount of redundancy they provide in cues to the child. If done sensitively, adults obtain evidence of a child's skill without producing noticeable errors. Adjustment of redundancy simultaneously supports the child's understanding and helps the adult determine the child's need for support. In early language learning, adults support verbal messages with enough redundant verbal and nonverbal information to ensure understanding. As infants begin to comprehend verbal messages, adults decrease the redundant information and explicitness of statements (Bellinger, 1979; Bernstein, 1981; Greenfield, 1984; Messer, 1980; Schneiderman, 1983; Snow, 1977; Zukow, Reilly, & Greenfield, 1982).

The adjustment of support also occurs with older children beginning to learn how to handle a task, with mothers providing opportunities for children to take greater responsibility and offering support that prevents noticeable errors. Mothers assisting 6- and 9-year-old children in a classification task often began by giving redundant verbal and nonverbal information to ensure correct performance (Rogoff & Gardner, 1984). They might simultaneously point at the correct shelf, repeat the category label for the shelf, and look toward the shelf. As the session continued, the redundancy was decreased, and when the children were unable to proceed, the redundant cues often reappeared. Difficulties and hesitation shown by the children seemed to help mothers adjust the rate at which children were given responsibility and to pinpoint problems. The partners seemed to seek a level of responsibility at which the children could extend their role without making errors of a magnitude that would require acknowledgment.

The mothers frequently employed subtle evaluation of children's readiness and adjusted redundancy and supportive cues accordingly (Rogoff & Gardner, 1984). The mothers and children used hesitation, glances, and postural changes, as well as children's difficulties in decision making, to adjust their relative responsibilities for problem solving. For example, one mother subtly escalated her cues in the face of her child's continuing hesitation:

> The mother encouraged her child to determine where the next items went. When the child hesitated, the mother turned slightly toward the correct location. When the child still hesitated, the mother glanced at the correct location and moved the item held in the air slightly toward its intended location. Finally, she superficially rearranged other items in the correct group, and with this hint, the child finally made the correct placement.

Thus the mother encouraged the child to assume greater responsibility and masked her assistance as random activity rather than correction of error, gently adjusting her support to the child's level of understanding.

The same kind of subtle evaluation of learners' readiness, with attendant support from an expert for taking the next step, is evidenced in the tutoring of chemistry, physics, computer science, and mathematics at the university level (Fox, 1988a, 1988b). A tutor makes use of the timing of the student's participation in the discourse to infer understanding, pausing to allow the student to take responsibility for an idea by anticipating or completing the tutor's idea. A tutor makes use of information about the number and length of each response opportunity that a student passes up, taking into account whether or not the information being discussed is new, the effectiveness of the tutor's invitation to respond, and what the student does during passed-up opportunities (e.g., looks blank or calculates). If a student passes up two or three opportunities, the tutor is likely to continue with an explanation; if no evidence of understanding occurs during the explanation, the tutor is likely to repeat or reformulate it.

Within a student's discourse, pauses in moving from one step to the next while working out a problem are taken by the tutor as an indication of lack of understanding, especially if the student provides other signs of "being stuck," such as laughter, sighs, and postural and gaze cues. What is *not* said by the student is as informative as what *is* said.

The student uses similar structure to interpret the tutor's response. If the tutor nods and agrees with the student, the student can infer that the answer shows understanding. But if the tutor hesitates after a student's turn, the student will interpret that action as meaning that the student's contribution was in some way incorrect or incomplete.

Although classroom situations involving many students may not allow such personalized equality and sensitivity of exchange, teachers may attempt to discern students' level of understanding by the looks on their faces, their responses to ridiculous suggestions, and their uptake of questions. And students, for their part, may be able to direct the teachers' comments by their looks of interest, questions, or boredom. Individual students may attempt to mask their disinterest or avoid eye contact with the lecturer, which provides further information if a lecturer is interested in discerning interest or understanding.

In Fox's tutoring situations, as in our research on mother–child instruction, both partners showed a preference for having the learner handle the problem before the tutor intervened, and for the tutor's intervention to involve a collaborative redirection of the learner's efforts. Correction of learner errors was avoided by the type of support provided by the tutor. For example, tutors used collaborative completion of statements as a way to find out what the student understood, with a rising intonation to cue the student to complete the statement (Fox, 1988b). If the student provided an inappropriate completion, the tutor could give the correct answer simply by completing her own sentence without appearing to correct the student.

A common form of tutorial assistance that avoids direct correction is to ask a "hint" question whose answer will help the learner progress if the learner can discern how the answer helps to solve the larger problem. The tutor provides support both for answering the question and for recognizing how the answer is a resource for solving the problem, assisting the learning in building a bridge to the problem's solution through the supporting connection of the hint question.

Fox (1988b) argues that these processes of diagnosis and repair used by human tutors are beyond the capabilities of computer systems, which lack the necessary cognitive flexibility and multiple interpretations of ongoing interaction in context:

> These processes involve not an abstract domain of knowledge—such as physics or chemistry—but rather a history of the preceding discourse, the ability to find alternative interpretations, based on another's utterances, of one's own verbal behavior and the ability to re-design one's own utterances to rule out undesired interpretations and guide the hearer towards the desired interpretation. These are extremely sophisticated processes. (p. 30)

Similarly, Schallert and Kleiman (1979) suggest that elementary-school students understand teachers better than they understand textbooks because teachers tailor their presentations to children's level of understanding and monitor students' comprehension to adjust messages. Schallert and Kleiman quote Socrates from the dialogue *Phaedrus:* "Written words seem to talk to you as though they were intelligent, but if you ask them anything about what they say . . . they go on telling you the same thing forever."

In summary, the subtle and tacit skills of determining a learner's current understanding and designing a supportive situation for advancement have been observed in interactions of parents and their infants and in interactions of adult tutors and child and adult learners. In these situations, interactional cues—the timing of turns, nonverbal cues, and what each partner says or does not say—are central to the achievement of a challenging and supportive structure for learning that adjusts to the learner's changes in understanding.

DEVELOPMENTAL CHALLENGES: "UPPING THE ANTE"
AS SKILL PROGRESSES

As children evidence increased skill in handling a process, their more expert partners can allow or even require them to take greater responsibility. Researchers in prelinguistic development have noted that adults carry on conversations with infants in which the adult's role as conversational partner is adjusted to the baby's repertoire, with adults stepping up their expectations as the baby's skills increase:

> Mothers work to maintain a conversation despite the inadequacies of their conversational partners. At first they accept burps, yawns, and coughs as well as laughs and coos—but not arm-waving or head movements—as the baby's turn. They fill in for the babies by asking and answering their own questions, and by phrasing questions so that a minimal response can be treated as a reply. Then by seven months the babies become considerably more active partners, and the mothers no longer accept all the baby's vocalizations, only vocalic or consonantal babbles. As the mother raises the ante, the child's development proceeds. (Cazden, 1979, p. 11)

Caregivers' provision of background knowledge to make the context of statements explicit, accomplished by clarifying their own and children's intentions and by specifying the referents of a statement, is reduced as children gain language facility (Ochs, 1979).

In early picture-book reading, mothers adjust their demands according to their children's level of skill. Mothers begin by carrying the whole conversation, primarily labeling the pictures with 12-month-olds (DeLoache, 1984). They increasingly seek information from older children. With 15-month-olds, mothers use a question format ("What's this?") but without seeming to expect an answer; they name the objects and ask children simply to confirm the label ("Is that an elephant?"). Or the mothers ask the questions and answer them, with the children contributing no more than their attention. Starting at about 15 months, children begin to label single, visible, clearly demarcated objects. Mothers at this point skip pictures with which they think their children are unfamiliar. With older children, mothers ask more inferential questions, requesting information that is not directly visible in the picture ("What do bees make?"). If children do not reply, some mothers give clues and now apparently avoid responding to their own question, instead helping children to get the right answer.

Mothers report that they intentionally teach their children and consciously adjust their input and demands. DeLoache (1984) suggests that the sensitive adjustment shown by the mothers is in the service of the immediate goal of communicating effectively with the child and of getting and maintaining the child's attention—a goal that may be compatible with the mothers' more distal goal of teaching. A similar adjustment by an adult to a child's skill in contributing to storytelling between ages 23 and 31 months is described by Peters (1986).

Similarly, while reading books with their mothers, children began to label pictured objects as they became familiar with them, with their increasing responsibility structured in a consistent fashion (Adams & Bullock, 1986). When children were 14 months, mothers did almost all the labeling of pictured animals. By age 26 months, children labeled almost as many animals as their mothers. However, by 38 months, the labels provided by the children differed according to conceptual structure: children gave well over half the basic-level names (e.g., bird), and their labels conformed to adult usage, but subordinate-level naming of atypical exemplars (e.g., penguin) showed roughly equal contributions by adult and child.

When children were 38 months, labeling of typical exemplars had become an active issue with the mothers, who worked on the children's use of adult labels. At the beginning of a 2-week study of book reading with 38-month-olds, the mothers labeled most of the typical exemplars, but by the end of the 2 weeks, the children contributed almost half the labels for typical exemplars. Adams and Bullock (1986) conclude that these organized shifts in relative contribution indicate that "semantic development is essentially a socially-distributed process" (p. 187).

Mothers also adjust to their children's skill level in assisting them in early numerical learning. Mothers working with preschoolers in a counting task adjusted the level of their assistance to the children's correctness (Saxe, Gearhart, & Guberman, 1984). When the children made accurate counts, the mothers shifted their directives to a superordinate level in the task structure so that the children had more responsibility for determining the subgoals for counting. When the children counted inaccurately, the mothers shifted to a subordinate level in the task structure, taking over management of the subgoals themselves.

An example of a child being encouraged to take over development and management of a mnemonic process is provided by a dyad working on a strategy for associating category labels with their locations, in the classification task of Figure 5.3 (Rogoff & Gardner, 1984):

> The mother devised a story incorporating the first three out of six category boxes, explaining, "We'll remember those things go there . . . we'll make a little story," as she invented mnemonics involving a daily routine. The child contributed slightly to the story for the fourth category, and invented part of the story for the last two category boxes.

Thus by the end, the child took over the responsibility for developing the story line, an activity that likely had mnemonic benefits. But the idea was the mother's, and during the course of instruction, she transferred it and its management to the child. It was clear that the mother was attempting to involve the child in developing the story, because she paused and looked at the child at junctures, pointing to the next box without developing that part of the story and encouraging the child to fill in the blanks in the story:

> Finally, the mother asked the child to tell the story independently as a review, ensuring that the child could manage the whole story structure.

The mother managed the mnemonic strategy so that by the end, the child was a major participant in the construction of the strategy.

Such transfer of responsibility has also been noted in classrooms. Pettito (1983) observed a fourth-grade teacher structuring a long-division lesson into stages that involved decreasing explicitness of formal steps, with adjustment according to the skills of individual students. Brown and Campione (1984) observed that in initial sessions of reading instruction, primarily the teacher modeled strategies for comprehension, but the teacher's demands for student involvement gradually increased as students began to perform parts of the task until finally they independently produced strategic behavior that resembled that modeled by the teacher. The students improved in both reading comprehension and guidance skills as they took on the roles practiced with the teacher; they gradually served as experts to one another (Brown & Reeve, 1987). Reviewing studies successful in training reading comprehension, Pearson and Gallagher (1983) stressed the importance of direct explanation and modeling of necessary skills, provision of guided practice, and careful release of responsibility for applying the skills from teacher to students.

Children's Adjustment of Their Level of Responsibility

Children collaborate with adults in arranging their own participation and level of responsibility. Adults' judgment of children's skills and support of their learning could not function without children clarifying the areas of need for greater responsibility or greater assistance. Indeed, children are active in directing the support of adults and the adjustment of that support as their skills develop.

CHILDREN'S GUIDANCE OF ADULT GUIDANCE

While adults assess children's current understanding of material and adjust their support of children's developing skills (see Wood, in press), children simultaneously adjust the pace of instruction and guide adults in their supportive efforts.

An example of an infant adjusting his level of responsibility and the pace of "instruction" in handling a challenging object is found in Rogoff, Malkin, et al.'s (1984) description of an adult and a 12-month-old working a jack-in-the-box (containing a bunny) together. Initially, the adult performed all aspects of manipulating the toy (turning the handle to pop the bunny out of the box, and pushing the bunny back into the box), while the baby concentrated solemnly on the actions. In the second episode of play with the jack-in-the-box, the baby attempted to push the bunny back into the box with the adult's encouragement and assistance. In the third episode, the baby began to participate in cranking the handle, and in the fourth episode the baby seemed to demand some independence in turning the handle, while the adult encouraged this involvement:

> The baby grabbed the box on its sides and shoved it back and forth on the tray, and the adult paused in cranking. The baby looked at the crank and slowly reached for it, confirming the adult's interpretation that he had been demanding a turn. Putting the baby's hand on the crank and turning the crank, the adult said, "Okay now, you do it." (pp. 40–41)

Over the course of this interaction, the baby eventually participated in winding the handle and pushing the bunny back into the box and closing it, while the adult supported the baby's involvement by winding the handle to near the end of the cycle and helping the baby to hold the lid down on the springy bunny.

Adjustments of level of participation and the nature of the activity can be managed by babies through eye contact, joint attention, smiles or cries, and posture changes. They can indicate interest by looking eagerly toward an object or event, leaning forward and gesturing, and making enthusiastic vocalizations. In a negative situation, or if an adult seems not to understand the baby's cues, the baby's activity may change from joint attention to listlessness, then gaze aversion, and finally turning entirely away (Rogoff et al., 1986). Kaye (1977a) found that 6-month-old infants' actions, especially gaze aversion, controlled their mothers' efforts to teach them to reach around a barrier. Older children can request greater assistance or greater responsibility through nonverbal and verbal indications of hesitation or readiness to take on more complex aspects of a task.

CHILDREN'S INVOLVEMENT IN ADULT ACTIVITIES AND RECRUITMENT OF ADULT ASSISTANCE

In addition to their contribution to managing joint interaction, children recruit adult assistance in their own activities and manage their participation in adults' ongoing activities that may not have interaction with the child as a focus. Children's attempts to learn from adult activities may go unnoticed by parents, who are likely to view children's attempts to "help" or be involved in adult activities as just an inevitable aspect of childhood.

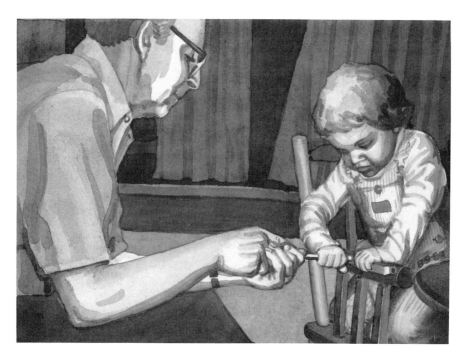

Figure 5.4   An eager 2-year-old attempting to assist his grandfather, who is tightening a screw in the highchair. (United States)

Babies seem to be automatically interested in whatever object an adult is handling, and try to grasp it themselves and perform similar actions with it (Eckerman, Whatley, & McGhee, 1979; Hay, Murray, Cecire, & Nash, 1985). Toddlers follow their parents around the house, trying to be involved in ongoing activities. Rheingold (1982) found that children aged 18 to 30 months spontaneously and energetically helped their parents or a stranger in the majority of the household chores that the adults performed in a laboratory or home setting. Many of the parents reported that they commonly circumvented their child's efforts to participate at home by trying to do chores while the child was napping, to avoid the child's "interference."

Their tendency to seek proximity to and involvement with adults assists infants and toddlers in acquiring information about the environment and about the activities of the person who is followed (Hay, 1980). Children's eagerness to be involved may force busy parents to give them some role in activities, allowing them to stir the batter, put tape on the present, carry the napkins to the table, help turn the screwdriver, and so on.

Such activities, although not designed for children's benefit, are likely to involve adults and children in roles that fit the characteristics of guided participation. For pragmatic reasons—such as to avoid broken eggs, torn wrapping paper, harm to the child, or damaged objects—the adult may try to keep the child from getting involved in an aspect of the activity that is too far beyond the child's skill. But the child is not likely to be satisfied with an aspect of the job that is too simple, and will insist on greater involvement if given an obvious make-work role. Thus even a reluctant adult and a child may collaborate on ensuring that the child participates in skilled activity at a safe but challenging level—working within the child's zone of proximal development for practical reasons.

An example of how a child may insist on involvement and manage her level of participation is provided by my daughter, who at age 3½ years was interested in learning to sew:

> I was getting ready to leave the house, and noticed that a run had started in the foot of my stocking. My daughter volunteered to help sew the run, but I was in a hurry and tried to avoid her involvement by explaining that I did not want the needle to jab my foot. I began to sew, but could hardly see where I was sewing because my daughter's head was in the way, peering at the sewing. Soon she suggested that *I* could put the needle into the stocking and *she* would pull it through, thus avoiding sticking my foot. I agreed, and we followed this division of labor for a number of stitches. When I absent-mindedly handed my daughter the needle rather than starting a stitch, she gently pressed my hand back toward my foot, and grinned when I glanced at her, realizing the error.

This incident illustrates the eagerness with which young children approach the possibility and the process of learning through involvement in adult activities. Children arrange for participation in the activity, and adults tacitly (sometimes unwillingly) provide access and information.

Along with young children's efforts to play an active role in adults' activities go their efforts to recruit adults to help them in their own activities (Heckhausen, 1984; Nelson-LeGall, 1985; Rogoff et al., in press). As with the division of labor in children's participation in adult activities, when children recruit adult assistance to complete their own goals, the assistance is likely to be requested for just those aspects of the task that they are not quite able to complete independently. Again, the pragmatics of such assistance are likely to place the level of support requested and provided, and the level of responsibility, within the zone of proximal development. Both adults and children actively manage their contributions to guided participation in explicit as well as tacit socially arranged learning.

6

Cultural Similarities and Variations in Guided Participation

The fundamental aspiration of the whole of modern child psychology . . . [is] the wish to reveal the eternal child. The task of psychology, however, is not the discovery of the eternal child. The task of psychology is the discovery of the historical child, of what Goethe called the transitory child. The stone that the builders have disdained must become the foundation stone. (Vygotsky, *Thinking and Speech*)

"The potential of every human being of becoming an artist," asserts the great French photographer Henri Cartier-Bresson, "remains unfulfilled without the individual's acquaintanceship and immersion into the artistic traditions of the past, and the distinctiveness of his culture." (John-Steiner, *Notebooks of the Mind*)

Most research on the zone of proximal development, scaffolding, and adult–child interaction has involved middle-class parents and children in North America and Europe. How, then, do the interactional processes observed in research with such samples relate to the broader spectrum of child-rearing practices around the world? How do observations made in nonindustrial societies or in other cultural communities in Europe or America compare and extend the theory? My use of the term *culture* indicates the organized and common practices of particular communities in which children live (which may differ from those of children's nations).

In this chapter, I suggest that guided participation may be widespread around the world, but with important variations in arrangements for and communication with children in different cultures. The most important differences have to do with the goals of development—what lessons are to be learned—and the means available for children either to observe and participate in culturally important activities or to receive instruction outside the context of skilled activity.

110

Universality of Guided Participation

The general processes of guided participation appear around the world. Caregivers and children make arrangements for children's activities and revise children's responsibilities as they gain skill and knowledge. These arrangements and adjustments facilitate children's extension of their existing knowledge to encompass new situations. With the guidance of those around them, children participate in cultural activities that socialize them in skilled roles.

Ethnographic accounts of teaching and learning in different cultures suggest that families structure children's activities and provide well-placed instruction in the context of joint activities, and that children are active participants in their own socialization (Fortes, 1938). For example, Mayan mothers in Guatemala help their daughters learn to weave in a process of guided participation (Rogoff, 1986). They divide the process of learning to weave into steps, providing guidance in the context of joint participation in the activity and adjusting their daughters' participation according to the girls' increasing skill and interest in progressing (Figure 6.1). Similar processes occur in the teaching and learning of weaving in Mexico and tailoring in Liberia (Greenfield, 1984; Greenfield & Lave, 1982).

Guided participation involves the structuring of children's activities and the offering of well-placed pointers as children participate in Guareño cultivation, animal husbandry, hunting, and fishing in the Orinoco delta of Venezuela:

> The traditional vocational education system of the Guareños is highly structured and systematic, with either individual or small group instruction. Guareños feel that a knowledge of the intricate flora, fauna, and landforms of their island home, as well as the skill required to manipulate the implements used to exploit their habitat, can only be gained through repeated physical practice. Hence, emphasis is placed on "learning by doing" through repeated practice over time rather than by simple watching and copying. Regardless of the complex of tasks to be taught, a teacher's first step is to familiarize his student verbally and visually with the physical elements of the appropriate location. The entire complex is demonstrated over a period of time; proceeding from simple to complicated steps, the complex is divided into individual tasks. Instruction is not only sequential but additive, so that at each succeeding step, tasks learned earlier are repeated. Finally, an entire task complex is learned, with only occasional verbal or physical correction needed. When competent, the learner is allowed to help the teacher and to experiment and use his own initiative, and the teacher eventually eliminates his need to fill that role. (Ruddle & Chesterfield, 1978, p. 393)

Children participate in the cultural activities of their elders, with their responsibilities adjusted to their own initiative and skill. Caregivers provide guidance in specific skills in the context of their use. For example, toddlers in India learn at an early age to distinguish the use of their right and left

(a)

(b)

Figure 6.1 Learning to weave on the backstrap loom, in a Mayan community in Highland Guatemala. (a) Women sitting in their courtyard chatting and weaving, observed by two little girls. (b) By about age 5, girls begin to set up their own backstrap looms, using bits of thread that they find and plaiting long leaves to make warp and weft. (c) Around age 7, girls are assisted in beginning to weave a simple belt with the loom already set up for them. This 7-year-old from the United

(c)

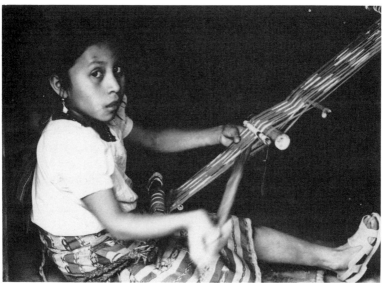

(d)

States is being taught by a Mayan woman, who has been explaining to the girl how the sticks are arranged, how the heddles are to be pulled to change the threads, and how the edges of the belt are kept straight. (d) By age 9, Mayan girls such as this one are weaving simple items independently, and by age 13, they are skilled weavers, handling all phases of weaving. (Photographs © B. Rogoff)

hands: the right is the clean hand used for eating; the left, the "dirty" hand used for cleaning oneself after defecation.

> If a child did not learn to eat with the right hand by participation and ob-
> servation, a mother or older sister would manipulate the right hand and re-
> strain the left until the child understood and did what was required. One
> of the earliest lessons taught a child of one-and-a-half to two years of age
> was to distinguish between the right and left hand and their distinctly sepa-
> rate usages. . . . Although we judged that the Indian style of eating re-
> quired considerable manipulative skill, we observed a girl, not quite two,
> tear her chapati solely with her right hand and pick up her vegetable with
> the piece of chapati held in the right hand. (Freed & Freed, 1981, p. 60)

These caregivers structured the situation as well as relied on children's participation, and the children achieved an impressive understanding of the difficult distinction between right and left.

An example of the close mutual involvement of expert and novice is also
provided in adult education for healing practiced by the !Kung of Africa.
The teacher regulates the learner's experience with the healing trance, supporting the ability to achieve and to control the trance through intimate joint
participation (Katz, 1982). The learner may physically hold onto the more
experienced healer around his torso, hanging over his shoulders; as the
teacher heals a person, the healing energy goes through the teacher's body
and into the learner's. The learner heals through the teacher, with the teacher
"carrying" the novice healer into expertise. While this education is between
adults, the joint participation and learning through osmosis that it exempli-
fies resembles the processes that may be especially available to young children, who spend so much of their time in intimate contact with more skilled
members of their culture.

In these accounts, which illustrate the ubiquity of social guidance and
participation in learning through structuring of activities for novices in close
involvement with others, there are also obvious cultural differences. The lessons to be learned differ from culture to culture, and the interpersonal arrangements for participation and for communication vary. The remainder
of this chapter discusses cultural variations in lessons to be learned and in
means of communication with children, in turn.

Cultural Variation in What Is Learned: The Goals of Development

The most important differences across cultures in guided participation involve variation in the skills and values that are promoted according to cultural goals of maturity. For researchers to attempt to understand development
without considering everyday activities and skills in the context of cultural
goals would be like attempting to learn a language without trying to understand the meaning it expresses.

As detailed in Chapter 2, cultures vary in their institutions and related
tools and technologies, and these cultural differences are closely linked with

the disparate performance on cognitive tests of individuals from different cultures. Cultural psychologists and sociocultural theorists have argued that basic to the differences across cultural (or historical) groups are the intellectual tools used, such as literacy and arithmetic (Cole & Griffin, 1980; Rogoff, 1981b; Rogoff, Gauvain, & Ellis, 1984; Scribner & Cole, 1981; Vygotsky, 1978, 1987). In like manner, speculations abound regarding the effect of computers on the thinking of children who learn to use them (Papert, 1980), and the influence of television on children's thinking and social behavior.

Along with differences in skills considered important (e.g., reading, weaving, sorcery, healing, eating with the right hand) and approaches valued (e.g., individual achievement, speed in performance) are differences in the situations available to children for the practice of skills and incorporation of values.

Skills for the use of cultural tools such as literacy begin to be practiced even before children have contact with the technology itself. American middle-class parents involve their children in "literate" forms of narrative in preschool discourse, as they embed their children in a way of life in which reading and writing are integral parts of communication, recreation, and livelihood (Cazden, 1988; Michaels & Cazden, 1986; Taylor, 1983). Picture books made of durable materials are offered to babies, and bedtime stories become a part of their daily routine.

Heath (1982, 1983) presents a fascinating comparison of middle-class, school-oriented practices for inculcating literacy with the practices of families from two communities whose children have trouble reading. Parents in a white Appalachian mill town taught their children respect for the written word, but did not involve book characters or information in the children's everyday lives; their children did well during the first years of learning to read, but had difficulty when required to *use* literate skills to express themselves or interpret text. Children of rural origin in a black mill town learned skillful and creative use of language, but were not taught about books or the style of analytic discourse used in school; they had trouble learning to read, which kept them from making use of their creative skills with language in the school setting. Early childhood in both of these communities did not include school-style reading and writing in the texture of daily life, and the children experienced difficulties with literacy in school.

The socialization of narrative style varies across cultural groups, with differences appearing as early as first or second grade in the kind of topical oral account that teachers value (Michaels & Cazden, 1986). The narrative styles used in "sharing time" (show and tell) by black and white children differ in the approval they receive from teachers, and in the extent they resemble the literate styles that teachers aim to foster. White children use a "topic-centered style" with tightly structured and marked discourse on a single topic, using temporal grounding, a statement of focus, and marking of structure through tone grouping and pausing. In contrast, the sharing-time narratives produced by black children use an episodic style with a series of episodes linked to an implicit theme, marking transitions through pitch contour, tempo, and temporal markers. When adults from the two groups were presented with segments of narratives from which identifying information about children's group membership was removed, they differed in their judgments of the excellence of the two styles. The white adults judged the white children's style as more skillful and indicative of greater chance of success in reading, while the black adults found the black children's narratives to be better formed and indicative of language skill and likelihood of success in reading. The adults' value judgments reflected their shared culture with the children, and presumably were based on their appreciation and understanding of the children's use of culturally bound narrative scripts that specify both what is interesting to tell and how to structure it.

Cultural Goals and Developmental Outcomes

The importance of understanding the variations in what children are expected to learn in different cultures is linked to the assumptions of this book that thinking and learning are functional efforts by individuals to solve specific problems of importance in their culture, and that developmental courses vary in their goals rather than having a universal endpoint to which all should aspire. Thus in understanding cognitive development, it is essential to take into account the particular problems that children are attempting to solve and their importance in the culture.

It may be important for preschoolers in a culture in which literacy provides a primary means of communication and is a requirement for economic success in adulthood to learn to attend to the nuances of differences between the colors and shapes of small two-dimensional representations. However, such a focus may not matter in other cultural groups, in which it may be more important for young children to learn to attend to the nuances of weather patterns or of social cues of those around them, to use words cleverly to joust, or to understand the relation between human and supernatural events.

It is easy for middle-class American and European researchers to focus on skills that are important in our own daily lives and in our community, not only because as humans we all tend to be ethnocentric, but also because in many other nations, skills such as literacy (and the arbitrary skills associated with a particular form of literacy and schooling) are adopted as national priorities in the attempt to change the countries' economic position. Researchers' judgments of the importance of literate (or other technological) skills for intellectual development can be misled by the worldwide export of these tools to other nations (or to economically disadvantaged communities in the United States and Europe) and by attempts to convert their inhabitants to a Euroamerican view of the natural world and literate ways of thinking and acting. We must be careful not to confuse the specific uses of skills with the economic power of their users. This point is clearer when we consider the respect that is now being given to socialization practices and cognitive processes of the Japanese, apparently because of their success in beating Americans at their own game (i.e., economic power and excellence in mathematical and technological skills).

To understand development, we must examine children's skills and interaction with their partners in terms of the function of such skills in achieving locally valued goals, conscientiously avoiding the arbitrary imposition of our values on another group. It is impossible to avoid judgments of good and bad courses of development if one is attempting to *influence* another group. But if the aim is to *understand* development, it is essential not to impose assumptions about the goals of development of one group on individuals from another. Interpreting the activity of people without regard for *their* goals renders the observations meaningless.

Coda

Does this dismiss the possibility that there are *bad* outcomes of development? No. The purpose of the previous section was to argue for the importance of avoiding the imposition of outside goals while interpreting the activities of a functional human group. In any group, there is some agreement about undesirable outcomes for individuals. Because we act according to consensus in issues of values, it is important to question whose consensus it is.

I suppose that there would be agreement across cultures that the survival of an individual is some measure of success, but that the survival (or gain) of an individual at the expense of the group would have negative connotations. But even using such criteria, there would be variation in the balance of individual and group goals. Some communities may try to raise children who would be willing and able to sacrifice themselves for the group's good. Other communities may try to prevent individuals from harming themselves or others at all costs—for example, by prohibiting individuals to allow themselves or others to die if something could be done about it, even if the resources required to keep one person alive led to great sacrifices in the well-being of others. (Here I am thinking of differences in community feelings about allowing old people to choose their time to die with dignity—or even assisting them in their choice—and of the priority given to preserving the life of a very sick premature infant at great expense to the group and other individuals.)

My aim is to suggest that judgments of good outcomes of development must be defined socially and that they differ according to many aspects of a community's functioning, including its economic surpluses (which provide leeway for making extra allowances for some individuals without jeopardizing the group), its system of subsistence and tools of survival, and its political, economic, and religious systems. (See LeVine, 1977, for a discussion of the relation between resources and cultural goals for child rearing.)

Wolff (1963) provides an engaging account of child rearing in a lower-middle-class Boston Irish family, characterized by bawdy and humorous "consistent inconsistency," illustrating the point that there are a variety of appropriate avenues through which parents and children achieve mutual regulation. Such varying approaches fit with the cultural and personal traditions of the parents, despite clashing with those of researchers.

Within any community, nonetheless, different families will vary in their success in meeting the goals of the community, because of differences in their genes, their family's position in the community, their material resources, and the chance circumstances of life. Presumably, even families living in the most difficult of circumstances are trying to do the best with what they have, but sometimes the best is just trying to make it to the next day. In hardship such as extreme poverty, poor health, or a history of habits that impede functioning (e.g., drug addiction or abusive relationships), it is unlikely that caregivers will be thinking of the welfare of children as a central priority.

Adults living in difficult circumstances still interact with their children, except in the most extreme cases. The interaction is unlikely to provide the children with guided participation in becoming successful members of the community from which researchers come. Likewise, the researchers' children might have more difficulty surviving hardship circumstances than do children who are socialized to them. The routine interactions with and arrangements for children provide them with guided participation in maneuvering the life style in which they are embedded. The value of a particular life style is a matter of judgment, difficult to disentangle from the values of the judges' upbringing.

An irritated whack on the side of a young child's head when the child asks a question is liable to teach a lesson that is very different from language lessons on forming questions in conversations with eager middle-class adults. The whack teaches children about monitoring the mood of an adult before initiating interaction, about forms of initiating interaction that are not permitted under certain circumstances, or about the appropriateness of whacking someone on the side of the head when irritated and big enough to get away with it. Children often do learn their lessons, and as adults they use the same practices in which they participated as children, as seen in intergenerational continuity of parent–child relations, child abuse, and alcoholism (Egeland, Jacobvitz, & Sroufe, 1988; Ricks, 1985). Fraiberg, Adelson, and Shapiro's (1975) title "Ghosts in the Nursery" captures well the notion that the practices of the parents often continue when the children become parents—happily or unhappily.

Whether the parental practices appropriated by children are regarded as valuable or problematic, the process is one of guided participation. The structuring of situations in which children participate and their engagement with other people support children's appropriation of the system of understanding in which they participate in daily life. In guided participation—whether following the middle-class model or any other, culturally sanctioned or not—it is a question of values to determine the appropriateness of the particular model.

If we are interested in understanding the processes by which children grow to be skilled in the activities of their elders, we must take the same approach in interpreting the processes of interaction and children's activities in families whose outcomes do not have our community's approval as with those who do. We must consider the circumstances and goals of the family and the community. If we feel that it is our responsibility to do something about how a family and its children are functioning, we will be better prepared to do so if we understand their reality from the perspective of their goals and constraints.

The aim of this book is not to make prescriptions for intervention or for child rearing, but this coda seems important to explain that in arguing for the universality of guided participation, I am not arguing for the universality of its middle-class form. Understanding cultural as well as individual variation is essential for understanding the process of guided participation and the process of development itself. To learn from variations, we must keep in mind the local goals of socialization. My assumption is that functioning cultural groups have goals and child-rearing methods that are appropriate for them. I return now to the discussion of cultural variation, to consider variation in the means by which caregivers and children communicate.

Cultural Variation in Communication with Children

Along with cultural differences in what is being learned go differences in how communication with children is structured. Cultural variations in communication strategies deeply influence the ways in which parents and children collaborate in children's socialization.

There are striking cultural differences in the explicitness and intensity of verbal and nonverbal communication, the interactional status of children and adults, and the company children keep (see Field, Sostek, Vietze, & Leiderman, 1981; Leiderman, Tulkin, & Rosenfeld, 1977; Whiting & Edwards, 1988). I suggest that these cultural differences fit together into patterns that vary in terms of the responsibility that adults take for teaching children in cultures in which children do not participate in adult activities, and the responsibility that children take for learning in cultures in which they have the opportunity to observe and participate in the activities of mature members of the society.

Explicitness of Verbal and Nonverbal Communication

An emphasis on explicit, declarative statements, in contrast to tacit, procedural, and subtle forms of verbal and nonverbal instruction, appears to characterize cultures that promote schooling (Jordan, 1977; Rogoff, 1981b, 1982a; Scribner, 1974; Scribner & Cole, 1973). Differences in the use of explanations may relate to cultural values that define the appropriate use of language, subtlety, and silence, as well as to the adequacy of other forms of communication for most purposes. For example, among the Navajo, who have frequently been characterized as teaching quietly by demonstration (e.g., Cazden & John, 1971), talk is regarded as a sacred gift not to be used unnecessarily.

Although researchers have focused on talking as the appropriate means of adult–child interaction, this emphasis may reflect a cultural bias that overlooks the information provided by gaze, postural changes, smells, and touch. Middle-class American infants have been characterized as "packaged" babies who do not have direct skin contact with their caregivers (Whiting, 1981) and often spend more than a third of their time alone, in a room separated from any other people.

Middle-class American infants are held approximately half the time as Gusii (Kenyan) infants. Whereas Gusii infants are held 80% of the time at 3 to 6 months, and about 50% of the time at 9 to 12 months, middle-class U.S. infants are held only 45% and less than 20% of the time at those ages. Significantly, U.S. babies are placed in holding containers (Figure 6.2a) for a proportion of time (39% at 4 months and 29% at 10 months) that, when combined with their being held by caregivers, adds up to almost the total holding time for the Gusii infants (Richman, Miller, & Solomon, 1988). Heath (1983) observes that the working-class U.S. black infants that she studied were almost never alone—they were held and carried day and night—and were seldom in the company of only one other person.

The separation of mainstream middle-class U.S. infants from other people may necessitate the use of distal forms of communication, such as noise. In contrast to U.S. children's use of distal communication, children who are constantly in the company of their caregivers may rely more on nonverbal cues, such as direction of gaze or facial expression. And infants who are in almost constant skin contact with their caregivers may manage effective communication through touch, by squirming and changing position. The availability of tactile and postural forms of communication may facilitate the toilet training reported as early as 4 to 8 months in some cultures where mother and infant have skin contact (and babies wear no diapers). Consistent with the suggestion that vocalization may be less necessary when there is close contact between adults and infants, Freed and Freed (1981) report work by Lewis in 1977 showing that U.S. infants and small children are less likely to vocalize when held on the lap and more likely to vocalize when out of their mothers' arms and off their laps.

Interactional Status of Adults and Children: Whose Responsibility Is Learning?

In some societies, young children are not expected to interact with adults as conversational peers, initiating interactions and being treated as equals in discussion (Blount, 1972; Harkness & Super, 1977; Schieffelin & Eisenberg, 1984). Instead, they may speak when spoken to, replying to informational questions or simply carrying out directions.

Draper and Harpending (1987) argue that the conversational distance between adults and children often observed in agricultural societies whose

(a)

(b)

Figure 6.2 Contrasting arrangements for holding and interacting with infants. (a) This 9-week-old American is held in a baby container, engaged in face-to-face conversation with her father. (Photograph © B. Rogoff) (b) This 11-month-old from the Ituri Forest of Zaire, carried on her mother's back, is able to observe what her mother sees and does. (Photograph courtesy of David Wilkie)

members have large families and practice narrow birth spacing is the result of the mothers' attempts to employ child caregivers. In this view, mothers make themselves unavailable to their toddlers and require toddlers to focus on others in the social world as their companions, making mother–child communication infrequent. In such settings, toddlers move in a circle of children whose world overlaps only partially with that of adults. However, I believe that this account is incomplete. In such groups, the children may not act as conversational peers of adults, but they may be very involved in the adult world as participants.

In the Mayan community in which I have worked, children seldom interact with adults as conversational partners, but engage with adults during their participation in adult activities, taught by demonstration (which includes

Figure 6.3 Children engaged with their mother in the context of participation in adult work. Two young Mayan girls help their mother carry water from a tap about a block from their home. (Guatemala) (Photograph © B. Rogoff)

talk) in context. Children are freed from direct supervision by adults by age 3 or 4 and then move around town with a multi-age group of children, amusing themselves by observing ongoing events and imitating their elders in play. Infants were always with adults and interacted with them (not necessarily in conversation) on 50% of the daytime occasions I observed. But by ages 3 to 4, children were less often with adults and interacted with them on fewer than 10% of the occasions, with further drops in adult companionship from age 5 throughout childhood (Rogoff, 1981a). Children participated in household work beginning by age 5, taking responsibility for sweeping, some food preparation, and child care.

When older children did interact with adults, it was in the context of participation in adult work. Adults were as likely as or more likely than peers to be interacting with 9-year-olds when the children were engaged in household or agricultural work, but were almost never involved with them when children were playing. Play was a domain for peer interaction, not adult companionship. Even in play, though, the children emulated adult roles: 66% of their play (excluding sports) involved imitation of adult roles. But of the 1708 observations of 9-year-olds out of school, native observers identified only 6 occasions as teaching situations.

Ochs and Schieffelin (1984) suggest that there may be two cultural patterns of speech between young children and their caregivers. In cultures that adapt situations to children (as in middle-class U.S. families), caregivers simplify their talk, negotiate meaning with children, cooperate with them in building propositions, and respond to their verbal and nonverbal initiations. In cultures that adapt children to the normal siutations of the society (as in Kaluli New Guinea and Samoan families), caregivers model unsimplified utterances for children to repeat to a third party, direct them to notice others, and build interaction around circumstances to which the caregivers wish the children to respond.

This contrast is useful for drawing attention to differing strategies of interaction with children, although it does not apply to all cultures. Watson-Gegeo and Gegeo (1986a) report that Kwara'ae (Solomon Islands) caregivers speak with children in both of the ways that Ochs and Schieffelin (1984) contrast: on the one hand, they converse with young children, simplify their speech, negotiate meaning, and respond to children's initiations; on the other, they model statements for children to repeat to others and direct children to notice other people and situations. The goal of Kwara'ae caregivers is to adapt children to the situation, but they argue that it is most effective to do so by starting from where the child is—although they do not go to the extent of entering into pretend play; this is children's domain (Watson-Gegeo & Gegeo, 1986b).

In all these patterns, the child participates in activities of the society, but the patterns vary in terms of the child's or the caregiver's responsibility to adapt in the process of learning or teaching the more mature forms of speech and action.

The adaptation of caregivers to children may be necessary in societies that segregate children from adult activities, thus requiring them to practice skills or learn information outside the mature context of use (Rogoff, 1981a). In the U.S. middle class, many school-age children do not even know what their parents' occupations are, much less how their parents carry out adult work and adult interaction. They are segregated from the occupational and recreational world of adults, and learn about skills they may eventually need in order to participate in their society as adults in a separate context specialized for the purpose—school. (In an age-segregated society, such lessons in development continue in adulthood, with classes in childbirth, handling toddlers, and adjusting to various phases of adulthood, since individuals face new phases of development without much opportunity to observe others at different phases and thereby to pick up examples and ideas of the next step directly.)

At home, young children in an age-segregated community such as the U.S. middle class seldom have much chance to participate in the functioning of the household, and may be segregated from human company by the provision of separate bedrooms, security *objects,* and attractive toys. Middle-class infants are in the unusual situation (speaking in worldwide terms) of being entirely alone for as much as 10 hours of a 24-hour day, managing as best they can to handle their hunger or thirst with a bottle and their need for comforting with a pacifier or blanky or teddy, and working, as Margaret Mead put it, to establish their independence in the transitions to sleep and waking in the night and at naptime (Morelli, et al., 1988; Ward, 1971; Whiting, 1981). During waking hours, their involvement with adults is focused on entertaining themselves while their parents get some work done or on parental interaction that is focused at the children's level, with adjustment of speech and activities to their skill and understanding.

In societies in which children are integrated in adult activities, the children are ensured a role in the action, at least as close observers. Children are present at most events of interest in the community, from work to recreation to church. They are able to observe and eavesdrop on the ongoing processes of life and death, work and play, that are important in their community. As infants, they are often carried wherever their mothers or older siblings go, and as young children they may do errands and roam the town in their free time, watching whatever is going on. As nonparticipants in ordinary adult conversation, they may be free to eavesdrop on important adult activities from which nonparticipant adults may be excluded.

Mayan children, for example, are present at all adult activities except for the birth of a baby. (Sleeping in the same room as the rest of the family, they are present for earlier phases of the baby's development, but were believed by adults "not to hear.") Once, when a Mayan friend was telling me about his marital unhappiness with great secrecy and requesting me to tell no one, an unrelated 10-year-old hung around in the room during the whole conversation, without my friend showing any concern about the child's presence.

In a Mayan community in Mexico, Gaskins and Lucy (1987) noted the

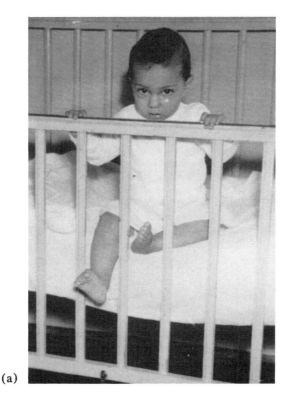

(a)

(b)

Figure 6.4 Contrasting sleeping arrangements. (a) This 9-month-old American is placed in a crib to sleep in a room by himself. (Photograph courtesy of Oscar Magarian) (b) This 15-month-old naps on a relative's back while she harvests peanuts in the Ituri Forest of Zaire. The baby is not strapped on. (Photograph courtesy of Gilda Morelli)

importance of children as providing extra eyes and ears for their mothers, who stay at home and extract information about village events from the children. Because children are exempted from many adult social norms, they have access to information unavailable to adults:

> Children can observe or enter a yard or home without causing anyone to take any special note. A child can linger to watch an ongoing activity without requiring any social engagement. Children are everywhere and little cognizance is taken of their presence. An adult watching in the same way would require the initiation of social interaction. By contrast the child is a "nonperson." (p. 6)

Hence children can be sent to spy on someone for their mothers' interest. Mothers' questions about the events serve to focus children's attention on the relevant features of ongoing activities, guiding the children in determining what aspects of events are significant. And, I would presume, children can use their prerogative to come and go and observe in order to gain access to informative situations for their own learning.

Ward (1971) offers an account of eavesdropping as a means of language learning in her description of a black community in Louisiana, in which children are expected to be seen and not heard:

> At any age a child visiting someone not seen daily will remain very quiet, perhaps observing and listening. At the first disturbance, he will be sent outside immediately. . . . Within the extended circle of relatives and very close friends, however, this stricture on speech is broken. The silent absorption in community life, the participation in the daily commercial rituals, and the hours spent apparently overhearing adults' conversations should not be underestimated in their impact on a child's language growth. (p. 37)

Nothing is censored for children's ears; youngsters go everywhere in the community, except to Saturday-night parties. Heath (1983) provides a similar account of a working-class black community in the Piedmont Carolinas.

Small children in the Louisiana community that Ward (1971) studied are not the conversational partners of adults, people with whom to "engage in dialogue." If children have something important to say, mothers will listen, and the children had better listen if their mothers speak to them. But for conversation, mothers talk to adults or, if desperate, to a child older than 8 years. A mother "will never find herself politely trapped, as will [a] middle-class . . . mother, by the verbal precocity of a three year old, with whom one cannot honestly discuss an interesting issue" (Ward, 1971, p. 46). These children are not encouraged to learn skills in initiating and monopolizing conversation with adults on topics of their own choosing (skills that are useful in middle-class schooling); they hold their parents' attention longer if they say nothing. Toddlers learn to amuse themselves, to sit very still and listen to adults talk—as long as 3 hours—and to amuse themselves with siblings and other children. With infants, adults play some language games involving questions of family structure. Questions between older children and adults involve straightforward requests for information; they are not asked for the sake of conversation or for parents to drill children on topics to which the parents already know the answers.

In conversations between mothers and young children undertaken at Ward's request, fewer than 5% of utterances were expansions of either partner's speech, contrasting with this common form of interaction in conversations between middle-class mothers and their children. However, the mothers did provide their children with language models involving expansion of their own simplified speech, varying the tonal pattern and choice of words to fill slots in sentences over series of statements that, Ward (1971) argues, offer a graphic presentation of syntactic choices for constructing statements. A mother's questions to little Scott provide an example:

What	Scott ate today	for dinner?
What	you ate	for dinner?
What did	you eat	for dinner?
What	you and Warren have for dinner? (p. 49)	

Mothers' speech to children, while not taking the form of a dialogue, is carefully regularized, providing precise, workable models of the language used in the community.

Heath (1983) reports that working-class black Carolina adults do not see young children as conversational partners. However, the toddlers are always surrounded by others and move through phases of echoing and experimenting with variation on the speech around them—at first ignored but gradually participating by making themselves part of the ongoing discourse, by breaking into adult conversation. Adults attempt to understand these comments and correct errors of fact or babytalk. Adults also encourage verbal facility by instigating and appreciating children's involvement in assertive challenging and in scolding exchanges by preschoolers with adults and other children.

Since children are not regarded as information givers, however, they are not asked questions for which adults already have an answer, such as questions of fact or detail. The questions that adults ask children most often encourage children to seek similarities across situations, based on the children's experience. Heath suggests that these analogy questions point to the significance adults give to metaphorical thinking and speaking. Flexible use of language, adapted to shifting roles and situations, characterizes skilled language use in this community. Heath (1983) quotes a woman speaking about how she expects her toddler grandson, Teegie, to learn to know and to talk:

> He gotta learn to *know* 'bout dis world, can't nobody tell 'im. Now just how crazy is dat? White folks uh hear dey kids say sump'n, dey say it back to 'em, dey aks 'em 'gain 'n 'gain 'bout things, like they 'posed to be born knowin'. You think I kin tell Teegie all he gotta know to get along? He just gotta be kéen, keep his eyes open, don't he be sorry. Gotta watch hisself by watchin' other folks. Ain't no use me tellin' 'im: "Learn dis, learn dat. What's dis? What's dat?" He just gotta léarn, gotta know; he see one

thing one place one time, he know how it go, see sump'n like it again, maybe it be de same, maybe it won't. He hafta try it out. If he don't he be in trouble; he get lef' out. Gotta keep yo' eyes open, gotta féel to knów. (p. 84)

In communities in which children are not conversational partners, children may be poorly prepared for the pattern of discourse used in school, but they become proficient in the language and other skills of their community. They are able to learn from observing and eavesdropping as ever-present members of the community, from their growing participation in daily activities from an early age, from the questions and directives and demonstrations of adults, and from their playful talk with other children. Children can do most of the work of socialization themselves, by watching their elders and gradually becoming more centrally involved, in a process that Benedict (1955) called "continuity of cultural conditioning."

With such opportunities to observe ongoing activity and to lend a hand when necessary, children from many cultures begin to participate in chores and other cultural activities from age 3 or 4, when they begin to see what to do, and assume responsibilities for child, animal, and house care by age 5 or 7 (Rogoff, Sellers, Pirotta, Fox, & White, 1975; Ward, 1971; Whiting & Edwards, 1988). Their role grows and their opportunities to practice are amplified by their interest in participation and by their caregivers' setting them tasks within their capabilities and guiding their contributions in the context of joint activity.

Mayan mothers, for example, report that 1- to 2-year-olds observe their mothers making tortillas and attempt to follow suit. Mothers give children a small piece of dough to use and facilitate their efforts by rolling the dough into a ball and starting to flatten it. The toddler's "tortilla," if it is not dropped in the dirt, is cooked by the mother with the other tortillas and eaten by the toddler or another family member. (It goes to the chickens if it is dropped in the dirt.) As the child gains skill in shaping tortillas, the mother adds pointers and demonstrates how to hold the dough in a position that facilitates smooth flattening, and the child can both witness the outcome of his or her own efforts and contribute to making meals. The child observes carefully and participates, and the mother, usually good-naturedly, supports the child's efforts by simplifying the task to make it commensurate with the child's level of skill and by demonstrating and giving suggestions in the process of joint activity. Five- and 6-year-old children are able to make some tortillas for dinner, and girls of 9 or 10 can handle the process from grinding the corn to rolling and patting the tortilla to turning it on the hot griddle with their fingers, preparing the family's dinner when necessary.

Pueblo Indian children have access to many aspects of adult life and the freedom to choose how and with whom to participate (John-Steiner, 1984). Their reports of their own learning stress their role as "apprentice" to more experienced members of the community, with observation and verbal explanation in the context of involvement in the task being learned. John-Steiner contrasts this sort of verbal explanation with the verbal instruction that occurs in the classroom, out of the context of productive activity. One woman describes an episode in teaching her daughter to make bread that demonstrates how verbal explanation is embedded in the process of carrying out the task:

> I told her, you forgot to put in your baking powder. And she said, how do you know? Because the bread is too hard and it won't rise. It was so dry and it is kind of shiny, that is how you can tell if you don't have baking powder. Then she said, she did put in some, but maybe she didn't put in enough of the baking powder. (p. 60)

In other communities that emphasize children's observation and participation, guided participation may involve adjustments by adults or more skilled children to facilitate children's efforts, sometimes with less emphasis on verbal explanation. Howard (1970) reports that Rotuman children have great opportunities to observe how essential tasks are performed, since they are frequently with working adults. The children are subtly encouraged to imitate, and if a child experiences difficulty, an adult may physically adjust the child's body position to correct an error or refine a movement, seldom offering verbal instruction. If children ask for verbal instruction, "they are likely to be told to watch a skillful adult in action" (p. 116).

Questions by children to adults may be rare in some communities (Heath, 1983). Learners' questions to a teacher may be regarded as impolite challenges, in that they involve a subordinate obliging a superior to respond. This implies that the subordinate has the right to hold the superior responsible for the information requested, as Goody (1978) observed in the apprenticeship of Gonja youths learning to weave.

Rather than relying on questions and explanations to organize their learning, observers may be skilled at picking up information through watching, on some occasions even without actually participating in the performance of a task. Nash (1967) reports that the method of learning to use the footloom in a weaving factory in Guatemala is for the learner (an adult) to sit beside a skilled weaver for some weeks, simply observing, asking no questions, and receiving no explanations. The learner may fetch a spool of thread from time to time for the weaver, but does not begin to weave until, after weeks of observation, the learner feels competent to begin. At that point, the apprentice has become a skilled weaver simply by watching and by attending to whatever demonstrations the experienced weaver has provided.

This example points up the power of active observation by skilled observers. Mainstream middle-class researchers, who rely less on observation, tend to think of it as passive. However, it is clear that children and skilled adult observers are very active in attending to what they watch. In the guided participation of children in cultures that stress children's responsibility for learning, children may have the opportunity to observe and participate when ready in the skills of the community and may develop impressive skills in observation, with less explicit child-centered interaction to integrate the children into the activities of society. (At the same time, I should note that they are also often involved in talk; theirs is not generally a silent, nonverbal world. The talk may involve directions to them rather than conversations, and explanations are likely to occur in the context of participation rather than as discursive lessons. Verbal activities as well as nonverbal skills are available for children's observation and participation.)

Skilled observation may allow skilled participation by young children. Sorenson (1979) notes that Fore (New Guinea) infants, whose caregivers are always accessible to them, have the responsibility of regulating contact, returning to "base" when they desire. They have access to all aspects of the environment, for both observation and involvement, and develop a realistic self-reliance. Adults intervene infrequently in their activities, to the point that the children handle knives and fire safely by the time they are able to walk. Sorenson states that he "continued to be surprised that the unsupervised Fore toddlers did not recklessly thrust themselves into unappreciated dangers, the way our own children tend to do" (p. 301).

Efforts to aid children in learning may thus vary in terms of the children's responsibility to observe and analyze tasks or the caregivers' responsibility to decompose the task and motivate the children. Dixon, LeVine, Richman, and Brazelton (1984) noted that Gusii (Kenyan) mothers gave their 6- to 36-month-old infants the responsibility for learning. They used clear "advance organizers" in instruction, often modeling the expected performance in its entirety, and appeared to expect the task to be completed exactly as specified if the children attended to it. This contrasted with the efforts of American mothers, who took the responsibility for teaching and making their babies learn. They concentrated on arousing the children's interest and shaping their behavior step by step, providing constant encouragement and refocusing.

There are provocative suggestions of cultural differences in children's efforts to observe. Guilmet (1979) reports that Navajo children quietly observed teachers more than twice as often as Caucasian children in the same classroom. Preliminary analyses suggest that Mayan toddlers are especially alert to the events going on around them (Rogoff, Mosier, Mistry, & Göncü, in press). For example, it was difficult for mothers and other adults to surreptitiously handle an object or communicate with one another without toddlers attending to the event.

> One 12-month-old was sitting on his mother's lap when she gestured behind him to an older sister to fetch a rag, indicating with her gesture where the rag was. The baby, who was engaged with another activity at the time, turned and looked in the direction of her point, behind him, without having been able to see her gesture.

Postural cues and changes in the attention and direction of gaze of others were used by the Mayan toddlers to keep themselves informed about what was going on around them. Preliminary analyses suggest that such sensitivity to social events at the periphery of their attention did not appear as frequently

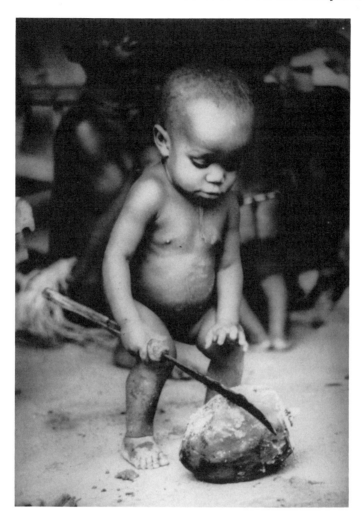

Figure 6.5   A baby of 11 months from the Ituri Forest of Zaire cuts a fruit with a machete, under the eye of a relative. This is not an unusual situation in this culture, where infants are generally able to observe and participate in skilled cultural activities, according to Wilkie. (Photograph courtesy of David Wilkie)

in a sample of middle-class toddlers in the United States (Rogoff et al., in press).

Different Social Partners of Children

In the previous section, variation in children's social partners was mentioned in passing. However, it is essential to recognize that along with differences in the roles of parents in varying cultures are differences in the roles of siblings and other children, grandparents, and the community in general.

In settings where mothers and fathers do not see themselves as conversational partners of children, other people do converse with children. The nuclear family, with one or two parents living in a separate dwelling perhaps hundreds of miles from kin, is a quite different child-rearing environment than that experienced by children who are surrounded by siblings, cousins, grandparents, and other related and nonrelated familiar people (Mistry, Göncü, & Rogoff, 1988; Watson-Gegeo & Gegeo, 1989; Whiting & Edwards, 1988).

Whereas middle-class American mothers consider it part of their role to play with their children, mothers in other cultures laugh with embarrassment at the idea of playing with their children, as this is the role of other children and occasionally grandparents (Rogoff et al., in preparation). When a toddler is playing, reported the Mayan mothers in our sample, it is time for a mother to get her work done. In our study, we brought novel objects for the toddlers to explore, and when we handed them to the mothers, they often demonstrated the use of the objects for an older sibling, with directions to play with them with the toddler.

Such a separation in roles has been noted by Ward (1971), in her description of the social partners of black children in the Louisiana community described earlier. The children watch and listen to adults; they play and talk and tumble with other children. Older children are involved in taking care of younger children, and teach social and intellectual skills: "Alphabets, colors, numbers, rhymes, word games, pen and pencil games are learned, *if at all,* from older children. No child, even the firstborn, is without such tutelage, since cousins, aunts, and uncles of their own age and older are always on hand" (p. 25). Similar observations have been made by Farran and Mistry (personal communication) in regard to siblings' and other relatives' roles with native Hawaiian preschoolers.

The supervision of the child cohort may be the responsibility of the whole community, without the need for any particular adult to be devoting attention to the pack of children. Ward (1971) states that caretaking and disciplinary duties belong to anyone who is near the child. Mistry and colleagues (1988) have made similar observations in a tribal village in India, where neighbors, related to the family not by kinship but by long association, make their opinions known concerning anyone's treatment of a child and take over with rights usually reserved for parents in the American middle class.

Hence one would expect cultural differences in the orientation of young children toward their parents as primary social partners (as in the American middle class) or toward the larger group. The sort of intimate face-to-face mother–infant interaction that is the subject of research on infant social interaction may be very unusual in cultural settings where infants are not being brought up as conversational partners of their mothers but as less individually and dyadically focused members of the community. Whiting and Edwards (1988) note that of the 12 cultural groups they studied, the U.S. middle-class mothers ranked highest in sociability with children—interacting in a friendly, playful, or conversational way, treating children at times as status equals—whereas mothers in the other communities stressed training or nurturant involvement with children, maintaining authority and dominance with respect to children.

Face-to-face interaction may be a prototype of parent–infant interaction in research on mother–child communication because of the didactic and dyadic role assumed by American middle-class parents, who rely on their own efforts to motivate children to learn, in contrast to caregivers and children in cultures in which children have the responsibility to learn and are involved with many other social partners in the process. There appears to be great cultural variation in the extent to which mothers rely on the face-to-face position for communication. Mothers in many cultures commonly hold their infants facing away from them (Heath, 1983; Martini & Kirkpatrick, 1981; Sostek et al., 1981).

Variation in infant positioning from facing the mother to facing the same way as the mother may reflect cultural values about the social world in which the child is becoming embedded, as well as the means of communication between parents and children. Martini and Kirkpatrick (1981) note that Marquesan mothers (in the South Pacific) appeared strained and awkward when asked to interact with their babies face to face. In everyday activities, babies are usually held facing outward and encouraged to interact with and attend to others (especially slightly older siblings) instead of interacting with their mothers. Martini and Kirkpatrick report that this is consistent with a general cultural value of embeddedness in a complex social world. Marquesan infants learn different lessons in their interactions from those learned by U.S. infants engaged in face-to-face interaction, but mothers in both societies provide guidance in developing culturally appropriate skills and values. Marquesan mothers actively arrange infants' social interactions with others; if babies appear to get self-absorbed, mothers interrupt and urge attention to the broader social environment:

> [Mothers] consistently provided the infant with an interactively stimulating world, first by interacting, next by encouraging and making effective his attempts to make contact, and finally by directing others to interact with the infant. Caregivers . . . shaped the infants' attention towards others and objects, and shaped their movements towards effective contact and locomotion. By the end of the first year, infants were becoming interactants able to accompany and learn from older children in an environment supervised by adults. (p. 209)

Like middle-class American children, children in other cultures learn and develop in situations of joint involvement with more experienced people in culturally important activities. Caregivers collaborate in children's socialization as they determine the nature of children's activities and their responsibilities in participation. They work together and in the process adapt children's knowledge to new situations, structure problem-solving attempts, and regulate children's assumption of responsibility for managing the performance of tasks. This guided participation includes tacit forms of communication and distal arrangements of children's learning environments, as well as explicit verbal interaction. The mutual roles played by caregivers and children in children's development rely both on the caregivers' interest in fostering mature skills and on the children's own eagerness to participate in adult activities and push their own development. Guided participation involves participation of children in skilled cultural activities with other people of varying levels of skill and status.

These joint socialization roles may be universal, although communities vary in the goals of socialization and in the means of communication. Observations of variations in guided participation across cultures draws our attention to

1. How the goals of mature contribution to the community organize the skills and values that children learn
2. The opportunities available to children for learning in the arrangements made for children's activities and companions
3. The responsibility that children take for learning from whatever activities they participate in, and the rich opportunities for observing and eavesdropping
4. The tacit but ubiquitous nature of children's guided participation
5. The unself-conscious nature of the roles of children as well as of their social partners in day-to-day arrangements and interactions

Observations in cultures other than those of the researchers may make such aspects of guided participation more apparent. However, I propose that these are features of guided participation that are common for U.S. middle-class children as well. They may be more common, in fact, than the explicit, didactic, self-conscious instruction and learning that has been the focus of research.

PART III

COGNITIVE DEVELOPMENT THROUGH INTERACTION WITH ADULTS AND PEERS

7

Explanations of Cognitive Development Through Social Interaction: Vygotsky and Piaget

> When I discuss and I sincerely seek to understand someone else, I become engaged, not just in avoiding contradicting myself, in avoiding playing on words, etc., but also in entering into an indefinite series of viewpoints other than my own. . . . It is a moving equilibrium. . . . The engagements . . . that I make by nature of cooperation lead me I don't know where. (Piaget, "Logique génétique et sociologie")

> Under conditions of cooperation, an activity that is initially shared by those participating in it emerges as an original and fundamental foundation for the development of *individual* activity. (Rubtsov, "The Role of Cooperation in the Development of Intelligence")

Part III discusses speculations and research on the role of social interaction in the cognitive development of individual children. What do children gain from social interaction, and under what circumstances? What aspects of social interaction contribute to children's advances? What is the significance of variations in social interaction, such as whether partners are adults or peers, the extent of their expertise, their authority or equality relative to the children, and the extent to which partners share in decision making? Are there differences in the role of social interaction depending on the age of the child?

These questions were addressed by Vygotsky and by Piaget, and they came to rather different conclusions. In this chapter, I describe the similarities and differences in mechanisms of social interactional influence on cognitive development posited by these two theorists, focusing on the importance of expertise versus equal status and the related question of the role of adults versus peers. I also address the differences in Vygotsky's and Piaget's assumptions about when in childhood social interaction can affect individual development. The next two chapters focus on research and specific speculations on the influence of interaction with adults and with peers.

I have suggested that the day-to-day engagement of children and adults in shared activities contributes to the rapid progress of children in becoming skilled participants in the intellectual and social lives of their society. With Vygotsky, I have argued for the influential role of children's engagement with more skilled partners. But such suggestions and evidence of the structure and tuning of adult–child interaction and arrangements do not necessarily demonstrate that adult–child involvement fosters children's individual learning and development. Features of adult–child interaction and arrangements may have little relation to children's learning. It is important to examine explicitly the influence of expertise of partners, of equality of status, of shared problem solving, of the structuring of children's efforts, and of the transfer of responsibility to children over the course of development.

As we do so, however, it is important to recognize that we are examining a very limited part of the question of the role of the social world in cognitive development. Part III focuses on social interaction per se; but as I have argued in Parts I and II, the social context includes much more than social interaction between partners. A primary aspect of the social context is at the level of society—the institutions, technologies, norms, and practices developed by and appropriated from previous generations.

In addition, children's social partners, especially their caregivers, make arrangements for children's daily routine, tasks, circumstances, and partners. Much of this is accomplished independently of social interaction between children and their partners. Consider the time spent by middle-class parents in choosing day care, schools, or summer camp; interviewing and scheduling baby sitters; arranging for playmates to visit; selecting and preparing children's food, clothing, toys, and furniture; and ferrying them to after-school activities. In other cultures, parents may arrange children's activities by assigning them to the care of a sibling, holding them responsible for certain tasks, or restricting or requiring their presence at certain events. Such arrangements for children have an impact on children's activities, but may not involve social interaction in the decisions or the work of arrangement.

Thus it is obvious and necessary to acknowledge the role of guided participation in learning and development. So much of what children are able to do requires their being embedded in their culture. They would certainly not learn English without exposure to that language, nor would they develop scripts for the events involved in eating in restaurants, playing Peekaboo, or reading books without involvement as observers or participants. Most of the skills studied in cognitive research are tied closely to the technology—the books, number system, language, logic—of the culture in which children develop and that children learn to master with the assistance of more skilled partners.

Like genes, social interaction and social arrangements are an essential aspect of child development, without which it would be impossible to conceive of a child developing. (Even the process of conception is inherently social!) The impact of social partners and of social conventions is a logical necessity that is not addressed by the bounded variables and interventions examined in correlational and experimental studies of the effects of social interaction.

Most research on the effects of a particular variable requires that other variables be held constant, but with questions of the impact of sociocultural experience, it is impossible to exert such control over the phenomenon without destroying it. As I have argued earlier, the particular actions and skills of an individual cannot be understood out of the context of the immediate practical goals being sought and the enveloping sociocultural goals into which they fit.

What of processes that appear to be very stable across wide variations in the human condition? Should they be considered as not having sociocultural involvement? No. It is a fallacy to think that sociocultural processes lead to variation and biological processes lead to universals. For example, it is obvious that variations in hair color and height have genetic bases. And it is clear that universal features of human activities and skills are founded on commonalities in the social environment that go with being human.

It is easier for us to recognize the role of sociocultural variation than that of sociocultural universals, which we tend to take for granted. Human problems and some of the constraints on their solution are held in common in all human situations. It is those that *vary* that capture our attention. For example, different groups vary in their solution to the problem of communicating (e.g., using English, Spanish, or sign language) or of calculating (e.g., on abacuses, calculators, or fingers). The relation to specific social experience is obvious in these differences; it is necessary to be surrounded by English speakers to learn English. It may be necessary to be exposed to some sort of language to learn the rudiments of grammar, even those aspects that may be common across languages. But, consistent with Trevarthen's idea of innate intersubjectivity, the basics of the potential for social communication, such as turn taking and attention to others' intentions, may be inborn features of being human.

Even panhuman processes are likely to rely on the support of the social world, however. There are similarities among human babies around the world, because of both our species similarities and the panhuman social environment in which babies are nurtured. Although variations in cognitive processes and in development make the role of variations in social context obvious, universals of cognition and development are based on universals of human cultural as well as biological heritage, which cannot be dissociated. They have evolved together over the history of our species.

The role of societal institutions and intellectual technologies is central to Vygotsky's theory, but barely appears in Piaget's theory (i.e., his statement that the hypothetico-deductive thought of formal operations is based on social convention). Thus the context of the discussion of specific forms of social interaction and their impact on cognitive development differs in the two theories.

Mechanisms of Social Influence

The theories of Piaget and Vgyotsky differ in the mechanisms proposed to underlie social influence, the phase of childhood seen as being open to social influence, and the ideal partner and role relations. It is to these differences that we now turn; further discussion of points of similarity and contrast is available in Tudge and Rogoff (1989). I speculate that the differences between the theories relate to differences in the phenomena the two theorists attempted to explain.

The two theories are based on different perspectives; Vygotsky focuses on the social basis of mind, while Piaget focuses on the individual as starting point. To understand cognition in social context, I believe that Vygotsky's perspective is essential; it cannot be reached by simply adding social context onto Piaget's individualist approach.

Both theories emphasize the importance of a common frame of reference, or intersubjectivity, in social interaction. However, consistent with the difference in centrality of the social and the individual in the two theories are differences in the locus of intersubjectivity. In Vygotsky's perspective, joint problem solving occurs *between* partners, whereas in Piaget's view, individuals work with independence and equality on each other's ideas.

In Vygotsky's theory, consistent with his emphasis on development as a process of learning to use the intellectual tools provided through social history, social interaction is expected to promote development through the guidance provided by interaction with people who have achieved some skill in the use of those intellectual tools. The model of most effective social interaction is thus joint problem solving with guidance by a person who is more skilled.

In Piaget's theory, children are seen as revising their ways of thinking to provide a better fit with reality when faced with discrepancies between their own ways of viewing the world and new information. Vygotsky (1987) characterized Piaget's theory as follows: "Development is reduced to a continual *conflict between antagonistic forms of thinking;* it is reduced to the establishment of a unique compromise between these two forms of thinking at each stage in the developmental process" (p. 176). For the most part, this conflict was considered solitary, but Piaget (1926) also speculated that social interaction could bring about cognitive conflict, resulting in efforts to reestablish equilibrium. According to Piaget, social influence fosters change through the induction of cognitive conflict and the logical operations carried out by children attempting to reconcile their differing views to achieve equilibrium in their understanding. The Piagetian model of most effective social interaction is thus cooperation between equals who attempt to understand each others' views through reciprocal consideration of their alternative views.

Piaget emphasized cooperation as the ideal form of social interaction promoting development because he believed that the social relations involved in cooperation are the same as the logical relations that children construct in regard to the physical world. He considered cooperation to be a parallel form of logic in which children discuss propositions that provoke cognitive conflict and its logical resolution, yielding equilibrium:

> Cooperation itself constitutes a system of co-operations: putting in correspondence (which is an operation) the operations of one partner with those of the others, uniting (which is another operation) the acquisition of one partner with that of others, etc.; and in case of conflicts, raising the contradictions (which presupposes an operational process) or above all differentiating the different points of view and introducing between them a reciprocity (which is an operational transformation). (Piaget, 1963/1977, p. 347)

Piaget (1977, pp. 160–162) laid out three conditions under which equilibrium is achieved in intellectual exchange. The first is that the partners have a common scale of intellectual values, allowing them to understand terms in the same sense. This involves a language and a system of ideas in which they converge, providing a key that allows each to translate into common terms the differing conceptions. The second condition is that the partners recognize a conservation of their propositions in which one does not contradict oneself, and in which the partners search for agreement on propositions or find facts that justify their difference in points of view. The third condition for equilibrium is that there is a reciprocity between partners such that the propositions of each are treated interchangeably. Piaget emphasized cognitive conflict as the working out of differences of opinion by coming to understand the other's perspective and by logically comparing the value of the two perspectives.

Vygotsky's model for the mechanism through which social interaction facilitates cognitive development resembles apprenticeship, in which a novice works closely with an expert in joint problem solving in the zone of proximal development. The novice is thereby able to participate in skills beyond those that he or she is independently capable of handling. Development builds on the internalization by the novice of the shared cognitive processes, appropriating what was carried out in collaboration to extend existing knowledge and skills.

Differences between the two theories in the model of social influence relate to important differences in the aspects of cognitive development that the theorists sought to explain. Piaget's emphasis was on children's qualitative shifts in perspective on logico-mathematical problems, whereas Vygotsky was interested in children's development of skills and information useful for the application of culturally developed tools for thinking. The resolution of cognitive conflict may be necessary for a child to discard an existing belief to consider one that is qualitatively different, to achieve a Piagetian shift in perspective, as when children realize that the quantity of water does not change when it is poured into a container of another shape. And interaction with an expert may be necessary to provide practice in skills and access to information required to become proficient with culturally developed tools for thinking.

Variation in Social Processes May Relate to What Is Developing

The nature of guided participation may differ according to whether a situation involves children's development of understanding and skill or of a shift in perspective. For present purposes, I refer to the development of understanding and skills as the integration and organization of information and component acts into plans for action under relevant circumstances (e.g., learning to tie shoes; to associate items to remember them, or to read). Shifts of perspective, for present purposes, involve giving up an understanding of a phenomenon to take another view contrasting with the original perspective. The problems that Piaget posed to children about whether quantities change when their shape is transformed are examples of shifts in perspective for children who make the transformation from nonconservation (the quantity of water changes when it is poured into a glass of a different shape) to conservation (the quantity of water does not change despite the change in its shape).

The purpose of making these distinctions is to facilitate discussion of different interactional processes that may contribute to the development of understanding and skills or shifts in perspective. The development of understanding and skills may occur with the aid of simple explanation or demonstration, but may involve fine-tuning of communication, when describing a skill out of context or providing a simple demonstration is insufficient. For example, simply telling a child how to tie a shoe is unlikely to be helpful, but helping the child hold the loops and suggesting a mnemonic for the sequence of events ("the bunny circles around and then goes down the hole") may provide the support, over a number of sessions, to assist the child in learning the skill. Similar examples could be drawn from other domains, such as mnemonic strategies, subtraction skills, and reading skills.

For social influences to enhance changes of perspective, however, it may be necessary to have greater shared communication. To see a problem from a qualitatively different vantage point requires a person to become aware that there is another perspective and that it may offer some advantages. For development of understanding and skills, individuals may more easily realize that there is information they do not know or tactics they could learn. But changes of perspective require dissatisfaction with one's current understanding of a problem. Social interaction may contribute to making the person aware that there are alternatives—for example, through the sort of cognitive conflict that Piaget posited to occur between peers who have different answers to the same question. Social interaction may then contribute to directing the individual to accept another view, through presentation of the alternatives and consideration of the merits of each.

But for such social effects to occur, some conditions must be satisfied: individuals must become aware of and interested in exploring alternatives to their own perspective, and there must be intersubjectivity between partners to explore the existence and value of the alternatives. True, interest is needed to develop understanding and skills, but there is no need to give up current

Figure 7.1   Child of 21 months being guided by her father in the development of a skill. (United States) (Photograph © B. Rogoff)

understandings to achieve "conversion"—a process that may require inter-subjectivity. Understanding and skills may develop through observing or eavesdropping on actions and statements that are not intended to communi-cate to the observer, but mutual engagement in the exploration of possibilities may be more necessary for changes in perspective to result from social inter-action.

Intersubjectivity in problem solving may also be important in fostering the development of "inaccessible" cognitive processes that are difficult to observe or explain—as with shifts in perspective as well as some kinds of understanding and skill. Communication of such processes may require skill-ful explanation and analysis. It is relevant to this argument that many tech-nologies of education are designed to make opaque processes more transpar-ent, and that many intellectual tools serve the purpose of communicating about abstract ideas or past, future, or imaginary events. For example, blue-prints and time-management charts facilitate planning by individuals, but their necessity may arise in social situations, to enable people to communi-cate concretely about abstract ideas and to coordinate their actions. Conven-tions used in diagramming, gesturing, and speaking are ways of facilitating mutual understanding by making events and ideas more concrete. Hence, learning to handle "inaccessible" problems involving nontransparent cognitive processes may rely on social conventions necessary for shared problem solving and on learning through joint participation in a process of osmosis, rather than on explanation or demonstration.

The difficulty of communicating some ideas or of negotiating mental responsibility in social groups may lead individuals to prefer to work alone. This preference may be based on expectations of greater effectiveness of individual effort, but it may also involve concern about the effort or risk of collaborative work—even though the collaboration may be more effective than individual work. Bos (1937) describes a pair of 12-year-olds who said that it is more difficult to work together than on their own "because it is not so easy to grasp the other's point of view" (p. 362). From discussion of these feelings, however, each realized that the other had the same concerns, and this understanding led to an intensive and harmonious collaboration.

> It is indeed easier quietly to pursue ones [*sic*] own thoughts than to formulate them convincingly, express them verbally and moreover assimilate proposals and ideas of the partner. This love of facility probably contributes to the opposition of people to endeavour with their mental power in active co-operation to arrive at a better achievement. (Bos, 1937, p. 362)

Through collaboration, partners may develop ways to communicate about difficult problems that advance the definition or solution of the problems.

Consideration of the different tactics one might employ in assisting a child to develop understanding and skills or shifts in perspective may clarify age differences in the impact of social guidance as well as differences between adult and peer partners—issues on which Piaget and Vygotsky differed.

What Phase of Childhood Is Sensitive to Social Influence?

Piaget and Vygotsky appear to be almost in opposition on the question of the age at which social influence contributes to cognitive development. For Piaget, development moves from the individual to the social, and for Vygotsky, development moves from the social to the individual.

According to Piaget, the young child is largely impervious to social influence because egocentricity blocks the establishment of reciprocity and cooperation in considering differing points of view. Thus, according to Piaget, it is not until middle childhood that children's intellect benefits from social interaction, when logical argument between children with varying points of view becomes possible. Young children would generally find it so difficult to consider the logic of another's point of view that they would either continue to see things from their own perspective or switch to the other person's perspective without understanding the rationale and hence without actually advancing developmentally.

The three conditions that Piaget (1977) set out for the achievement of

Figure 7.2 Children of 5 and 6 years in a tug of war, illustrating that, as Piaget pointed out, young children sometimes have difficulty coordinating their efforts. (United States) (Photograph © B. Rogoff)

equilibrium are not possible with egocentrism. First, there is not a common scale of reference in terms of language and ideas to allow a durable exchange of ideas. Second, there is not sufficient conservation of propositions (commitment to sticking to what you have said before) to oblige children to take account of what they have said or agreed to in order to apply these propositions in subsequent propositions. And third, there is not reciprocity between the partners to allow coordination of propositions.

Piaget (1977) specified that at the stage of concrete operations (from about 7 to 11 or 12 years), children become able to cooperate and to coordinate points of view. "Thus the child becomes capable of discussion—and from this internalized discussion, and that conducted with oneself, which is reflection—of collaboration, of arguments that are orderly and understandable by another" (p. 157). Piaget suggests that cooperation provides an impetus to order thought in logical operations that involve a system of propositions that are free from contradiction and are reversible: "Thinking in common promotes non-contradiction: It is much easier to contradict oneself, when one thinks for oneself (egocentrism) than when some partners are there to remember what one has said before and the propositions that one has agreed to admit" (Piaget, 1977, p. 157).

The importance of social interaction and the role of society becomes more obvious in the next stage, formal operations: "Things are even clearer in the formal stage, which begins after 11–12 years, since hypothetico-deductive thought is above all thought supported by a language (common or mathematical) and is thus collective thought" (Piaget, 1977, p. 158).

Vygotsky's approach contrasts with Piaget's in its assumption that from the beginning the child is a social being, involved in social exchanges that guide the development of higher cognitive processes:

The child's rich and complex social contact leads to an early development of means of social connection. It has been clearly demonstrated that simple though unique reactions to the human voice are present in the third week of life (i.e., the presocial reactions) and that the first social reactions appear by the second month. . . . Laughter, babbling, pointing, and gesture emerge as means of social contact in the first months of the child's life. . . . However, the most important event in the development of the child's thinking and speech occur at approximately two years of age. . . . This critical moment, the moment when speech becomes intellectual and thinking verbal, is marked by two clear and objective symptoms. . . . First, the child who has attained this level of development begins to *actively expand his vocabulary* by asking the name of each new thing he encounters. Second, these efforts result in an extremely rapid increase in the child's vocabulary. (Vygotsky, 1987, pp. 110–111)

In contrast with Piaget, Vygotsky assumes that social guidance aids children in learning to communicate and to plan and remember deliberately from the first years of life. This guidance provides children with the opportunity to participate beyond their own abilities and to internalize activities practiced socially, thus advancing their capabilities for independently managing problem solving.

Newson and Newson (1975) cite Vygotsky's perspective in their argument that from earliest infancy, children are guided in development by social interaction.

Knowledge itself originates within an interaction process (highly active on the part of the infant) between the infant himself and other, more mature, human individuals who already possess shared understandings with other communicating beings. Furthermore, these shared understandings are embedded in a uniquely human way of conceptualizing the world in spatial and temporal terms. In short, the child only achieves a fully articulated knowledge of his world, in a cognitive sense, as he becomes involved in social transactions with other communicating human beings. (p. 438)

Through such dialogues-of-action, the infant becomes thoroughly familiar with the role of a skilled communicator, participating in forms of communication long before he is able to understand the full content of what is being communicated. (p. 445)

Vygotsky argued that rather than deriving explanations of psychological activity from the individual's characteristics plus secondary social influences, the unit of analysis should be social activity, in which individual functioning develops (Wertsch, 1985). Piaget's approach was the reverse—to focus on the individual as the unit of analysis, with social influence overlaid on the individual's activity, after the child becomes able to take another person's perspective. These differences in the timing and centrality of social influence may relate to Vygotsky's focus on development of understanding and skills in using cultural tools and Piaget's focus on qualitative shifts in perspective.

Peers Versus Adults: Equal Status Versus Expertise

The two theorists attributed varying degrees of importance to the roles of adults and peers. Piaget (1926) emphasized peer interaction, with its exploration of cognitive conflict between companions of equal status. An example is provided by two 5-year-olds quarreling over drinks of soda that had been poured into glasses of different shapes (an everyday situation resembling Piaget's conservation task). An adult had attempted to pour equal quantities for the two children, but since Valerie's glass was tall and thin, and David's was wide and flaring at the top, the quantities were not obviously equal. Valerie attempted to convince David of the fairness of the distribution:

> "Yours is fatter and mine is thinner, that's why it looks like I have more. See, I have to squeeze my hand to get it into my cup, but not into yours. [She squeezes her fingers together and puts them into the opening of each cup to demonstrate.] It's just that mine is thinner so it looks like it has more."

The children proceeded to quench their thirst. It is such interaction between peers, Piaget argued, that can lead children to reconsider their ideas.

In contrast, Piaget felt that children's discussions with adults are unlikely to lead to cognitive restructuring because of the unequal power relations between adults and children. Only when children are able to discuss problems as equals are they likely to take into account new ways of thinking. Interaction with an adult, Piaget held, is essentially unequal; it is an asymmetric interaction in which the adult has the power, and this disrupts the condition of reciprocity for achieving equilibrium in thinking (Piaget, 1977, p. 165). "The child's socialization with his fellows is greater than, or at least different to, his socialization with adults alone. Where the superiority of the adult prevents discussion and co-operation, the playfellow provides the opportunity for such social conduct as will determine the true socialization of the intelligence" (Piaget, 1926 [3rd ed., 1959], p. 258). When peers have different perspectives, no such asymmetry exists: "Criticism is born of discussion, and discussion is only possible among equals: cooperation alone will therefore accomplish what intellectual constraint [caused by unquestioning belief in the adult's omniscience] failed to bring about" (Piaget, 1932, p. 409).

According to Piaget, the effect of lessons from adults is for young children to abandon their own ideas for those presented, since their ideas are poorly formulated and exist only as an "orientation of the spirit" that cannot compete with the views of adults. But in such cases, children agree without examining the idea, and they do not learn to verify for themselves. Not until adolescence do children learn to discuss as equals with their teachers, when they have "conquered their internal liberty" (Piaget, 1928/1977, p. 230).

Although Piaget argued that children's interaction with adults does not promote their cognitive development, his focus was on the use of adult authority. He allowed for the possibility that adults may be able to interact with children in a cooperative fashion that permits the sort of reciprocity required for children to advance to a new level of equilibrium:

> It is despite adult authority, and not because of it, that the child learns. And also it is to the extent that the intelligent teacher has known to efface him or herself, to become an equal and not a superior, to discuss and to examine, rather than to agree and constrain morally, that the traditional school has been able to render service. (Piaget, 1928/1977, p. 231)

For Vygotsky, ideal partners are not equal, but the inequality is in skills and understanding rather than in power. For this reason, interaction with either adults or peers can bring about cognitive growth. But for cognitive development to occur in the course of interacting with a peer, the partner should be "more capable" (Vygotsky, 1978).

Vygotsky's emphasis on interaction with more skilled partners is necessary to his theory, since such interaction is conceived as the means by which children begin to use the intellectual tools of their society. Thus the partner must be someone who knows more about the tools than does the child. By the same token, Piaget focused on changes in perspective, from one view of a problem to another, based on his interest in understanding qualitative transitions in the philosophy of science and logic.

The contrast I made earlier between developing understanding and skill and shifting perspective thus seem to relate to the status and relative expertise desirable for children's partners. A similar perspective is offered by Damon (1984) and Subbotskii (personal communication, 1988), who suggest that different types of learning may be differentially facilitated by equal or by more expert partners. Focusing on the relative advantages of interaction with more expert peers (in tutoring) and equal peers (in collaboration), Damon (1984) suggests that

> peer tutoring may be used whenever students need to acquire information or skills that do not extend beyond their conceptual reach. Learning historical facts, practicing word attack skills, becoming adept at multiplication tables, even figuring out how to make use of a computer . . . draw upon features of basic understanding that the child has already developed. . . .
> Peer collaboration, on the other hand, . . . is an ideal technique for encouraging children to wrestle with intellectual challenges in difficult new principles. Learning to communicate accurately through written and spoken language, grasping the logic behind scientific formulas, and realizing the political rationale underlying a societal governance system can all be fostered in a collaborative peer interaction context. Such intellectual accomplishments stretch the boundaries of children's mental abilities. Consequently, they flourish best under conditions of highly motivated discovery, the free exchange of ideas, and reciprocal feedback between mutually respected equals. These are precisely the characteristics of collaborative interchanges between children. (p. 340)

Intersubjectivity: Theoretical Convergence and Differences

The theories of Piaget and Vygotsky share an emphasis on the importance of partners' understanding of each other. For Piaget, the partners must have a common language and system of ideas, and must grant reciprocity in attempting to examine and adjust for differences in their opinions. Piaget emphasized logical consideration of alternative perspectives provided by coming to understand another person's point of view.

For Vygotsky, the child is assumed to be interested in gaining from the more expert partner, who is seen as responsible for adjusting the dialogue to fit within the child's zone of proximal development, where understanding is achieved with a stretch leading to growth. Both perspectives are similar in stressing the importance of a match between partners involving shared thinking, and the importance of the child's understanding as the point of departure.

The role of shared thinking has received attention in the Vygotskian tradition in Wertsch's (1984) writings on "intersubjectivity," building on the work of Rommetveit (1985). It also appears in the work of Perret-Clermont and Schubauer-Leoni (1981) in the Piagetian tradition. The notion of intersubjectivity seems inherent in Piaget's view of social influences, but has been overlooked by some Piagetian scholars who focus on cognitive conflict as quarreling. Both theories and, increasingly, the literature on social influences focus on the role of intersubjectivity in social interaction (Forman & Kraker, 1985; Rogoff, 1986; Tudge & Rogoff, 1989; Youniss, 1987).

Despite the agreement between the two theories on the importance of sharing perspectives or thinking together, there is an essential difference in their conception of intersubjectivity. It relates to the contrast between them in the centrality of their focus on the social versus the individual. For Vygotsky, shared thinking provides the opportunity to participate in a joint decision-making process from which children may appropriate what they contribute for later use. For Piaget, the meeting of minds involves two separate individuals, each operating on the other's ideas, using the back-and-forth of discussion for each to advance his or her own development. This discussion is the product of two individuals considering alternatives provided socially, rather than the construction of a joint understanding between partners.

Forman (1987) discusses this distinction in collaborative problem solving in Piaget's and Vygotsky's theories. In Piaget's theory, collaborative problem solving is explained by deriving both cognitive and social processes from the same central intrapsychological process, whereas in Vygotsky's theory, the correspondence between cognitive and social processes is due to the derivation of individual cognitive processes from joint cognitive processes in social contexts.

These differing interpretations are accompanied by differences in the proposed mechanisms of cooperation. Forman (1987) contrasts intersubjectivity as a process that takes place between people from the Vygotskian perspective, with perspective taking or decentering as individual processes working on socially provided information from the Piagetian perspective.

A similar distinction also appears in the work of Rubtsov (1981), who observed that children's difficulties with the class-inclusion problem are sometimes resolved while collaborating with agemates, and these advances persist after the interaction. Rubtsov appears to agree with Piaget in focusing on parallels between the organization of joint activity and the organization of thought, but emphasizes the facilitation provided by the social arrangements and shared activity: "The relations determining the logic of an intellectual structure consist of compact condensed forms of mutual relationships among the participants in cooperation" (p. 59).

Thus although both theories—and the research deriving from them—emphasize cooperation in cognitive activity, they differ in the extent to which the process of cognitive development is seen as occurring in this cooperative interaction. For Piaget, the cooperation provides information for the individual to use in becoming aware of differing perspectives and in resolving the differences between them. In the Vygotskian perspective, in contrast, the individual makes use of the joint decision-making process itself to expand understanding and skill. Cognitive development from a Piagetian view is a product of the individual, perhaps sparked by having to account for differences in perspective with others, whereas cognitive development from a Vygotskian point of view involves the individual's appropriation or internalization of the social process as it is carried out externally in joint problem solving.

Piaget's view is thus a limited version of social impact on the individual's cognitive development; in taking the individual as the basic unit, it does not reach a collective perspective on the social context of cognitive development. It is important, as far as it goes, but does not make the necessary shift in perspective to encompass the social construction of meaning. To understand how individuals are embedded in the social world, it is necessary to grant that meaning is more than a construction by individuals. Of course, it is essential also to consider the process by which socially constructed meaning is used by individuals. This is the question of internalization, which has been raised by a variety of theories but deserves much more attention than it has received. In Chapter 10, I address the question of how individuals appropriate socially constructed meaning to advance their own cognitive development.

The remaining chapters consider speculations and research on the roles of adults and peers, of expertise and equality, and of intersubjectivity. Intersubjectivity may vary according to the status roles of partners. It may be that involvement in each other's thinking is limited to situations in which partners treat each other's ideas and skills as equally important. However, when the status of partners differs greatly, as when one partner is an expert or has more authority than the other, an asymmetrical intersubjectivity may operate, with partners involved in joint decision making and understanding, but one is more responsible for stretching to reach the other's ground. This contrast is especially important because of the cultural differences across communities in the status roles of caregivers and children, who may engage as peers in mutual conversations or may share in joint activity with asymmetrical roles— with both types of intersubjectivity supporting children in developing the skills and perspectives of their society.

8

Evidence of Learning from Guided Participation with Adults

> David, age 7½ months, was at a restaurant with his parents and seemed
> to be getting bored. His mother handed him a dinner roll, although until
> then he had eaten only strained foods, zwieback toast, and Cheerios.
> David happily took the roll, examined it, looked up at his mother, and
> said, "Da?" as he held the roll up near his mouth. His mother replied
> automatically, "Yes, you can eat it."

> The child acts (or is made to act) as if he or she had a plan or strategy
> before it is possible to devise and carry out that strategy independently.
> The child does not first master a strategy that guides action and then be-
> gin to act, but first acts and then begins to master the strategy that guides
> the action. . . . The child begins to regulate his or her own activity by
> becoming aware of what has already been going on for some time under
> the direction of others. (Wertsch, "Adult–Child Interaction and the Roots
> of Metacognition")

> The fluency with which Mozart composed seems to be the outcome of
> his particular, intensive apprenticeship, of his opportunities to internalize,
> while still very young, the musical possibilities developed before his time.
> (John-Steiner, *Notebooks of the Mind*)

This chapter examines research on the consequences of children's interactions
with adults for their cognitive development. In the routine and recurrent interactions between adults and children are many thousands of opportunities
for guided participation in solving everyday problems. We tend to overlook
the numerous, implicit everyday opportunities for children to gain understanding and skills of the world around them. As Rheingold (1985) argues, development is largely a process of becoming familiar. It may be through repeated
and varied experience in supported routine and challenging situations that
children become skilled in specific cognitive processes. For example, Ferrier
(1978) and Newson and Newson (1975) argue that the opportunity for language development occurs in routine participation in shared experiences and

efforts to communicate as caregivers and infants carry out the thousands of diaperings, feedings, baths, and other recurring activities of daily life.

The advances that appear with development may build on these many opportunities to stretch knowledge and skills. In this perspective, development is built on learning, and, at the same time, learning is based on development. Children contribute to their own development through their eagerness and management of learning experiences as well as through their building on the knowledge and skill they have already developed. At the earliest ages, this "knowledge" includes their reflexes and aspects of behavior necessary for eating and protection, as well as primordial schemas for social interaction and learning systems such as language (Slobin, 1973). Soon, however, children's inborn behavioral and motivational repertoire is modified by experience, with their history reflected in the knowledge they bring to each new situation.

The research evidence on the influence of children's interaction with adults on their cognitive development provides clues about the means by which specific features of guided participation facilitate individual development. This literature goes beyond asking whether there is a relation between social interaction and children's individual skills to begin to address questions of how and under what circumstances social interaction may guide cognitive development.

There are important limitations, however, in this body of research:

1. It extracts for observation one session or a few sessions in children's lives to examine its (their) impact on individual development; it does not do justice to the repeated and adjusted nature of routine interaction in children's lives.

2. It focuses on dyadic situations, overlooking the richness of routine social situations. An apprenticeship model would involve not only a novice and an expert, but also other novices and experts jointly engaged in the same activity over time.

3. It involves situations in which adults are in charge and are focused on interaction with children. Thus it does not represent the many occasions in which children and adults are in each other's presence without interaction as their agenda, and the many times that the interaction is initiated and controlled by children seeking assistance, entertainment, or companionship. In keeping with the adult-initiated nature of the observed situations, there is little research on how children initiate and direct interaction or guide the assistance of others.

4. It concentrates on social interaction without considering the larger social context of arrangements for children and the societal context of the interactions and the cognitive skills. Skills in language, object manipulation, memory, and planning are, of course, closely tied to their application in cultural practices. The research on social interaction ignores the nature of the cultural tools used in the skills studied, overlooking the tools of language for categorization and analysis of events, technologies for constructing and analyzing objects, taxonomies for organizing lists of information to be remembered, and conventions such as maps for planning efficient routes in advance

of actual navigation. In its emphasis on one cultural setting, the research examines the types of interactions (dyadic, often face-to-face) and specific cognitive skills that are of importance in that setting—Euroamerican middle class. It does not address the relations between interaction and cognitive skills in other settings.

5. In its frequent reliance on speed of development as a measure of the impact and excellence of social interaction, it reflects an assumption that the earlier that children develop a particular competence, the more skilled they will become in the long run and the better they will compete in life. This assumption is not universal; in many cultures, the pace of development is not a matter of concern except for the very extreme cases in which children lag substantially behind what is expected. It is reasonable to question the assumption that faster is better, held by professionals as well as by the public. Piaget criticized it in identifying it as "The American Question." Children who are hurried to attain a recognizable competence in, say, number skills or reading may attain superficial evidence of skill (e.g., counting, knowing the alphabet, decoding written words) that does not help or, indeed, even hinders the development of deeper understandings in those domains, such as concepts of numerical properties or reading for comprehension.

6. The research situations are managed by an investigator who sets the problem, the goals, and the rules for the participants, removing these activities from analysis and limiting the roles of the participants, who might otherwise define their own problem or goals or rules.

With recognition of these limitations in the research—some an inevitable consequence of finite resources and time for programs of research, some a reflection of biases in approach—let us examine the relation between children's keeping with the adult-initiated nature of the observed situations, there is litsocial interaction with adults and their language development, skills in object exploration and construction, memory, and planning. These topics cover most of the available literature examining the role of social guidance and cognitive development. I do not review much of the research on the relation between social context and IQ, and between teaching and classroom learning, because it often does not closely examine either social interaction or cognitive processes. My preference is for research that investigates the processes of social interaction and cognition, rather than that which deals with summary scores that are often attributed to individuals as general characteristics.

Language and Conceptual Development

Language Development

The relation between social interaction (or adult "input") and children's language development has received a great deal of attention. Many early studies correlated some features of maternal language with children's language skill, often including variables without predicting on a conceptual basis which ones should correlate. It is not surprising that shotgun correlational studies yield inconsistent results.

Researchers in this area disagree about what to make of the pattern of negative and positive correlations between linguistic input and children's language development. (See Hoff-Ginsberg & Shatz, 1982, and Snow, 1984, for reviews.) Some scholars conclude from research that fails to document relationships between linguistic input and child language acquisition that social interaction has little impact on language development (e.g., Bates, Bretherton, Beeghly-Smith, & McNew, 1982). However, this conclusion assumes that the methods used have been adequate to answer the question.

Camaioni, de Castro Campos, and DeLemos (1984) argue that the reason many studies have not found a relationship between social interaction and language is that they have reified both the social and the linguistic as separate, given categories rather than as processes in formation. They suggest that an adequate examination of the question requires scholars to

1. Look at social interaction and language as constitutive processes rather than as rules operating on already given categories
2. Consider language as a means to structure reality through social or communicative functions (stressing that linguistic activities are, right from the start, intersubjective processes)
3. Adopt linguistic models whose basic unit of analysis is not the single utterance but the *dialogue*

Similarly, John-Steiner and Tatter (1983) point out that approaches that assume the social and individual aspects of development are separable rend apart the inherent unity of social and individual contributions. They argue that the limited findings of studies that test influences of separated social and cognitive processes on language development show the futility of separating these aspects of development, rather than diminishing the credibility of the mutual roles of individual and social features of development.

John-Steiner and Tatter (1983) stress that language development occurs within a system in which the primary goal is a functional one—achieving understanding between child and caregiver. With communication as the goal, child and caregiver together structure their interaction and advance their understanding of each other, with adjustments in adult speech and progress in language development as by-products.

These views, which stress that language development occurs in the process of functional communication, recast the question of social impact on language development. Instead of separating input (i.e., characteristics of maternal speech) from output (e.g., tests of children's vocabulary or grammatical skill), they focus on features of the communication of social partners with the child and on the child's skill in communication. Early language use involves conversations and propositions that are built in dialogue between people. Even infants in the one-word period build discussions with adults through taking successive turns that layer comments on topics of joint attention, as in "Shoe" . . . "Is that your shoe?" . . . "On" . . . "Oh, shall I put on your shoe?" (Greenfield & Smith, 1976; Scollon, 1976).

Consistent with the perspective that language development occurs in the

Figure 8.1   Mother and 12-month-old sharing attention to an object. (United States) (Photograph © B. Rogoff)

context of functional communication, research shows a relationship between the extent and responsivity of adult–child interaction and the language development of children (Hoff-Ginsberg & Shatz, 1982; Snow, 1984). For example, mothers' frequency of and responsivity in interaction are related to infants' and toddlers' greater communicative competence (Hardy-Brown, Plomin, & DeFries, 1981; Olson, Bates, & Bayles, 1984). The extent to which mothers encourage attention to objects and events, and label the objects at which infants point, is associated with vocabulary size (Adamson, Bakeman, & Smith, in press; Masur, 1982; Papousek, Papousek, & Bornstein, 1985). Snow (1984) and Moerk (1985) argue that a great deal of speech addressed to children is sensitive to their linguistic skills and is contingent (both temporally and topically) with their previous utterances, and that the more children experience such contingency, the greater the facilitation of language acquisition.

Several studies demonstrate the importance of joint attention that focuses on children's interests rather than requiring children to refocus their attention. Tomasello and Farrar (1986) found that the extent of mothers' references to objects that were already the focus of their toddlers' attention correlated with the children's vocabulary 6 months later, while the extent of object references that redirected the children's attention was not related to vocabulary development. In addition, in an experimental study, toddlers learned words better if their attention was already focused on the objects of reference than if the words were presented when the children were not attending to the objects (Tomasello & Farrar, 1986).

Similarly, preschool children who heard new vocabulary items (Spanish labels for toys) contingent on their own expression of interest in the toys were better able to produce the newly learned words than were children who heard the labels at the same time as the experimental children, with timing unrelated to their own attention and interest in the toys being named (Valdez-Menchaca, 1987). Three-month-old infants interacting with adults who responded contingently to their vocalizations produced utterances that seemed more speech-like (syllabic) to adults than the utterances of infants whose partners interacted with them equally often but not contingently (Bloom, Russell, & Wassenberg, 1985). Recasts of children's comments enhance language development if they occur in smoothly continuing discourse (Nelson, Denninger, Bonvillian, Kaplan, & Baker, 1984). Snow (1982a) summarizes:

> A major facilitator of language acquisition is *semantic contingency* in adult speech. Adult utterances are semantically contingent if they continue topics introduced by the preceding child utterances. Semantically contingent utterances thus include a) expansions, which are limited to the content of the previous child utterance, b) semantic extensions, which add new information to the topic, c) clarifying questions, which demand clarification of the child utterance, and d) answers to child questions. (pp. 3–4)

It is noteworthy that the adult's semantically contingent speech builds from the child's comments, hence stressing the involvement of the child's interests and skills in the shared process. In addition, middle-class parents tailor their feedback in conversation to their children's contributions, responding differently to 2- to 3-year-olds' well-formed or ill-formed utterances: they expand, correct, or ask clarifying questions in response to children's ill-formed utterances, and extend the topic or move the conversation on more frequently in response to well-formed utterances (Demetras, Post, & Snow, 1986; Moerk, 1985; Penner, 1987).

Hoff-Ginsberg (1986) argues that maternal speech contributes to language acquisition by providing the child with data that illustrate regularities in the language: "These data feed into the child's proclivity to look for regularities in the system, to extract those patterns, and to use them as a basis for generalizations" (p. 160). In the process of communication, adults provide data and structure, of which children make active use.

Research on the communication environment of twins, who generally have to divide parental resources, supports the idea that the extent of parents' conversation and attention focusing may relate to children's language development. Papousek et al. (1985) report research by Bornstein and Ruddy suggesting that the lag in vocabulary learning of 12-month-old twins (compared with singletons) may result from the fact that each twin receives half as much maternal verbal input and encouragement of attention to objects, properties, or events in the environment during the first year as would a singleton. Since twins did not differ from singletons at age 4 months in manipulation, vocalization, and looking, their lag at age 12 months may reveal the effect of having to share the interactional energy of their mother. Tomasello, Mannle, and Kruger (1986), reporting similar findings, suggest that the economics of interacting with two babies at once reduces the opportunities for interaction for each baby and may account for the slower language development of twins compared with singletons.

The tailored responses of middle-class adults communicating with young children, focusing their attention, and expanding and improving the children's contributions appear to support children's advancing linguistic and communication skills in ways valued by their community.

Conceptual Development

Research on conceptual development similarly illustrates the role of communication in advancing knowledge and gives evidence that children's level of understanding provides an important starting point for adult–child discussion of concepts.

Children's conceptual development was enhanced in a study that encouraged mothers to provide more advanced concepts in conversation as they read picture books to their 3-year-olds over a period of 2 weeks (Adams, 1987). To encourage the mothers to discuss concepts and use taxonomic labels, some of the books were designed with the pictures of animals arranged with taxonomic families together. The mothers hedged and modified their children's labels and made statements of class inclusion, providing taxonomic information, when using the books that were organized by family. The children whose mothers read those books showed advances in their categorization of animals to a level approaching adult usage, compared with children whose mothers read books with the same pictures arranged randomly. Thus social interaction that encouraged discussion of category hierarchies induced children to progress toward appropriately handling a body of culture- and domain-specific knowledge.

In a study of understanding of the concept of seriation, Heber (1981) found improvement in 5- to 6-year-olds' seriation skills in a condition in which an adult engaged each child in dialogue about the child's seriation decisions, especially when the dialogue encouraged the child to specify the rationale for decisions (to an "ignorant" puppet) or guided the child in discussing relations of "more" and "less." In contrast, there was no improvement in the seriation skills of children who received a didactic explanation of the rationale, worked with peers of equal skill, or worked independently, compared with children who received no opportunity to work on the problem. The fact that the conditions that encouraged development involved dialogue is consistent with the idea that benefits of social interaction derive from shared thinking in intersubjective communication.

Figure 8.2   Adult and toddlers labeling pictures in a picture book. (United States)

Object Exploration and Construction

Adult support appears to encourage children's attention to objects and exploration, and infants' and older children's skills in handling objects, especially if the adults' support is contingent on the children's efforts.

Children's attention and skill with objects can be channeled by adults' highlighting of events during social interaction. The active and supportive involvement of an adult in children's exploration of novel objects led to more exploration by 3- to 7-year-olds than did the simple presence of the adults (Henderson, 1984a, 1984b). Adult object demonstration, focusing of the infant's attention, and collaborative engagement with objects relates to infant attentiveness, skill, and learning of new uses of objects (Bornstein, 1988; Hay, Murray, Cecire, & Nash, 1985; Hodapp, Goldfield, & Boyatzis, 1984;

Parrinello & Ruff, 1988; Rogoff, Malkin, & Gilbride, 1984). An intervention to increase the level of maternal focusing of her infant's attention (by having an encouraging observer comment on the effectiveness of the mother's natural efforts to stimulate her infant) produced greater exploratory competence by the infants as much as 2 months later (Belsky, Goode, & Most, 1980).

Kaye (1977a) found that mothers' attempts to teach 7-month-olds to reach around a barrier to grasp a toy were tailored to the infants' motivation, attention, and competence. The mothers modeled detouring or simplified the task when the infants looked back at the toy after having just looked away but not when the infants were reaching for it. They simplified the task when the infants were not succeeding at it or were not interested in it. When infants had been close to success but were becoming fretful, the mothers moved the infants' hands around the screen toward the toy. Simplification of the task enhanced the infants' success in the training phase, although not in a posttest.

Puzzle Construction

In a series of studies with preschool children on the task of constructing complex block pyramids, Wood and his colleagues have found that adults sensitively tailor their support of children's efforts according to the children's skill and that such contingency may help children to advance their skills.

The level of assistance by a tutor who was instructed to help the children only when they had run into difficulty was adjusted to the children's ages (Wood, Bruner, & Ross, 1976). With 3-year-olds, the tutor's efforts focused on maintaining the children's attention to the task. With 4-year-olds, the tutor could concentrate on pointing out the nature of mistakes. With 5-year-olds, the tutor was needed only to check the construction or to help with critical difficulties.

When mothers helped their 3- to 4-year-olds in the same task, most of them tailored their instruction to their children's needs, guiding at a level that was near the limits of the children's performance, taking into account the children's responses to the most recent instruction, and adjusting the specificity of instruction according to whether the children had been successful on that step (Wood & Middleton, 1975). Whereas the *number* of interventions by mothers did not relate to the children's performance, children performed best on the posttest of independent construction if their mothers had intervened in their region of sensitivity to instruction and had adjusted appropriately to their success.

The type of sensitivity shown by the mothers in tailoring their scaffolding (Wood & Middleton, 1975) was effective in improving 3- to 4-year-old children's performance when a tutor followed the mothers' patterns in systematically accommodating the contingency of her instruction to children's needs (Wood, Wood, & Middleton, 1978). Children who were taught contingently, with the tutor moving to less intervention after success and to more intervention after failure, were more capable of carrying out the task in the posttest than were children who were taught according to scripts that focused on modeling the whole task, describing the task, or arbitrarily switching between these levels of intervention. In these studies, children's skills in particular situations can be seen to advance as a result of supportive guidance provided in social interaction.

Children's Remembering and Planning

Planning and memory activities have been suggested as tasks in which collaboration and guidance may be especially fruitful (Brown & Reeve, 1987; Hartup, 1985; Lomov, 1978). Adults may be able to carry out metacognitive or metamnemonic roles that are beyond children, while demonstrating to the children how such processing can be accomplished. Wertsch (1978) argues that the regulation supplied by adults while assisting young children is a form of metacognition, with shifts across development moving from executive control by the adult (with step-by-step commands for carrying out a task); to questions and suggestions aimed at revealing to the child the overall strategy or the next step; and, finally, to general executive assistance by the adult, with children handling the details of carrying out strategies.

DeLoache (1983) notes that mothers' memory questions (regarding names or attributes of objects) during picture-book reading with toddlers are structured to elicit the best the children can do, but with some requests for information that are too difficult for the child. When the child fails to respond, the mother quickly answers her own question, providing a model that may be especially effective in its timing and filling a slot that allows the child to compare a well-formed response with whatever "inchoate thought" the child has formulated in answer to the question.

Correlational data suggest a link between parental memory demands and children's memory skills. Two- and 3-year-old children whose mothers made frequent memory demands on them evidenced better performance on memory tests up to a year following the observation of maternal memory demands (Ratner, 1984). Children whose mothers managed conversations about past events by rephrasing and elaborating their previous questions when the children were 2½ years old recounted more information in a more coherent narrative when they were 4 years old (Fivush, 1988).

Although these suggestions of connections between joint mnemonic activity and children's memory skills are intriguing, it is important to remember that correlational links allow multiple explanations. Children who remember skillfully are likely to act differently in joint mnemonic activities from children who are less skilled in memory tasks.

Experimental data examining the relation between collaborative memory or planning activities and children's subsequent independent performance do not yield entirely consistent results that would support the assumption that social interaction automatically fosters development. The inconsistencies across studies suggest that it is not the presence of a partner that matters, but the *nature of interaction* between the partners. The child's partner's skill in the task and the achievement of joint problem solving seem to be critical. The variation in results may have to do with young children's difficulties in participating in joint decision making in planning, although they can benefit from social guidance in more concrete tasks, such as remembering categories or lists of items.

The rest of this chapter is divided into a discussion of research with young children (ages 4 and 5) and older children, since the inconsistencies appear in studies with the younger children. The research with both age groups underlines the importance of considering shared decision making, with intersubjectivity between the partners, rather than just comparing groups that vary in the presence or expertise of partners.

Guided Participation and Young Children

Studies with young children have occasionally found no benefits from having an adult partner present when compared to the success of children working alone (Kontos, 1983). In our research, we have found that 4- and 5-year-olds benefited from working with adult partners in memory tasks but were no more effective in learning to plan routes than were those who worked alone.

MEMORY TASKS

Several memory studies with young children have shown that the children benefit from working with supportive adults. A pilot study compared the free recall of 4-year-olds whose parents were either encouraged to assist them in learning a list of items or instructed to simply present the list without elaboration, as in standard laboratory procedures (Mistry & Rogoff, 1987). In both conditions, the parents were constrained as to number and order of item presentations. The children whose parents were instructed to provide strategic assistance performed slightly better than those whose parents were instructed to simply present the list. Children who recalled more items were somewhat more likely to have had the memory goal emphasized by their parents, to have labeled the items, and to have received more parental suggestions about strategies to use to organize the items.

In two studies that varied the support of an adult experimenter, 5-year-olds benefited from guidance in learning and remembering the organization of common items (Göncü & Rogoff, 1987, in preparation). The experimenter followed scripts designed to adjust the extent of guidance in determining category labels and the extent of children's participation in decision making. The children remembered the classification scheme better in the individual posttest if the adult had offered any type of guidance on category rationales (whether suggesting that the child find categories or explaining, demonstrating, or collaborating with the child in determining the categories) rather than having children work alone or simply providing feedback on the placement of individual items.

Figure 8.3   Four-year-old planning a maze route with her mother's assistance. Videotaping was done with a hidden camera pointed through the glass of the maze. (United States)

PLANNING TASKS

Maze Routes. Two studies found that 4-year-olds who solved practice mazes with their mothers' assistance were no more skilled in planning maze solutions as matched children who worked alone in the practice session (Radziszewska, Germond, & Rogoff, in preparation). During the practice session, children either worked by themselves, with their mothers seated nearby, or solved mazes with their mothers' assistance. In the practice phase, children in the two groups were yoked in pairs to ensure that they practiced on an equal number of mazes.

In both the original study and a replication (designed to decrease instructions from the experimenter that we thought might have made the mothers' help unnecessary), children who had worked alone and those who had had their mothers' assistance in the practice phase solved an equal number of mazes in the posttest, with an equal degree of planfulness. We are currently doing a third version of this study, with mazes differing in the degree to which planfulness is appropriate, to learn whether task variation in the need for advance planning makes the assistance of mothers more useful to the children in distinguishing when to plan in advance and when to plan opportunistically, a skill that is difficult for 4-year-olds (Gardner & Rogoff, 1988).

Grocery-Store Routes. Another study involving young children in spatial planning revealed a similar absence of differences between children who had worked alone and those who had worked with a partner. Five-year-olds were asked to devise routes to pick up grocery items (presented in a pictorial list) without backtracking through the aisles of a three-dimensional model store (Gauvain & Rogoff, 1989). Children who had worked alone on planning efficient routes through the store performed as well on a later test as children who had worked with peers or with their mothers. Simply having a partner did not make children more likely to plan routes efficiently.

The children who actually shared decision making in their interactions with partners (rather than working independently or dividing the task into independent turns), however, did perform better than both the children who had worked alone and the children who had had a partner but had not worked jointly. These results, although correlational, support the idea that intersubjectivity between partners is an important aspect of interaction. The presence of a partner may be irrelevant unless the partners truly work together in problem solving.

AN EXPLANATION: DIFFICULTY OF SHARING THINKING IN SOME TASKS

Piaget's suggestion that young children have difficulty coordinating problem solving with another person (Azmitia & Perlmutter, in press; Piaget, 1977) appears to be a plausible explanation for the lack of benefits of social interaction for young children in the planning tasks—unless decision making is shared. But an explanation based solely on egocentricity at a young age would not explain the fact that adult guidance benefits young children's memory performance (as well as their language and conceptual development and object exploration and construction).

The nature of the tasks is crucial to consider. In some situations, the presence of a partner may serve as a distraction, requiring attention to be focused on the division of labor and on social issues rather than providing support. Some tasks may be difficult to coordinate with another person, and this may be especially true for young children.

The spatial planning tasks that we have used may be particularly difficult for young children to work on collaboratively. Some cognitive processes, such as planning, may be less accessible both to reflection by the individual and to discussion or joint attention in action. Planning tasks involve limitations in the concrete contexts for description and instances to "point to" in conversation or demonstration, since they deal with future events. It may be more difficult to share decision making or understanding of a problem that deals with abstract concepts or future events than to achieve intersubjectivity in dealing with concrete, present referents. Perhaps it is easier for young children to work with others on memory tasks, learning information that is physically presented without the need for complicated interpersonal understanding, than it is on planning tasks, which require discussion of future possibilities and strategies for dealing with the efficient coordination of several possible actions.

There do not seem to be general difficulties for young children in profiting from social interaction, as they benefit from guided participation in remembering as well as in language and conceptual development and object exploration and construction. I attribute the findings on difficulties in guided participation in planning to task-specific challenges for young children in sharing problem solving in the development of efficient plans and dealing with coordination for the future, which contrast with greater ease of establishing intersubjectivity in concrete tasks involving objects to be remembered, referred to, and handled appropriately. This is supported by the evidence that young children who actually shared decision making in planning routes through the grocery store performed better in subsequent independent planning. Simply being with a skilled adult may have no direct link to children's learning. Interaction in which the adult and the child manage to achieve intersubjectivity in decision making, with adult guidance, may relate to better subsequent performance by young children.

Further evidence for the importance of intersubjectivity for cognitive benefits of social interaction is provided by the observation that a joint focus of attention during conversations in a museum between mothers and young children—with joint discussion—led to greater memory for the information discussed, no matter which member of the pair initially focused attention on it (Tessler, cited by Fivush, 1988). Details that the children pointed out but that did not become a focus of joint discussion were not as well remembered by the children.

If we investigate the extent to which children actually participate in specific, sophisticated thinking in social interaction, we may be able to delineate features of social interaction that are influential in cognitive development. Just as research on language development points to the importance of joint attention and of expansions of young middle-class children's attempts to communicate, building on children's interest and level of skill, research on the development of memory and planning skills suggests that a crucial aspect of social interaction is the extent to which children participate in a shared thinking process with the support of a more skilled partner. This notion is supported by research on remembering and planning with older children.

Guided Participation and Older Children

The studies of remembering and planning undertaken with older children compare interaction with middle-class adults (as skilled partners) with that with peers (as less skilled partners). Such a comparison provides a control for having a social partner and facilitates the examination of memory and planning processes that are made public when they are performed socially. Partners in problem solving provide information to each other on decision making that can be used by researchers to infer decision-making processes.

The research with older children is consistent in showing advantages of working with a skilled partner in memory and planning tasks. Adult partners consistently evidence greater sensitivity, demonstration, and modeling of sophisticated strategies than peer partners. Since peers have been purposefully used as less skilled partners in these tasks, the results are unlikely to apply to situations in which peers are skilled or in control. We take up the question of the value of peer interaction in the next chapter.

MEMORY TASKS

In tasks involving learning a classification system to organize sets of common objects, 6-year-old children performed better after having had the assistance of adults than of 8-year-old children (Ellis & Rogoff, 1982, 1986). The adult teachers almost always explained the tasks before beginning to place items, referred to the need to categorize, and provided category rationales for the groups of items; less than half of the child teachers did so. Most of the adult teachers prepared their learners for the memory test through rehearsal and mnemonics for the classification system, while very few of the child teachers provided explicit preparation for the test beyond admonishing their partners to study. The children whose mothers offered guidance and who participated in working out the organization of items and in preparing for the test remembered the items and the conceptual organization better in the individual posttest (Rogoff & Gauvain, 1986).

The example given in Chapter 5 involving joint development of a mnemonic strategy for remembering the locations of the categories (Rogoff & Gardner, 1984, using the same data as Ellis & Rogoff, 1982, 1986) illustrates the mnemonic support that mothers provided. The mother created a temporal mnemonic for the locations of the first groups of objects, thinking aloud as she suggested making up a little story organized according to daily routine. Then she reviewed the categories and enlisted the child's help in creating the story for the remaining groups. She provided guidance and invention in suggesting the mnemonic and getting the child started on it, and she and the child collaborated on the level of the child's participation in producing the mnemonic. Once the child showed some grasp of the mnemonic, the mother turned it over to the child to manage for further review.

Most of the child teachers appeared insensitive to their partners' need to learn, providing little guidance and almost no preparation for the test (Ellis & Rogoff, 1986). More than half of them did not include the learners in the task, placing the items themselves without explanation and often without even looking to see if the learner were watching. Others required the learners to perform the task with minimal guidance, having them guess the location of items without explanation. The peer dyads did not evidence the intersubjectivity and shared decision making observed with the adult–child dyads; they appeared to focus on the immediate task of sorting items.

When the child teachers did try to guide the learners, their hints were not effective for placing later items in the group or for the long-term goal of communicating the category structure in preparation for the test. For example, one child who wanted the learner to put an item in a white box pointed to the background of the photograph of the item. This hint was effective in getting the item placed, but would have been of little help for other items in the group or for the test. The child teachers had difficulty formulating hints that were useful but still allowed the learner some independence in solving the problem, failing to interject helpful information at the level the learner needed. (On occasion, it appeared that this was the child teachers' idea of the role of a teacher, as they used schoolteacher intonations to praise the learners' correct guesses.)

Similar contrasts between the teaching interactions of adults and children teaching younger children have been found by McLane (1987) and Koester and Bueche (1980): the child teachers seemed to focus on accomplishing the concrete task rather than ensuring that their partners understood the rationale, and they usually did too much (taking over the performance of the task) or too little (insisting that their young partners "figure it out" without giving them guidance in doing so). Child teachers may have difficulty coordinating communication when the cognitive task is unfamiliar or especially challenging.

The learners' interaction with the adults in Ellis and Rogoff's (1982, 1986) study appeared to involve more effective guided participation: the adults attempted to orient the children to the task, to provide links between current knowledge and the new situation, and to structure the task, and the children participated in guided decision making with their roles collaboratively adjusted so that they were involved at a level that was challenging but within reach. The interactions involving child teachers did not show these features of guidance, and the learners who were paired with child teachers made more attempts to direct the teaching, especially by trying to become involved in the task when the child teachers took over all the responsibility and excluded the learners. These results support the idea that interaction with skilled partners is useful for children's learning in the memory task through guided participation in skilled problem solving.

PLANNING STUDIES

In the first study in this series, Radziszewska and Rogoff (1988) found that 9-year-old children gained more skill in errand planning from collaborating with parents than with 9-year-old partners. Partners were given a map of an imaginary downtown (Figure 8.4) and two lists of errands and were asked to plan a trip to get materials for a school play. Each partner had a list with five items to be picked up, such as uniforms from the Theatrical Supplies store and paintbrushes from the Paint Shop or the Shopping Center. The dyad had to coordinate their planning of the route so the driver could make one trip efficiently (to save gasoline). To produce an optimal route, subjects needed to devise a plan incorporating the stores that had to be visited (i.e., to get items that were available from only one store), and to decide which of two alternatives would be more efficient to include for items that could be bought at a choice of stores. The map was the same for all

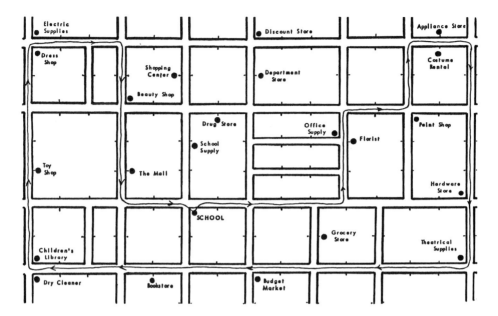

Figure 8.4 Map of imaginary downtown for errand-planning task, showing an optimal route. (Reprinted by permission of the publisher, from Radziszewska & Rogoff, 1988, copyright 1988 by the American Psychological Association)

trials, and the optimal route was similar, but the lists of items were different for each trial. Partners planned two trips together; then each planned a trip independently.

The collaborative planning of adult–child dyads was much more sophisticated than that of peer dyads. The peer dyads planned by making decisions on a step-by-step basis, as is common in children's individual planning (Magkaev, 1977). They usually proceeded by identifying the store closest to the current location and checking to see if it was on either of the lists; much less efficient routes were the result. Adult–child dyads planned longer sequences of moves, averaging 4.9 stores per move decision compared with the peer dyads' average sequences of 1.3. Almost half of the adult–child dyads planned the whole route at once, whereas none of the peer dyads did so. Adult–child dyads were also twice as likely to explore the layout before making moves, often marking the choice and no-choice stores with different colors and symbols to facilitate planning an optimal route. Furthermore, adult–child dyads were 11 times as likely to verbalize planning strategies.

During collaboration with adults, children usually participated in the more sophisticated planning strategies organized by the adults. Statements of strategy came primarily from the adults, but the sophisticated planning decisions were made jointly by the adults and children. Differences in the performance of the children who performed well and those who performed poorly after collaborating with adults appeared to relate to the extent of shared and guided decision making with the adults during collaboration.

The interaction between peers resembled that between adults and children in dyads in which the children subsequently performed poorly. They were also similar to the peer teachers in the study by Ellis and Rogoff (1986) who focused on immediate actions with a step-by-step approach and poorly communicated their problem-solving strategies. The more skilled peer partners often dominated decision making, ignored their partners, and communicated little.

It appears that planning with a skilled partner provides an opportunity for children to practice skills that are in advance of those that they can manage independently, and that such collaboration enhances children's later independent planning. Children who had worked with adults produced routes that were about 20% shorter than those of children who had worked with peers, and they applied specific aspects of the sophisticated planning strategy they had practiced with adults. For example, 14 of the 16 children from adult–child pairs started the individual trial by searching for and marking the choice and the no-choice stores on the map, as was common in their collaborative trials, whereas only 1 of the 16 children from peer dyads marked the stores in advance of making moves.

Although the differences in performance that resulted from having had a peer or adult partner were striking, both during collaboration and in independent performance, the advantage of working with adults could be attributed either to adults' greater skill in the planning task or to guidance and children's participation in the collaborative planning decisions. The next study examined the roles of the child's partner's expertise in the planning task and of guided participation in planning.

Radziszewska and Rogoff (manuscript) replicated their earlier study (Radziszewska & Rogoff, 1988) and added a condition in which peer partners were individually trained to employ the optimal strategy in the errand-planning task, prior to their collaboration with target children. A pretest determined that the errand-planning efficiency of the trained peers approached that of the adults. During collaboration, dyads with a trained peer partner and dyads with an adult partner evidenced equally sophisticated planning (i.e., planning sequences of moves rather than single steps), and both groups showed more sophisticated planning than dyads with an untrained peer partner.

The results suggested that expertise in errand planning as well as availability of guidance and participation in skilled decision making contributed to the effectiveness of working with adults. Target children who had collaborated with adults performed best, and those who had worked with trained peers performed no better than those who had worked with untrained peers.

Despite the adults' and the trained peers' similar planning strategies and efficiency during collaborative errand planning, the adults more frequently communicated the optimal strategy to target children. In addition, more than half of the adult–child dyads evidenced strategic thinking aloud during collaboration, whereas none of the peer dyads (with trained or untrained partners) showed strategic thinking aloud. Almost all the children working with adults were active participants, observing or participating in decisions, whereas fewer than half of the children working with trained peers were active participants. Children who worked with untrained peers often collaborated, but without a partner skilled in errand planning, such involvement was least effective for the target children's learning. The children who performed best in subsequent independent errand planning had the benefit of participating in skilled planning decisions, with guidance: posttest performance by target children was related to the production of efficient routes on collaborative trials, active involvement of children in planning decisions, and discussion of decisions and of the optimal strategy in joint planning.

Together, the results with younger and older children suggest that intersubjectivity in remembering and planning is a central feature of social interaction that allows children to take advantage of the bridging, structuring, and transfering of responsibility that were suggested as processes involved in guided participation. Children appear to benefit from participation in problem solving with the guidance of partners who are skilled in accomplishing the task at hand.

Caveats in the Comparison of Peers with Adults

The initial purpose of using peers in the studies just discussed was as a less skilled comparison group for the skilled adult partners. The results may not represent the positive aspects of peer interaction in activities in which children are more skilled or in situations they regard as being in the domain of peer (rather than adult–child) activities, such as play and exploration. Hence the findings reported in the sections on older children's remembering and planning—that interaction with adults is more sensitive and instructive and that children learn more from their interactions with adults than from those with peers—must be qualified as limited to adult-world tasks in which adults are more skilled.

The generality of the results with regard to peer interaction is also limited to middle-class groups, not only because the adults' strategies and the tasks used are tied to such groups, but also because the role of peers varies greatly across cultures. In many cultures, children play a more central role in the socialization of other children than they do in the American middle class. In such cultures, children who have served as caregivers of younger siblings from the age of 4 or 5 and who work and play in mixed-age groups responsible for their own functioning may have the opportunity to develop skills in guiding other children; such skills are less available to middle-class U.S. children, who have little responsibility for other children and more limited contact with children of ages different from their own.

The value of cooperative classroom learning, in which peers work together on academic tasks and provide one another with motivation, guidance, and feedback (Damon, 1984; Slavin, 1987), also suggests that in circumstances in which children have practice in interaction, they may be very helpful to one another. Peers can serve as guides in academic activities in the classroom, especially if such interaction is encouraged in the classroom social structure, giving children experience as onlookers and in coordinated parallel activity, guidance, and collaboration (Aronson, Blaney, Stephan, Sikes, & Snapp, 1978; Cooper, Marquis, & Edward, 1986). When teachers encourage and support peer interaction, children may develop skill in academically useful forms of interaction.

Researchers will have to address the naturalistic interaction between peers in tasks they do well or choose for themselves—tasks that peers might teach each other or collaborate on when away from adult influence. As an approximation of this situation, Tudge and Rogoff (in progress) are investigating peer and adult–child collaboration on learning two spatial-planning computer games. The 9-year-old children were more comfortable handling the computer games than were the adults, although all participants began the study as novices. We are analyzing the progress in skill and in collaborative processes as peer and adult–child pairs gain expertise in the games over repeated sessions and examining the way, once the participants have become somewhat proficient, each teaches other novice children to play the games. Both games involve complex spatial planning, but one was presented as educational and the other as recreational, to see whether children take more control of the recreational game and rely more on adults in the educational game.

We expect that the collaboration and teaching processes, and perhaps the children's subsequent individual performance, may differ from those observed in the studies in which children were under the direction of adults, participating in tasks in which adults are more skilled. For, rather than being merely unskilled foils for comparison with skilled adults, children play special roles in one another's cognitive development.

9

Peer Interaction
and Cognitive Development

Eight-year-old Luisa asks what her mother is reading and is not satisfied with the reply that it is an old Swiss man's views on how children's thinking relates to their social interactions. Her mother expands, "Like, do you learn better from grownups or from other kids?"

Luisa replies, "From other kids, as long as they know it. Cuz if they didn't know it, you wouldn't learn it."

Mother: Why do you learn best from other kids?

Luisa: Because kids know how to teach kids in a fun way. I like to learn, but in a fun way.

Luisa's friend (also age 8) joins in, and Luisa prompts her mother to ask him about learning better from grownups or from other kids. He replies, "From a grownup, probably, because grownups explain things better. Sometimes. Depends on the grownup" (he laughs).

Then Luisa's 5-year-old sister claims to learn better from other kids, but can't explain why. When Luisa expands on the question, asking "What if you could choose having kid or adult teachers?" her friend interrupts, "I know what I'd choose! . . . But not cuz I'd learn better. . . ." (he laughs) "Kid teachers probably wouldn't make so many rules and stuff."

Luisa's 5-year-old brother asserts that he learns more from grownups, because they know more than kids. Luisa adds, "Sometimes!" but he insists, "ALWAYS they do. My teacher knows more than me."

Luisa then turns the tables on her mother: "Why do you want to know all this? . . . Why are you being so nosy?" (she laughs) "You owe me 4 cents. . . . A penny for my thoughts!"

So far, we have considered guided participation in which children interact with partners who are more skilled than they. Most of the research has involved adult partners. In Vygotsky's perspective, skilled peers may serve a function like that of adults in interaction in the zone of proximal development. It appears from the findings reviewed in Chapter 8 that while peers *can* be expert in cognitive problem solving, adults are more likely to be.

As discussed in Chapter 7, however, Piaget proposed that influential so-

Figure 9.1 Toddlers pause from their activity when they become aware of being watched. (United States) (Photograph courtesy of Oscar Magarian)

cial interaction occurs between partners of similar status. In Piaget's view, peers promote the advancement of one another's cognitive development through attempts to resolve cognitive conflict or discrepancy deriving from differences in their perspectives.

This chapter first discusses the roles of cognitive conflict, expertise, and equality of status between peers, making comparisons with adults. (I use the term *peer* broadly to refer to companions of roughly equal status, whether related or not, to include sibling and neighbor groups of generally similar age and status, not just the unrelated same-age classmates that have been a primary focus of peer research.) Then I take up in some depth the intersubjective thinking of peers who solve problems together. In peer argumentation and discussion of ideas, the process of building consensus and common ground can lead the partners to a more considered view than either of them contribute independently. Finally, I consider the role of peers when children interact in "peer culture" rather than in studies or activities managed by adults. Although children are familiar with adult environments, they are likely to treat a situation differently if they are in charge of it rather than being given a task by adults. They are probably more playful and exploratory and less goal-oriented when involved in a purely peer activity, as suggested in the epigraph to this chapter. That children are sensitive to the presence of adults is evidenced by the reduction of interaction of 5-year-old and 8-year-old peer dyads when they were in the presence of adult observers (Brody, Stoneman, & Wheatley, 1984). To understand the role of peer interaction in cognitive development, it is necessary to examine situations in which children are in charge of their own activities.

Conflict, Relative Expertise, and Status

Expertise and Cognitive Conflict Between Peers

Scholars working in the Piagetian tradition have taken seriously what Piaget had to say about the cognitive conflict induced by peer social interaction and have argued that it is effective in bringing about cognitive growth in children's understanding of conservation problems when children are asked to come to a joint decision about the equality of some material after it has been reshaped (Bearison, in press; Sigel & Cocking, 1977). Some scholars working in the Piagetian tradition also cite the influence of Vygotsky's ideas on their work (Doise & Mackie, 1981; Perret-Clermont, Brun, Saada, & Schubauer-Leoni, 1984).

Although Piaget's speculations on the benefits of peer interaction focused on the cognitive conflict occurring when children of equal status bring different perspectives to bear on a problem, interaction between conservers and nonconservers is not really interaction between equals, since according to Piaget's theory the conserver has a better understanding of reality, not just a different understanding of reality, than the nonconserver (Tudge & Rogoff, 1989). Hence it is possible that within Piagetian research, benefits derive from working with a partner who has more advanced skills, consistent with the Vygotskian position. Since in Piaget's view, cognitive conflict provides an impetus for children to seek equilibrium at a higher level, some authors suggest that children would be most likely to change their thinking when faced with a perspective that fits reality better than their own, especially if it involves problem solving at a level *just* beyond that of the child (Azmitia, 1988; Kuhn, 1972; Mugny & Doise, 1978; see also Tudge & Rogoff, 1989). The benefit of a partner whose perspective is not too far in advance of that of the child is also consistent with Vygotsky's concept of interaction within the zone of proximal development, where an expert and a novice work together at a level just beyond that of the novice.

Although working with a partner who is slightly more skilled may be most effective, working with a partner equal in skill, or even one less advanced, may still yield progress (Forman & Kraker, 1985; Glachan & Light, 1982; Light & Glachan, 1985; Rubtsov, 1981; Rubtsov & Guzman, 1984–1985). In some studies, however, there is no progress, as when partners are equal in understanding of seriation problems (Heber, 1981), or there may even be "regression," as when children interact with less advanced partners on balance-beam problems (Tudge, 1985). The significance of relative expertise of partners is not yet resolved, but it appears that even within Piagetian tasks, the benefits of social interaction may relate to the expertise of the child's partner.

Role Relations: Relative Status of Partners

Few studies have explicitly compared the processes and outcomes of working with partners of differing role status. The studies described in Chapter 8, comparing adults and children as partners in learning memory and planning skills, suggest that interacting with adults may be more advantageous to children than working with peers for learning these skills. Interaction with adults appears to have advantages because of the adults' expertise in the tasks and the greater likelihood of children's guided participation in the skilled activity (Ellis & Rogoff, 1982, 1986; McLane, 1987; Radziszewska & Rogoff, 1988, manuscript). Similarly, mothers are more likely to support infants' conversational skills through responding contingently and constructing exchanges around the infants' nonsocial actions than preschool siblings, who are less contingent and less likely to involve the infants' interests (Vandell & Wilson, 1987).

It is possible that Piaget's view stressing equality of status is instrumental for social interaction to encourage a change of perspective, while Vygotsky's emphasis on expertise is useful for tasks that involve the development of skills, as suggested in Chapter 7. The possibility that expertise and equality of status differ in importance according to task is being investigated (Radziszewska & Rogoff, in progress) in a comparison of adults and peers as partners in Piagetian tasks that require a shift of perspective and in an errand-planning task involving the learning of skills.

A few studies suggest that equal status may facilitate balanced discussion and yield cognitive progress in logic problems, supporting Piaget's suggestion. Light and Glachan (1985) found that peers who discussed each other's perspective were more likely to progress in their individual level of logic than were those who did not discuss the problem or whose conversations focused on assertions of status, although the consideration of each other's perspective did not depend on the children's initial level in the game.

Similarly, children may be freer to examine the logic of arguments when interacting with peers rather than with adults. Children of 7 and 11 years expressed logical arguments more with their peers than with their mothers (Kruger & Tomasello, 1986). Although mothers requested idea clarification more than did peers, children produced more self-generated clarifications of logic when interacting with peers and were more likely to make comments based on their partners' logic when talking with peers. Kruger (1988) found that 8-year-olds who had discussed moral dilemmas with their peers progressed more in their moral reasoning than did children who had discussed the dilemmas with their mothers. The more interactive logical discussion of partners' ideas that characterized peer conversations were positively correlated with progress in moral reasoning.

Children aged 2 to 4 years, however, were less likely to respond to and expand one anothers' comments than their mothers' comments, and their mothers, in turn, were more responsive partners than were their peers (Martinez, 1987). The difference between this study and Kruger and Tomasello's studies (1986; Kruger, 1988) may be attributed to the ages involved. With the preschool-age children of the Martinez study, an adult partner may be better able than a peer to provide the support for achieving intersubjectivity.

At the same time, preschool-age peers may offer one another opportunities to manage conversation that are less available in interaction with adults (Garvey, 1986). French (1987) suggests that mother–child conversation is both more controlled by and supported by mothers, whereas conversations between preschool peers provide more opportunity or even necessity for reciprocal involvement and for the children to initiate and sustain discourse.

Consistent with the notion that adults' authority role impedes children's equal participation are observations that when kindergarten teachers reduced their questioning of reticent children while still allowing the children the floor, the children's spontaneous contributions doubled (Evans & Bienert, 1987). In an experiment in a Soviet kindergarten that involved adult educators acting like peers with the children (avoiding use of authority and demonstrating uncertainty and errors), the children's classroom activities became more creative and independent (Subbotskii, 1987).

It will be important to examine differences in adult–child interaction based on the status roles taken by adults. Piaget assumed that the authority of adults impedes collaborative discussion. However, in many studies of adult–child interaction, adults do a great deal to diffuse their greater authority in order to bring about a more equal interaction. Extremes of adults acting as peers can be observed in caricature with some uncles, parents, or teachers who appear to regress in age as they jump about on the floor and pretend with young children. And as Hazen points out (personal communication), adults lose their authority by taking this peer role, as children become less likely to accept limits and to "mind" after interacting with adults as playmates.

Although the authority role of adults in Piaget's Switzerland may have been somewhat softened in many American classrooms and homes in recent decades, authority differences between adults and children still prevail. We may present our relative status to children less directly, but we still use (or attempt to use) our authority and greater status when it comes to the bottom line. Consider the use of authority by an adult, and its lack of impact on a child's thinking, in the following example:

> David, age 5½ years, was riding in the car with his mother and counting, "sixty-seven, sixty-eight, sixty-nine, sixty-ten, sixty-eleven (etc.)." His mother tried to explain that after sixty-nine, the numbers switch to seventy, then seventy-one, and so on, and that the number David called sixty-ten was called seventy.
>
> But David insisted that it was called sixty-ten. His mother tried to explain the number system again a few times, but ended up asserting, "There's no sixty-ten. It's called seventy. I know because I know more about numbers than you."
>
> David came back with an appeal to a higher authority, "Well, *I* know someone who knows everything about numbers and *HE* told me that it's sixty-ten!"

Mother challenged David to reveal his authority, "And who was that?" but gave up the argument when David replied with confidence, "God!"

The appropriateness of adults acting like the equals of children varies across cultures, with some communities interested in maintaining the status difference and relegating to peers and siblings the kind of playful and equal-status interaction that may be regarded as appropriate for parents and teachers in other communities.

The status issue seems to underlie some differences in educational prescriptions, with differing emphasis on adult questioning and directing of children versus adult facilitation of children's activity. For example, Sutter and Grensjo (1988) contrast explorative learning based on activity theory with more traditional classroom practices. They stress that an "exploratory learning" teacher takes part in a living dialogue, and suggest that this means departing from the shelter of formal authority based on power (which they characterize as demoralizing to instruction) and shifting to authority based on professional competence. Similarly, Wood (1986) points out that in classrooms in which teachers exert control through commands and questions, children respond tersely, whereas when teachers substitute noncontrolling talk, such as commentary on their own ideas, and increase the amount of time allowed for students to respond, children are more active and equal participants.

Such transformations in adults' roles may fit with societal goals for children's behavior and children's learning in some cultural groups (such as in academic families in the United States), but since they may conflict in others, it is worth noting that the status roles of partners relate to many aspects of social order and social interaction other than simply children's learning of a particular cognitive lesson. The crucial factor may be the extent to which partners share in problem solving and establish a common ground for their interaction, from which they may proceed regardless of asymmetries in their status, expertise, or particular viewpoints.

Shared Problem Solving and Intersubjectivity

A number of studies from both Piagetian and Vygotskian traditions focus on the sharing of decision making or perspective as an important factor in effective peer interaction. The most productive interaction appears to result from arrangements in which peers' decision making occurs jointly, with a balanced exploration of differences of perspective (Bos, 1937; Glachan & Light, 1982; Light, Foot, Colbourn, & McClelland, 1987). "It appears that in a balanced pattern of conflict, partners are able to monitor each other's reasoning and, thereby, enact mutually coordinated roles in attempting task solutions" (Bearison, Magzamen, & Filardo, 1986, p. 69).

The importance of intersubjective, joint problem solving in peer interaction has been noted with a variety of labels: "social interdependence" (Mugny, Perret-Clermont, & Doise, 1981), "transactive" discussion involving reasoning about one's partner's reasoning (Berkowitz & Gibbs, 1985), and "coopera-

Figure 9.2   Two 4-year-olds collaborating on a sand construction using a digging implement in a playground. (United States)

tion in joint actions" (Rubtsov & Guzman, 1984–1985). Forman has examined the cognitive benefits of cooperative activity by groups of adolescents, arguing that communication between partners allowed the "co-construction" of hypotheses by means of a sharing of different perspectives (Forman & Cazden, 1985; Forman & Kraker, 1985).

Research supports the notion that shared problem solving underlies the benefits of peer interaction. Children working together on a logic game made significant advances in skill from pre- to posttest if they discussed their differences of opinion, but not otherwise (Light & Glachan, 1985). Preschool children who worked together on an errand-planning task performed better in subsequent independent planning than children who worked alone only if they shared in decision making (Gauvain & Rogoff, 1989). Similarly, children who gained most from peer interaction on mathematics, spatial, and balance-beam tasks more frequently shared ideas about the logic of the tasks with each other, focusing on solutions and strategies for handling the problems rather than on each other's role or behavior (Damon & Phelps, 1987).

The collaborative process seems to lead to a level of understanding unavailable in solitary endeavor or noncollaborative interaction. Lomov (1978) claims that collaboration in remembering well-learned spatial layouts or verses of poetry produces a level of meaning unavailable in individual efforts to recall the information, with the strategies qualitatively different from those employed by a person remembering alone. Similarly, Mugny and Doise (1978) noted that children's collective performances on a Piagetian task were superior to the performances of group members taken individually when the children were paired with peers both more advanced and less advanced than themselves.

Several accounts of communication and joint problem solving provide a window on such processes of transformation of understanding resulting from the establishment of intersubjectivity and collective thinking. The first deals with argumentation as a form of reaching shared understanding, and the second involves collective judgments of the identity of artwork.

Argumentation to Achieve Shared Understanding

Miller (1987) refers to argumentation as the central form of social exchange that brings about shared thinking in a way that advances individuals' knowledge and perspective. The principal feature of argumentation that takes it beyond other forms of social interaction is the need to find a collective solution to an interindividual problem of coordination. Such discourse "has a built-in capacity to release processes of collective learning" (p. 231).

Miller proposes that three cooperation principles of argumentation provide the coordination that leads participants toward a set of collectively valid statements: generalizability, objectivity, and consistency. A statement is justified (generalizable) if it has been immediately accepted by the participants or if it can be traced back to other statements that have been immediately accepted. What belongs to the realm of the collectively valid may change for a group according to the principle of objectivity: if a statement (or a transition between statements) cannot be denied, it belongs to the realm of the collectively valid for the participants. Miller points out that this principle for change is usually called on implicitly if the participants in argumentation differ in experience and knowledge. However, if both participants can defend their viewpoints, they may have extended their knowledge through an extension of the collectively valid, even though they are in an "argumentative deadlock." Consistency, the third principle, precludes the acceptance of such contradictions in the realm of the collectively valid. In other words, when such contradictions are detected, the participants must seek a change in the collectively valid to resolve the contradiction.

Miller (1987) claims that this collective process in children's argumentation with adults and peers functions as a basic developmental mechanism. He gives the example of 5-year-olds arguing about the behavior of a balance scale, with one child centering on weight as the principle for explaining what will balance, and the other focusing on distance from the fulcrum as the crucial factor. In insisting on their own prespectives, the children clarify the problem to themselves and to each other in their co-construction of the argument. If the children get to this point in argumentation, they arrive at two equally justified standpoints that exclude each other. The principle of consistency requires them to change the collectively valid to resolve the contradictions.

> Even if these children do not yet have any idea of what these changes will eventually look like, i.e., even if the structurally higher level knowledge remains undefined (transcendent) relative to their already attained knowledge, they nevertheless know where it has to be found. It must be a structural solution of the contradiction between their mutually exclusive points of view—a contradiction they have created themselves and which now begins to determine their ascension to a higher level of knowledge. (p. 237)

Miller's (1987) concept of argumentation differs from Piaget's principles for achieving equilibrium in intellectual exchange in that Miller emphasizes the co-construction of both the statements of the differences and the search for resolution of contradictions, whereas Piaget stressed reciprocal symmetrical efforts by individuals to reason out differences. In addition, Miller does not focus just on discussions of logic or physical or moral laws, as did Piaget. He uses the term *argumentation* broadly to include any discussion that involves divergence of understanding, such that participants have to resolve what is being talked about in order to proceed. Tacit forms of such argumentation can be seen in the adjustments of partners to share a focus of attention and an interpretation of a situation in intersubjective communication of the most mundane sorts. Miller states that he has evidence that these cooperation principles determine the argumentation of children as young as 2 years. At the same time, he also describes a developmental progression in the adequacy of efforts to justify viewpoints in which argumentation is more effective in the later years of childhood.

Corsaro and Rizzo (1988) analyze a compelling example of a *discussione* among three 5-year-old Italian boys, in which they simultaneously negotiate meaning about friendship and future skill development in a skilled display of argumentation. They implicitly discuss their shifting and competitive alliances with one another in the context of explicit statements about honoring secrets between friends, originality in production of toy spaceships, and their own future developmental goals in which they anticipate abandonment of play for school activity, leading to adult occupations.

Argumentation is simply the effort to come to a closer understanding, and this closer understanding for Miller (1987) leads to the "collectively valid." Thus argumentation that extends the collectively valid and the individual's understanding involves not only shifts in perspective, but also the development of task definitions and appropriate strategies for problem solving as well as the establishment of facts and working definitions for describing and classifying reality. In contrast with Piaget's stance that progress is made toward a more adapted and logical view of reality, the establishment of the collectively valid is a local construction, varying from group to group according to the views and definitions expressed by the groups' members.

Collective Advances in Judgments of the Identity of Artwork

A deep examination of how individual participation in a collective process goes beyond individual contributions is provided by Bos (1937), who observed joint problem solving and its impact on individual perceptual judgments. Bos asked 11- to 13-year-olds to group sets of five or six pictures by different artists on the same subject (e.g., portraits of women, portraits of men, the Annunciation). The children worked in pairs or individually in two sessions. Their achievement was rated from perfect sorting of paintings; through good sorting with only minor errors, such as putting together two artists from the same school; some correct judgments along with some serious errors; a weak thoughtless result that nevertheless contained one good combination, such as putting two Rembrandts together but grouping each van Eyck with an Italian painter; to no single correct combinations.

Children who worked collectively in the second session achieved more than they had individually in the first session, with collective accomplishment at least as high as the best individual performance of either partner, and most substantially higher. A comparison group of children who worked individually in both sessions improved less, with only one-quarter of them improving to the extent of most of the children working collectively. Children who worked collectively first and then individually performed slightly better on their individual judgments than children who had initially worked alone.

An illustration of how the collective process exceeds the contribution of each individual involves a 12-year-old boy and a 12-year-old girl considering the series of portraits of women (three paintings by Rembrandt, including two of the same person at different times and one family group, and single portraits by Dürer and Memling):

> The girl proposes to combine both portraits by Rembrandt of the same woman (pictures A and B), but the boy disagrees and counter-proposes to combine B with Rembrandt's family portrait. The girl hesitatingly agrees, but asks what they should do with picture A, "Doesn't that also belong to it?" The boy sticks to his opinion that it does not belong because it has entirely different eyes. But the girl is not convinced and after casually looking at the remaining pictures, the boy is obliged to mount fresh arguments: "The portrait on picture A represents an entirely different type of person,

and her dress has no pleats either like in picture B." When that does not convince the girl, he adds that the woman of B has much more expression. The girl admits that there are differences between A and B, but still they are very much alike. As she cannot justify her opinion convincingly, she turns to the boy's proposal (to combine B with Rembrandt's family portrait) and charges that in those two pictures the faces are painted in a quite different style. But her attack on the boy's proposal does not work, and her own proposal does not gain influence.

The boy shifts his rationale and justifies his grouping on the basis of the similarity of the dresses and the light in the pictures. This leads the girl to examine the light in all the pictures, and she hesitatingly proposes to combine the three Rembrandts, but then retracts it because of the differences she had noted between B and the family portrait. The boy takes the idea over, "yes, perhaps they all three belong together," but since they lack a convincing rationale they cannot reach a decision. They begin again to study the pictures and to look for new points of view. The boy becomes convinced that A and the family group belong together because of a comparison of the way the hair is done and the jewelry, and the girl agrees. This solution was not originally proposed by either of the partners; they are both satisfied with it. The other two pictures by Dürer and Memling provide no difficulty; both children agree that there is no similarity at all between them, "they belong to different periods." (summarized from Bos, 1937, p. 363)

Bos concluded from this interaction that because of their mental contact, the children achieved a higher level of thinking than either could have independently:

> Because of the purposeful insistence [*sic*] of the children to convince each other of the fairness of their arguments and to respect the opinion of the other they were driven to an analytical work, which at times stood in the way of a correct solution. . . . Both came to a new way of thinking, arrived at fresh viewpoints, so that in this case it would be impossible to establish the individual share of each partner. The same things happen in cases where, in lively exchange of thoughts, adults discuss a problem. Through the interpretation of the other, which is rejected by us, we arrive at ideas, which in their turn are taken over, eventually are further elaborated, and thereby lead to a result. Whom shall we give credit for the solution? It was fortunate, that our young candidates did not bother about the authorship and after intensive collaboration, simply declared, that they had worked out the problems *together*. (pp. 363–364)

Bos (1937) characterized such cases of intensive collaboration as uniformly involving increased mental activity of the children. Their concentration and systematic way of working appeared to benefit from the collaboration. When the attention of one partner sometimes lagged, it was revived by the new views and proposals of the other. Because collaborating children are committed to state their opinion convincingly, they seek and find new criteria. Although this analytic working process at times overcomes the correct solution, it is typical of the rationalizing effect of the collaboration, in which the observations and arguments of the partners bring them to viewpoints that in mental isolation neither would have reached.

Bos also examined the interactions of 6- to 9-year-old children judging the appropriate seriation of pictures into a story. She found that although they were not able to mount such argumentative discussion, these younger children were able to establish an intimate mental contact by use of a descriptive method that yielded the same effects as the intense cooperative activity of the older children.

Not all the older children managed such cooperative activity, however. Half of the dyads used this collaborative working process, and another quarter worked collectively, taking one another's opinions into account only in rejecting them, without discussion or justification. The remaining quarter of the dyads worked individually in alternating participation in the execution of the task, *being* together but not *working* together. (Similar proportions were observed for the younger children in the seriation task.)

The extent of collaboration related to the extent of progress in the task in the Bos (1937) study, as in the studies reviewed earlier that examined the degree to which partners actually share in decisions and in understanding each other's task definition and perspective (e.g., Gauvain & Rogoff, 1989; Glachan & Light, 1982; Light & Glachan, 1985). Children who actively collaborated achieved a level of performance that was 76% of the maximum score possible; those who disagreed without discussion achieved 56% of the maximum; and those who were together but did not work together reached only 42%. The younger children in the seriation task showed the same pattern.

An examination of the data involving the younger children supports the idea that children who make good judgments in a task are also more skilled in collaboration *and* that children who collaborate attain greater leaps of skill. The significance of children's initial skill level in making collaboration possible is supported by the fact that children who later managed to truly collaborate had had a higher level of performance in the earlier individual session (45% of the maximum) than those who merely disagreed without discussion (33%) and those who worked individually while paired (29%).

The significance of collaborative problem solving in promoting children's thinking is supported by the greater improvement over their prior individual scores of those who truly collaborated (an improvement of 42%, to reach 86% of the maximum) than of those who disagreed without discussion (improving by 31%, to reach 64% of the maximum) and those who never managed to collaborate at all (improving by 17%, to reach 46% of the maximum).

Hence it appears that there is some advantage to simply having a partner for achievement of a higher level of problem solving, but the greatest advantage is available to individuals who manage, partially as a result of their own skill, to share problem solving and thus co-construct a more sophisticated approach.

The factors that Bos (1937) credited for the greater advantage of collaborative work are initiative, critical faculty, and concentration. In joint work, the will to take the initial step, which can be problematic in individual work, flows naturally from the pressure of having a group goal. Joint work also stimulates initiative by freeing an individual from the heavy responsibility of ensuring that the first step is the right one, as the presence of a partner promotes a more open attitude toward the work, making it easier to take risks. A critical approach is more easily applied in a collective situation, since judging another's work is easier than judging one's own because a partner can notice features of a solution that have escaped the attention of the person proposing it. Concentration is facilitated in the collective endeavor, as the partner may take up the task when one individual gives up temporarily. (In fact, in the collective condition, even when the partners did not attend to each other's efforts, the young children almost always completed the task; in the individual condition, the young children frequently left the task incomplete, giving in to a moment of slackness that in collective work could be corrected by the partner's efforts.)

> In the process of collaboration where the work is divided between two persons, initiative, criticism and concentration can function as factors determining achievement *even when the individuals concerned would not achieve such a productive process.* This explains the apparent paradox that out of two negatives a positive is born. (Bos, 1937, p. 408)

Thus in collaboration, the partners engage in a creative process in which the achievement of intersubjectivity leads to new solutions. In addition to this type of collaboration, oriented toward a serious goal imposed by adults, it is important to consider the role of children as playmates and companions, doing childish things that adults do not regard as having a purpose.

The Unique Roles of Peers

In nonacademic and nonlaboratory situations where children meet naturalistically, they may serve as important cognitive facilitators for one another. Because researchers do not have easy access to such situations, they have received little attention. But children spend far more time in direct interaction with one another than with adults. Siblings and other child companions are available at home, in the neighborhood, at school, most everywhere that children go. Children without siblings may have to recruit their parents to play with them, but only until their parents discover that inviting a friend to the house gets them off the hook.

In many cultures that differ from the American middle class, the importance of children's interaction with other children is even greater. In many societies, child care is largely carried out by 5- to 10-year-old children, who tend infants and toddlers (Watson-Gegeo & Gegeo, 1989; Weisner & Gallimore, 1977; Wenger, 1983; Whiting & Edwards, 1988; Whiting & Whiting, 1975). Children may carry a younger sibling or cousin around on their back or hip to be entertained with the sights and sounds of the community and the play of the other children. If the young one becomes hungry, the child caregiver may return to the mother to allow the child to nurse. Adults are avail-

Figure 9.3   A group of children cooking and serving a make-believe meal modeled after what they are learning to do in actual food production, here using leaf tortillas and dirt meat. Notice the mix of ages, and the infant and the toddler being tended by older children as they play. (Guatemala) (Photograph © B. Rogoff)

able to supervise the child caregivers, but the entertainment of young children falls to other children. Whiting (1979) notes that Kenyan graduate students at Harvard were surprised to see American children seeking interaction with their parents in preference to siblings.

Sibling caregiving may provide the young charges with special intellectual opportunities, especially in communities in which such caregiving arrangements are commonplace. Watson-Gegeo and Gegeo (1989) state that Kwara'ae (Solomon Island) sibling caregiving provides infants with a great diversity of cognitive and social stimulation, both from their mobility and from their skill, which is moderate at age 3 and requires no supervision after age 6 to 7. Heath (1983) notes that the playsongs invented by working-class black girls are tailored to language teaching for young children, with nonsense wordplay, number counting, and naming body parts—topics handled in middle-class adult–child interaction through nursery rhymes and routines but not included in adult–child interaction in the Carolina working-class black community that Heath studied.

Children's groups around the world generally include a mix of ages that may provide various benefits, including the opportunity to practice teaching and nurturance with younger children and the opportunity to imitate and practice role relations with older children (Whiting & Edwards, 1988; Whiting & Whiting, 1975). Howes and Farver (1987) found that toddlers who played with 5-year-olds engaged in more complex social pretend play than those who played with agemates. They were more likely to imitate and participate in activities with 5-year-old partners and were more active in constructing social pretend play when interacting with same-age partners.

The segregation of children by age is an unusual circumstance, speaking globally, that requires sufficient numbers of children together in a small territory in order to ensure sufficient numbers of children of the same age (Konner, 1975). Age segregation even with many children available, and even in an urban setting in the United States, is uncommon outside of bureaucratic institutions such as school or camp, where age groups are formed for adults' convenience (Ellis, Rogoff, & Cromer, 1981; Rogoff, 1981a). Nonetheless, a large proportion of American children's time is spent in such age-graded bureaucratic institutions.

From the cross-cultural evidence, it appears that the importance of peers may derive from their availability and from the different levels of status and expertise that they represent. Peer interaction may provide children with the chance to practice role relations as well as to observe more skilled partners who are likely to be more available than adults.

Even the youngest children may use other children as models. Children observe other children and may attempt to follow their lead from infancy. An example of imitation of a playmate is Piaget's famous account of his 16-month-old daughter's fascinated observation of another child's temper tantrum—and her mimicking of the tantrum in similar circumstances the next day. Imitation of a peer by an infant is also evident in an episode involving 12-month-old David, who was fascinated by an 11-month-old visitor's pacifier:

> David tried but was unable to take the pacifier out of the visitor's mouth, and then went over to a basket of toys and looked for an aged pacifier that had long been sitting there unwanted. (It was his sister's from 3 years before; David had never used a pacifier.) David proceeded to try out the pacifier in imitation of the visitor. Over the next few days, David continued to put the pacifier in his mouth and occasionally offered it to his mother as well.

Social Play and Exploration

What do children do when they are on their own together? Research tells us little about this, and even less about the cognitive aspects of peer interaction. The involvement of adults changes the nature of peer interaction, especially when the adults take charge. And without adults (such as experimenters) taking charge, it is difficult to study the cognitive features of peer interaction with any form of control. In laboratory and school situations, even games must be played by the rules established or enforced by adults. Such tasks lack the playful, exploratory features of peer interaction that may occur when children are on their own ground, and that may be an advantage that peer interaction could offer over interaction with adults. It may be the *absence* of external control, the freedom to play with the rules themselves and to recast the goals of an activity from moment to moment, that is unique and valuable in peer interaction.

Playful exploration among children may be especially important for developing new solutions to a problem, as information obtained by goofing around with the materials may suggest novel, creative solutions to problems down the line. "Creative and productive thought . . . [is] nourished by encouragement and fueled by both wonder and tension. . . . New work is born out of the playfulness of the young, and the freshness of perception that does not wilt after childhood" (John-Steiner, 1985, p. 45). Hence it may be important in studying the character of peer interaction to use tasks and situations in which peers feel enjoyment and freedom, and to observe long enough to determine the long-range advantages that may come from wandering exploration along the way.

Many researchers have attributed an important role to play in children's cognitive development, but they have often focused on solitary play. However, even in the absence of play partners, play often involves social practices, as children try new activities and work through ideas without the pressures that may accompany more formal attempts to learn a skill (Bruner, Jolley, & Sylva, 1976). And as Cooper, Marquis, and Edward (1986) note, even solitary activity may involve social negotiation. Children insist to others that they know what to do and would prefer to do it alone, and caregivers suggest activities that encourage leaving the caregivers alone (this may be a primary function of toys!).

Vygotsky suggested that development occurs in play, which is the "leading activity" (the central goal) in development during the preschool years, from 3 to 7. Vygotsky emphasized the affective, motivational aspects of play, suggesting that in play children enjoy ignoring the ordinary uses of objects and actions in order to subordinate them to imaginary meanings and situations. Children experiment with the meanings and rules of serious life, but place these meanings and rules in the center of attention—for example, in the case of two sisters focusing on the rules of sisterhood as they "play sisters." In such play, with pleasure, imagination, and involvement in devising and implementing rules, children free themselves from the situational constraints of everyday time and space and the ordinary meaning of objects or actions, to develop greater control of actions and rules and understanding. As such, play "creates its own zone of proximal development of the child. In play a child is always above his average age, above his daily behaviour; in play it is as though he were a head taller than himself" (Vygotsky, 1967, p. 552).

Role play and dramatic play may be arenas for children to work out the "scripts" of everyday life—adult skills and roles, values and beliefs—and to learn to take the perspectives of others (Hartup, 1977; Hollos, 1980; Piaget, 1926). Play appears to be important in the development of novel, adaptive behavior as well as in the socialization and practice of established skills (Lancy, 1980; Vandenberg, 1980). Forbes, Katz, and Paul (1986) note that play provides opportunities to create and manipulate meaning frameworks in which fantasy action is understood, fostering the development of "structurally integrated representations of social interaction" (p. 250). They state that "through active manipulation of representations in the course of original fantasy creation, the child comes to know the nature of the socially accepted world in a much fuller way than might be possible if play were to consist of simply recreations or recapitulations of observed social phenomena" (p. 262).

Sylva, Bruner, and Genova (1976) claim that the essence of play is the dominance of means over ends: "Freed from the tyranny of a tightly held goal, the player can substitute, elaborate and invent" (p. 244). Play provides practice in assembling bits of behavior into unusual sequences; it simulates features of nonplay activity with a lessened risk of failure and reduced frustration in the face of unanticipated events. Play allows players to be vulnerable to the world around them, to notice the "irrelevant" possibilities and details of things and events. A rich history of play may prepare a person to solve problems opportunistically, in an organized and flexible way.

Creativity may be fostered in play with peers, to the point that each age-graded generation develops an ethos that builds on that of the parental generation, at times with an explosion of creativity that recasts values and goals of society, as with the political and social impact of the generation that came to maturity in the 1960s. Bretherton (1984a) refers to the creation of "what ifs" and the functioning in subjunctive, simulative modes of peer interaction as a source of creativity and understanding.

In addition, children playing together actively negotiate meaning. The accomplishment of joint play requires children to work together to maintain intersubjectivity as they collaborate on a play scenario (Bretherton, 1984b; Göncü, 1987). Young partners in play may be demanding in regard to the meaning of one another's actions, and their insistence may help them with issues of communication, scripts, and plans. In the following example, 25-month-old Valerie clarifies her intentions in play with her twin brother, who adjusts his actions accordingly:

> Valerie and David were playing with toy dishes with their mother, but with slightly different scripts. Valerie was offering her mother pretend drinks in a cup, which her mother pretended to slurp up, and David was using a cup and a plate to pretend to serve his mother, handing her the setting.
>
> Then Valerie offered David a pretend drink. But instead of pretending to drink, David took the cup from Valerie and placed it on a dish he was holding, preparing to serve.
>
> Valerie grabbed the cup back, and in an exaggerated fashion, looking at David, she *pretended* to pretend to drink. She then put the cup to David's lips (as she had the first time), and he followed her suggestion and slurped his pretend drink.

In such negotiations, children may practice making their intentions known and understanding the intentions of others. They may correct each other on scripts for routine events at which they are playing, and they may consider alternative approaches offered by their companion to similar situations. While young children may often play in parallel, their collaborative play is charac-

terized by demands for clarity of communication and for following or negotiating agreed-on scripts and rules of play.

Compared with young children, middle-class adults may find it easier,
when they are so motivated, to subordinate their wishes to the play devised
by a child or to support and extend the child's play with suggestions and cooperation. However, they are not likely to seek out such interaction to the extent that child partners are, and are likely to quit long before a child would.
For example, my son at age 2½ did not manage to engage me in play when
he suggested, "Pretend you're a lady, Mom?" A similar line, with its rising intonation marking it as an invitation to pretend play, would likely work with
a peer, as with the two sisters observed by Vygotsky who played at being sisters. Mothers report that it is very tiring to have to pretend to be 3 years old
to keep their children entertained—but 3-year-olds can keep up play with
one another for hours!

Furthermore, differing roles are taken by adults compared with young
companions in play. Dunn and Dale (1984) found marked differences in
the play of 2-year-olds at home with their older siblings or with their mothers: children playing with siblings engaged in pretend games involving transformations of role identity, location, or psychological state, whereas their play
with mothers was more likely to involve labeling or acting on a replica object. In addition, the play of siblings commonly involved close meshing of the
partners' actions in complementary pretend roles, whereas mothers generally
observed and supported the play without entering it by performing pretend
roles or actions.

Thus peers may fill important roles seldom taken by adults, in play and
playful approaches to the work of children. Peer interaction may foster exploration and imagination without immediate goals, which in the long run
may lead to insightful solutions to unforeseen problems. Peers may motivate
one another and channel the choice of activities. And compared with busy
adults, peers certainly offer common availability and time.

10

Shared Thinking
and Guided Participation:
Conclusions and Speculations

The word in language is half someone else's. It becomes "one's own" only when the speaker populates it with his own intention, his own accent, when he appropriates the word, adapting it to his own semantic and expressive intention. Prior to this moment of appropriation, the word does not exist in a neutral and impersonal language (it is not, after all, out of a dictionary that the speaker gets his words!), but rather it exists in other people's mouths, in other people's contexts, serving other people's intentions: it is from there that one must take the word, and make it one's own. (Bakhtin, *The Dialogical Imagination*)

At bedtime one night, soon after Valentine's Day and a chicken-pox outbreak in his school, 5-year-old David explained to his mother that love is like chicken pox: you're not supposed to go to school when you have it. But in all seriousness, he confessed that he goes to school anyway. (His mother made some inquiries at school and verified that his teacher had told the class that love is contagious!)

Development . . . [is] a process of children's appropriation of their culture. Children enter into a social system and, by interacting and negotiating with others, establish understandings that become fundamental social knowledge on which they continually build. (Corsaro and Rizzo, *"Discussione* and Friendship")

In these final pages, I summarize the primary points made in previous chapters and extend them with speculations on topics that flow from the approach of this book. I consider ways in which we conceptualize the individual "residue" of shared thinking—as external ideas imported to an internal plane or as a natural product of participation in joint thinking. I discuss creativity in the process of guided participation, with active individuals seeking their own understanding. I speculate on the value of challenge as well as sensitivity of children's partners, especially in terms of degree of familiarity between partners. I consider asymmetries between partners in guided participation, with unequal responsibility for developing cultural skills, ranging from dialogue to observation managed by children. Finally, I conclude with a discussion of the interdependence of children and their caregivers in development.

Review of the Argument

The central aim of this book is to explore the idea that children's cognitive development is inseparable from their social milieu in that what children learn is a cultural curriculum: from their earliest days, they build on the skills and perspectives of their society with the aid of other people.

I have considered thinking as it serves effective action in the interpersonal and physical world, as people solve problems that inherently involve dealing with specific circumstances. Cognitive development consists of coming to find, understand, and handle particular problems, building on the intellectual tools inherited from previous generations and the social resources provided by other people. Development involves children's progress toward local ideals of mature thinking and action, rather than progress toward a universal goal. Both cognition and development must be studied with an understanding of the particulars of the goals being sought and of the circumstances and tools available, since these particulars are the substance of both thinking and developing.

By nature, people are active in their attempts to come to a better understanding of their world. Also by nature, their world is structured by decisions and inventions made by earlier generations and by the arrangements and involvement of their companions. Rather than viewing children as developing spontaneously, I have argued that human development is channeled along specific courses by the sociocultural activities of individuals and their social partners.

The mutual engagement of children and their companions provides support for development. Neither the individual nor the social environment can be analyzed without regard to the other, as the actions of one have meaning only with respect to those of the other. Both children and their partners are responsible for managing circumstances; together, they use the intellectual tools in the organized activities that have been inherited from their predecessors. In their use of societal tools to reach goals and solve culturally defined problems, they also adapt the traditions and agreements that constitute the institutions, norms, and technologies of their community. The picture is one of interdependent goal-directed activity.

As participants in sociocultural activity and users of societal definitions of intellectual goals and techniques, we take the activities and definitions for granted unless we have the opportunity to observe them from a vantage point outside our own society. Research done in other societies draws to our attention what we overlook in our everyday practices with our own societal institutions and tools for thinking. We note that political, economic, and religious institutions as well as the less formal routine practices of society define and organize individual goals and approaches to problems. Foremost among these, when cognitive development is considered, is the Euroamerican institution of schooling, which promotes an individually centered analytic approach to language, mathematics, and other tools of thought and stresses reasoning and learning with information considered on its own ground, extracted from practical use.

Like other societal institutions, schooling provides practice in the use of specific tools and technologies for solving particular problems. Such tools include mnemonic devices; language genres, such as essayist prose and story problems; and formats for calculation and record keeping, such as arithmetic and writing.

Societal institutions and tools of thought carry with them values that define important goals to be reached, significant problems to solve, and sophisticated approaches to be used in addressing the problems and reaching the goals. The values differ in their emphasis on independent versus interdependent performance, social responsibility versus technological advance, analysis of freestanding puzzles versus synthesis of patterns in practical contexts, speed of action versus considered deliberateness, and many other contrasts.

Children enter the world embedded in an interpersonal system involving their caregivers and others who are already involved with societal institutions and technologies. Through guided participation with others, children come to understand and participate in the skilled activities of their culture.

Guided participation involves collaboration and shared understanding in routine problem-solving activities. Interaction with other people assists children in their development by guiding their participation in relevant activities, helping them adapt their understanding to new situations, structuring their problem-solving attempts, and assisting them in assuming responsibility for managing problem solving. This guidance of development includes tacit and intuitive forms of communication and distal arrangements of children's learning environments; it is often not designed for the instruction of children and may not involve contact or conversation. The model is one of routine arrangements and engagements that guide children's increasingly skilled and appropriate participation in the daily activities valued in their culture.

Children's own eagerness to participate in ongoing activities and to increase their understanding is essential to their learning in social context. Children observe, participate in, and manage social activities in which they advance their skills and understanding. From early infancy, children seek and share meaning with their caregivers and other partners.

Guided participation characterizes the social arrangements and engagements of children around the world, with important differences in the lessons to be learned by children and in the nature of their specific social arrangements and engagements. The most notable differences have to do with the goals of development, consistent with differences among societies in the skills and understanding expected of mature members. In addition, there are important cultural differences in the explicitness of verbal and nonverbal communication, the availability of proximal communication with caregivers, the orientation of children toward parents or toward siblings or other caregivers, and the adaptation of children to the adult world or vice versa. I suggest that in cultures in which children are segregated from participation in and observation of adult activities, it may be more necessary for adults to engage in child-centered communication and to explicitly teach adult skills. Accordingly children of different cultures may vary in their skill in learning through active observation or through adult–child conversation. The variations as well as the similarities across cultures in the arrangements and interactions of children are central to the rapid progress of children in becoming participating members of their communities.

The metaphor of apprenticeship stresses children's active role in learning the lessons of their culture, through guided participation with more skilled companions. This view emphasizes the importance of partners' expertise and of skill learning in development, consistent with the perspective offered by Vygotsky. Vygotsky focused on interaction in the "zone of proximal development" as a crucial context for cognitive development, with children advancing their skills and understanding through shared problem solving with more experienced partners. Piaget offered a different perspective, emphasizing the role of cognitive conflict between same-status peers.

Thus although both theorists posited a role for social interaction in cognitive development, their perspectives differed, possibly because of the sphere of intellectual activity that each was trying to explain: Vygotsky was interested in development of skill in the use of societal intellectual tools—especially language—for handling intellectual problems, whereas Piaget was interested in the transformations of perspective that characterize advances in mathematical and physical reasoning.

In addition to differences between Vygotsky's and Piaget's theories in the centrality of the sociocultural context of thinking and in mechanisms by which they portray social interaction as influencing cognitive development—support of an expert versus cognitive conflict between peers—the two theories differ in the process of collaboration they posit to occur between partners. Vygotsky focused on shared problem solving, in which the partners collaborate to reach a joint solution to problems, whereas Piaget focused on reciprocal examination of logical statements by partners. With Vygotsky, the cognitive process is shared between people; with Piaget, the social process provides individuals with the opportunity to see alternatives and to explore the logical consequences of their own positions, in a meeting of minds as opposed to a shared thinking process.

Research that examines the relation between adult–child guided participation and children's development points to the importance of achieving a shared focus of attention, with children's participation and social guidance building on the children's perspective. Evidence supports the idea that caregivers' contingent recasting of children's efforts to communicate, shared attention, and discussion of events on which children have focused facilitates middle-class children's language development. Studies of exploration and construction of objects point to the importance of contingent and sensitively challenging support for children's efforts, with shifts over time in the level of support according to the skill or hesitation exhibited by children in their continuing problem-solving efforts. In investigations of learning to plan, research suggests that school-age children profit from guided participation with partners who are skilled in planning. Research with younger children, however, raises the possibility that even with skilled partners, young children may have difficulty sharing in the planning process, and hence benefit less from social interaction in planning tasks. Shared remembering, however, appears to be possible for young as well as older children, and children's remembering seems to benefit from their engagement in remembering with skilled partners.

The role of peer interaction in supporting cognitive development was central to Piaget's theory and has received some empirical support in research on peer discussion of Piagetian problems. However, interaction with peers appears to be less effective than interaction with adults in the development of skill in planning and remembering in tasks in which adults are more skilled than children.

In situations in which children are skilled and in charge, however, peer interaction may hold special significance. The interaction of children who differ in age provides opportunities for leadership or emulation, whereas the interaction of peers of equal status allows for equality in the comparison and explanation of ideas. In addition, peer interaction may encourage an exploratory approach, with opportunities to examine and manipulate the rules of daily life in the imagination. And, not to be overlooked, peer interaction is motivating and available.

Several questions have appeared throughout the book that I want to tie together with concluding speculations:

1. How can we conceptualize the process by which individuals profit from social engagement—as internalization of external models or activity or, as I will suggest, as appropriation inherent to the process of participation in shared activity?
2. How does individual creativity tie in with guided participation in the use of societal tools for thinking?
3. In the processes of guided participation, what is the role of partners' sensitivity and challenge?
4. What are the sources and importance of asymmetries in the roles of children and their partners in managing guided participation?

I conclude with the argument that children and their social partners, especially their caregivers, are interdependent rather than independent. The social engagements and societal channeling of cognitive development are inherent to the interdependence of humans.

Individual Appropriation from Shared Thinking

How can shared problem solving result in changes in the skills of an individual? The concept of internalization has been used in a variety of theoretical

Figure 10.1   A 20-month-old participating in a book-reading session, contributing what he has already appropriated from familiar routines involving the number system to provide a count-word. (United States)

approaches, including internalization of action on objects for Piaget, internalization of social activity for Vygotsky, and internalization of modeling in social learning (Aronfreed, 1968; Bandura, 1986; Zinchenko, 1985). The processes of transfer of "external" activity to the "internal" plane have received insufficient specification in most approaches referring to internalization.

   The work on social learning and socialization appears to conceive the process of internalization as one in which individuals are regarded as separate from one another and are considered to learn a lesson from observation or participation and then to internalize it, so that it becomes a part of their own bag of tricks. There are arguments about whether the lesson is brought inside unchanged or is transformed in the process of being internalized, and discussion of the kind of model or reinforcement that is necessary to get children to bother to internalize the external model. But the underlying assumption is that the external lesson is brought across a barrier into the mind of the child. How this is done is not specified, and remains a deep problem for these approaches.

However, the problem of specifying the process of internalization may be a problem only if priority is given to the internal or individual functioning, with the internal given responsibility for bringing something across a barrier. If, as I suggest, individuals are seen as appropriating some aspects of activity in which they are already engaged as participants and active observers, with the interpersonal aspects of their functioning integral to the individual aspects, then what is practiced in social interaction is never on the outside of a barrier, and there is no need for a separate process of internalization.

To act and communicate, individuals are constantly involved in exchanges that blend "internal" and "external"—exchanges characterized by the sharing of meaning by individuals. The "boundaries" between people who are in communication are already permeated; it is impossible to say "whose" an object of joint focus is, or "whose" a collaborative idea is. An individual participating in shared problem solving or in communication is already involved in a process beyond the individual level. Benefiting from shared thinking thus does not involve *taking* something from an external model. Instead, in the process of participation in social activity, the individual already functions with the shared understanding. The individual's later use of this shared understanding is not the same as what was constructed jointly; it is an appropriation of the shared activity by each individual that reflects the individual's understanding of and involvement in the activity.

The process of appropriation from shared activity, in contrast to the process of internalization of external activity, can be likened to the utilization of air and water in the functioning of an organism. We tend to think of air and water as being outside us, substances that we must take in for survival. But they are constantly being exchanged inside and outside each living cell of our bodies. The air and water are filtered and transformed to fit the needs of the body. The exchange is constant, does not require attention, and is already in place when a human being is still only one cell.

By analogy, humans are social creatures, living in a social sea. Human exchange is necessary for the survival of the newborn (and of the species) and continues with expanding consequences as the organism grows and becomes capable of more complex exchanges and learning. Thus social exchanges are themselves the medium for social activities to be transformed and used by individuals according to their understanding and involvement. It is within social exchanges that we should look for the advances in individuals' ways of thinking and acting that build on cultural history through the practices of individuals with their social partners. In the words of Wertsch and Stone (1979, p. 21), "The process *is* the product."

Children's participation in communicative processes is the foundation on which they build their understanding. As children participate in ongoing activities, they adjust to the social sense of their partners and incorporate the skills and perspectives of their society. As they are assisted in problem solving, they are involved in the views and understanding of the skilled partner, in the process of stretching their concepts to find a common ground; as they collaborate and argue with others, they consider new alternatives and recast their ideas to communicate or to convince. In these activities, children advance their ideas in the process of participation. It is not a matter of bringing to the internal plane a product that was produced externally. It is a matter of social engagement that leaves the individual changed.

Communication and shared problem solving inherently bridge the gap between old and new knowledge and between the differing understanding of partners (whether their understanding is at the same or at different levels), as individuals attempt to resolve contradictions or search for the common ground of shared understanding.

In his discussion of argumentation as the forum for individuals to advance their thinking through collective processes, Miller (1987) stresses that

> although [a] joint argument will be mentally represented in individual minds, the process of construction proceeds by interlocking the cognitions of all the participants in such a way that a structural whole (the joint argument) can result. Thus, each participant's thinking becomes more and more an integrative part of what everyone else thinks in the group, and therefore neither the meaning nor the mode of construction of each participant's cognition can be explained as isolated, individual mental entities. It is the mode of operation of this coordination device which explains the genesis of individual thoughts (in a collective argumentation). For example, if a participant of an argumentation changes his opinions, acquires some new information, or tries to resolve the contradiction between two different standpoints and if it can be shown that these mental activities are linked up with the collective process of argumentation, then they are most probably not that subject's isolated mental activities. They are released, determined, or even made possible by the mode of operation of this coordination device, which in sense surpasses the potentiality of individual subjects and represents a "reality *sui generis,*" a social reality. (p. 235)

In such coordination of discourse, the product is jointly produced and individually appropriated. Most of us can recognize such a process as one in which we have participated in work groups or family discussions, where individuals' ideas are tested and stretched and become part of a joint construction. The participants gain in understanding and may have difficulty determining "whose" idea an insight was; many claim an insight as their own and cannot trace it to the group discussion. Indeed, it was theirs, but not theirs alone. The insights of such coordinated discussion are theirs as participants in the process.

The product of such social interaction, far from being a copy of what is already invented or available in the thinking of either partner, involves a creative process in which the effort to communicate propels the partners together to develop new solutions through social means, with the partners each bringing their own understanding of the values and tools of the culture to the interaction. Leont'ev (1981) stresses the creative, constitutive role of participants in social interaction in developing new understanding. He claims that the very form of mental reflection of reality changes in the course of each person's development in each new generation, as he or she participates in practical activity developed in human society:

> Consciousness, or the subjects' reflection of reality, of their own activity, emerges. But what is consciousness? "Consciousness is *co-knowledge*," as Vygotsky loved to say. (p. 56)

> The process of internalization is not the *transferal* of an external activity to a preexisting, internal "plane of consciousness": it is the process in which this internal plane is *formed*. (p. 57)

Creativity and Guided Participation

Many people seem to regard social processes as fostering a reproduction of knowledge, a following of previous examples. But while individual development and thinking are channeled by societal institutions and tools, individual appropriation of social practices occurs in a creative process. In this sense, information and skills are not transmitted but are transformed in the process of appropriation. Social activity serves not as a template for individual participation but as a stepping stone, guiding the path taken but not determining it. For as individuals participate in social activity, they choose some aspects for attention and ignore others, and they transform what is available to fit their uses. Just as the meaning of conversation depends on both the information offered by the speaker and the interpretation by the listener, processes of guided participation depend on the structure provided by social activity and on its appropriation by the individual.

I have tried to deal with this issue in this book by emphasizing the active role of children and of their social partners in guided participation, as children seek information and manage and make use of social guidance and societal arrangements. Children contribute in very important ways to the unfolding of social interaction; they also, as a class, contribute to the social practices of society.

The presence and needs of children as a class are central to societal institutions that have developed specifically for children (such as schools and day-care settings). In addition, the need of parents to provide for children has been significant in the development of many other institutions, such as gender roles and production systems adapted to family structure. As sociobiologists would point out, the activities of adults are motivated in some large part to ensure the survival of their genes. The roles of men and women reflect their differing responsibilities and risks in regard to their offspring— hence gender differentiation in work roles (with women's work around the world almost always closer to home to accommodate nursing babies) and in institutions, such as marriage and family, designed to ensure cooperation in the support of children. The point is that as a class, children are active in creating culture, not just in using it.

Individuals transform culture as they appropriate its practices, carrying them forward to the next generation in altered form to fit the needs of their particular generation and circumstances. The shifts in societal practices over decades and centuries result from the transformation of institutions and technologies to fit current needs. For example, whole generations change the arrangements of men's and women's roles according to the needs in the work force associated with men going to or returning from war, and these shifts are associated with changed norms for child care (e.g., whether or not Rosie the Riveter is needed in the work force or is expected to fill an idealized role of motherhood at home as the men return to the jobs). Similarly, migration choices of parents influence the availability of nearby kin to share in child care. In such situations, the decisions of individuals, as they manage current circumstances, transform institutions and practices from generation to generation.

What of the strikingly creative ideas of individuals? Society continues to be transformed by the advent of new technologies, such as the wheel, television, the computer, and atomic energy. They arise from the efforts of creative individuals, from the power of new ideas. How does such creativity fit with guided participation in sociocultural activity?

First, it must be recognized that such creativity builds on the technologies already available, within existing institutions. A creative idea is in some sense a reformulation of existing ideas; there is nothing completely new under the sun. Something completely new would not even be recognized. Creative approaches are ideas that forge a new connection between ideas and tools that are already familiar: "Creativity lies in the capacity to see more sharply and with greater insight that which one already knows or that which is buried at the margins of one's awareness" (John-Steiner, 1985, pp. 51–52).

Second, individual creativity occurs in the context of a community of thinkers (artists, inventors, scientists), where more than one person is working on the solution of a particular problem or within the particular genre of expression. These communities may not be particularly organized, and they may be competitive or supportive. They may not even coexist in time—as exemplified by the use of Vygotsky's ideas in this book, by Michelangelo's study of ancient sculpture, or by the creative grounding of the cello virtuosity of Pablo Casals in his daily morning exercise of playing pieces by Bach (John-Steiner, 1985). Exceptionally creative writers, painters, and physicists discover their own teachers from the past, with

> a recognition of the importance of an intense and personal kinship that results when the work of another evokes a special resonance in them. Once such a bond is established, the learner explores those valued works with an absorption which is the hallmark of creative individuals. In this way, they stretch, deepen, and refresh their craft and nourish their intelligence, not only during their early years of apprenticeship, but repeatedly, throughout the many cycles of their work-lives. (John-Steiner, 1985, p. 54)

Figure 10.2   Two 4-year-olds planning the decoration of a rock, as they write and draw on it with chalky rocks, creating temporary rock art. (United States) (Photograph © B. Rogoff)

Many of the creative individuals who John-Steiner studied had shared the interests of their parents in formative ways. An example is Noam Chomsky's involvement in the study of language during his childhood as he assisted his father in research on medieval Hebrew grammar and gathered an informal familiarity with a historical framework that would become fruitful in his work in linguistics. Similarly, Wolfgang Amadeus Mozart was immersed from an early age in music with his father, an experience that John-Steiner likens to the rich language environment to which all children are exposed.

The mutual involvement of people working on similar issues is part of the social context of creativity. Dialogue, collaboration, and building from previous approaches often provide the catalyst for putting two ideas together that would not have occurred without the need for the individual thinker to carry out, explain, or improve on an approach.

The analogical thinking that is so powerful in creative thought is central to the achievement of intersubjectivity, as participants in a dialogue stretch to make their perspectives mutually comprehensible. The need to make new connections between ideas may be an inherent aspect of communication, sparking ideas for elaboration and discovery by the individuals involved.

An example of making such connections between ideas in the context of dialogue is provided in a discussion between two young sisters and their mother:

> One night, over a pizza, Valerie (age 4) asked her mother out of the blue, "How did we all get alive? How did you and me and David and Luisa and Dad get alive?" Her mother, unsure about which "Where do we come from" question this was, returned the question, asking Valerie what she thought.
>
> Valerie amended the question, "How did *your* mom get alive?"
> Her mother answered playfully, "From her mom and dad."
> Valerie asked how *they* got alive. From their moms and dads. And so on and on and on.
> Then Luisa (age 7) volunteered that long ago there weren't any people; "the only people were apes," and we came from them.
> So her mother provided versions of the story of Adam and Eve and then the idea of evolution—that early people were different from us, and that some people think that the early people came from apes.
> Valerie suggested that the apes came from dinosaurs, and before that there was nothing.
> Her mother suggested that dinosaurs came from salamanders, which came from fishes, which came from tiny one-celled animals. The mother and children spent some time discussing one-celled animals, how they live without arms and legs and heads, and other aspects of their lives.
> Then, trying to stump the children and to reintroduce some mystery, the mother asked, "Where do you think the one-celled animals came from?" To her surprise, Luisa answered with joy, "From ENERGY!"
> The mother asked Luisa how she had come up with that, and Luisa said, referring to a conversation two weeks earlier, "Well, Grandpa told me that molecules [they had been discussing water molecules] were made up of atoms, and atoms were made up of doodle-doodles [electrons, protons, neutrons, in Grandpa's terms], and those were made up of doodle-doodle-doodles [quarks, neutrinos], and *they* were made from ENERGY, just energy. So, I just figured that energy is what the one-celled animals came from!"

Sensitivity and Challenge in Guided Participation

To what extent is it necessary for guided participation to involve sensitive support from other people? Earlier chapters presented many examples of parents expanding contingently on their children's ideas, supporting their children's stumbling efforts, and participating in finely tuned interaction with their children. We have raised the question of conflict in discussion of peer interaction, with a resolution that the conflict has to be evenly explored to be valuable.

The value of sensitivity of guidance, like so many other phenomena in psychology, may be curvilinear. In other words, it is possible to have so little sensitivity of support that children are left to their own devices to discover the regularities of their world, like feral children abandoned in the forests who do not develop skills in the use of human tools. Or in some clinically aberrant patterns of parent–child interaction characterized by mismatched communication, children may become convinced that there are no regularities. Conversely, it is possible to have so much sensitivity on the part of eager parents that children are kept from having to learn to handle the rough spots of life. Children who are protected from error to an extreme degree may have difficulty understanding a process or handling their own errors when some eventually occur.

In my emphasis on the transfer of responsibility for problem solving in guided participation, I intend to make the point that children's partners collaborate in offering children adjusted support that provides both challenge and sensitive assistance. The freedom to err in manageable (or even graceful) ways is inherent to a transfer of responsibility.

This view contrasts with extreme views that stress the necessity for maternal sensitivity, as in the attachment relationship between mothers and infants. More sensitivity is not necessarily better. While it may be important for children to experience a benevolence in their interactions with others, variation in the sensitivity of support may be necessary for children to stretch their understanding and skills.

A minimal benevolence between partners may be necessary to establish the openness for communication, and a degree of familiarity (with either the individual or the class of individuals) may be important for the partners to determine a common ground for communication and to understand the interests, goals, and skills that can be expected of each other. An example of difficulties arising from insufficient familiarity between partners occurs with white teachers who are unfamiliar with the episodic narrative style favored in some black communities. Teachers have difficulty supporting such sharing-time narratives and, instead, interrupt the narratives or dwell on peripheral features of the content rather than on the episodic theme (Michaels & Cazden, 1986), derailing rather than assisting the children.

Many other examples could be found of the difficulties experienced by children who are grounded in one system and attempting to function in another system that does not involve sufficient familiarity with their backgrounds to allow sensitive support. If differences in values and practices are handled with respect, children can benefit from learning new cultural systems while maintaining their "home" approach. Unfortunately, children dealing with two cultural systems often face a less supportive contact between them. The dominant culture may be seen as competing with that of the home culture, with a goal of eradicating the features of the home culture rather than using them to build an understanding of the new approach. This eradication mentality, stemming from differences in status between two cultural approaches, may make it rare for children to have the opportunity to become bicultural (an opportunity that would be advantageous for majority as well as minority children). Rather, many children end up not becoming skilled in any culture, whether because their home culture is devalued and potential links are not exploited to help them learn the ways of the dominant culture, or because their home culture itself suffers such economic stress that the culture loses its strength and coherence, as may be the case for many very poor children.

Whether children are learning one culture or two, guided participation requires some benevolence and familiarity. A common ground for interaction is necessary for achieving intersubjectivity and joint problem solving, as I have argued throughout this book. Piaget and Vygotsky agree on the importance of partners' mutual understanding. For Piaget, the partners must have a common language and system of ideas, and must grant reciprocity in attempting to examine and adjust for conflicting opinions. For Vygotsky, collaboration in the zone of proximal development relies on support based on children's starting points to aid children in reaching greater understanding.

The importance of good will and common ground between partners is often taken for granted in research, in that most researchers seem to try to pair friends or acquaintances, and researchers are just beginning to distinguish the difference in perspective involved in cognitive conflict compared with quarreling and negative interaction.

It is important to consider the comfort of children's social relationships explicitly, however, as children's social interactions are not always benevolent, even with a teacher and certainly not always with peers. Cazden (1988) discusses the challenges faced by teachers in maintaining both control and face-saving with their students, and argues that teachers differ in their management of authority and benevolence. In the context of discussing the difficulties faced by minority children in school, Erickson (1987) points out that learning requires risk taking, since learning involves functioning at the edge of one's competence on the border of incompetence: "If the teacher is not trustworthy, the student cannot count on effective assistance from the teacher; there is high risk of being revealed (to self and others) as incompetent" (p. 344).

Although a degree of sensitivity and ease in establishing intersubjectivity are important, they must be balanced by sufficient challenge to allow and encourage change. Both common ground and differences in perspectives and ideas are needed for communication. Otherwise, communication would not be necessary or interesting, and there would be little impetus for partners to develop greater understanding or to stretch to develop a bridge between alternative views. Somewhat unfamiliar partners may play an important role in forcing children to stretch their understanding. With an easy interaction, there may be less need for children to work to make themselves understood. For example, the idiosyncratic and telegraphic language sometimes developed by twins who interact primarily with each other may result from having so much shared understanding that there is little need to elaborate or to attend to the linguistic conventions of the larger social group.

The interactions of young children with their peers may challenge them to stretch their understanding and take account of one another's perspectives in order to use shared frames of reference with partners who are similarly unskilled in supporting others' communication. In the earliest phases, the establishment of intersubjectivity between toddlers is facilitated by caregivers' suggestions for considering the peer partner's perspective and by the children's interest in involvement (Budwig, Strage, & Bamberg, 1986). Rudimentary forms of peer engagement frequently involve repeating each other's acts with glee or inventing playful variations on a theme. This provides shared affect and a frame for elaboration, and expands to include conversations and cooperative activities involving continual adjustment to achieve shared perspectives.

An example of the cognitive stretches involved in peers' efforts to achieve shared understanding is available in Gearhart's (1979) observations of 3-year-olds who were planning episodes of playing store. The children advanced in their planning of aspects of the play script that they had tried unsuccessfully to coordinate with their partners. Through interaction, the children learned that their partner had a separate plan, and that coordination of plans is necessary to make play run smoothly. The children developed more explicit and sophisticated plans over the course of repeated play episodes, addressing directly the shortcomings in their plan and its communication that had impeded joint action in earlier episodes.

Siblings may similarly force each other to work to be understood and to understand. Whereas a skilled and familiar adult may fill in the blanks left by a young child in communication or may adjust to a young child's limited perspective, sisters and brothers may be more demanding. They may have more difficulty making inferences about the young child's meaning, and they may be less concerned with smoothing or overlooking the roughness in a younger sibling's cognitive and communicative efforts. Although remarks from siblings may at times be intended as critical, often they may simply involve straightforward identification of a problem. The instances of sibling straightforwardness may help a young child become aware of difficulties. An example is provided in the following interaction between two young sisters:

> Valerie (23 months) stood in her highchair and jabbered excitedly about her Mickey Mouse place mat. She picked it up to show the rest of the family and continued commenting on it. But she held it facing her. Neither of her parents took the trouble to point out this difficulty to her. But her 4½-year-old sister said gently, "We can't see it," and Valerie looked down at the place mat and turned it around so it faced her intended audience.

Like interaction with peers or with siblings, interaction with traditional fathers may impel children to advance their communication skills. Fathers who are relatively little involved with their young children are likely to have somewhat limited shared understanding with them and may stimulate them to stretch to explain themselves and to understand their fathers (Mannle & Tomasello, 1989). As partners who may be somewhat unfamiliar with their children but who are more skilled and knowledgeable than peers or siblings, fathers may simultaneously necessitate children's taking greater responsibility for their communication and provide direction in development of adult forms of understanding. Fathers may be responsible for introducing new vocabulary and more complex linguistic forms, and may be more likely to initiate and dominate play rather than follow children's initiative (Snow, 1984). Such interaction may provide both impetus and resources for children to go beyond their own understanding.

Thus children are likely to profit from benevolent interactions with people who are familiar enough to establish some common ground with them in order to allow communication to proceed, but with some variation in sensitivity and familiarity of partners. Intimate partners give children the experience of complex sharing of ideas with people who do not require much background to be explained in order to proceed with a new thought. Less familiar partners may provide the challenge to develop new ways of expressing notions that could otherwise be taken for granted in interactions with a very familiar and skilled partner.

Asymmetries in Responsibility for Intersubjectivity and Learning

In much of our discussion of intersubjectivity, the prototype of intersubjective communication involves a relatively even mutuality between partners. This is the central feature of Piaget's ideas of collaboration, and is characteristic of the give-and-take attributed in much of the literature to the interaction of middle-class parents and children. Differences in assumptions about symmetries in responsibility of partners for adjustment to each other may underlie arguments on the innateness of intersubjectivity (discussed in Chapter 4) and the presence of intersubjectivity between adults and children in cultures with asymmetrical means of communication.

The prototype of intersubjectivity in the literature is a symmetrical dialogue (verbal or nonverbal), in which each partner accords the other equal latitude and in which exchanges resemble smooth and fair turn taking between partners of equal status engaged on the same topic. However, there are a variety of arrangements of intersubjectivity to consider, varying in symmetry of responsibility.

Joint decision making by partners varying in skill involves asymmetry in the management of problem solving and in the lesson learned. A skilled partner has a clearer idea than a novice of the eventual goal and sophisticated means of reaching it, and thus is likely to provide direction in problem solving. A skilled partner may also assist a novice in appropriating the new information that arises during joint problem solving, helping the child to understand the relevance of actions in which the child participates. Wertsch and Hickmann (1987) suggest that the transition from joint activity to individual regulation is a process in which "the child becomes 'aware' of the *functional significance* of the behaviors he has been performing under the guidance of an adult, in the sense of grasping how these behaviors constitute appropriate means to reach a particular goal" (p. 262). Wertsch and Hickmann note that the mothers they studied often provided "reflective assessments" at the end of episodes, pointing out to their preschool partners how the actions related to the goal. These organizing features of adult–child interaction may distinguish them from the sort of intersubjectivity available to peers of equal expertise.

Although our focus has been on the development of children through guided participation, children's partners, in adjusting to the children on whom we have focused, also develop. Change may be symmetrical in peer interaction, but in interaction between children with different levels of skill and understanding and status, and between adults and children, the skilled partners also develop through the mutual engagement.

More skilled partners often gain understanding of the process they attempt to facilitate. This is evidenced in the peer-tutoring literature that seems to find at least as much benefit for the tutor as for the tutee, and in the experience most people have had in understanding a topic through attempts to teach it. Skilled partners gain an understanding not only of the topic, but also of the process of communication and of the needs and skills of the children with whom they interact. This may be most apparent in the development of new parents resulting from their experience in testing hypotheses on how to handle their first child. This experience is often useful in their handling of their second child, since they have greater understanding of child rearing and have developed strategies for dealing with problems. In short, for children as well as for their social partners, engagement in shared thinking yields the opportunities for development of greater skill and understanding.

Observing and Eavesdropping as Active Social Activities

As was discussed in Chapter 6, there is important cross-cultural variation in the relative responsibility of adults and children for learning the lessons of culture, and in the appropriateness of adults and children interacting as peers. In some cultures, guided participation relies on the close involvement of partners in which the work of development is asymmetrical, as where the child is given the responsibility for learning the facts, skills, strategies, and perspectives of the culture, with great opportunities for observation but with little mutuality in dialogue with adults. In other cultures, adults may take major responsibility for structuring lessons and motivating children to learn through peer-like interaction on the children's level, which may accompany age segregation that limits children's chances to be integrated into adult activities. Even within European and American settings, it is important to consider asymmetrical intersubjectivity, with children gaining a great deal from observation. Observation may be a very important and commonplace way for a novice to be involved in skilled processes.

Variations in individuals' efforts to observe relate to their learning, as shown in Azmitia's (1988) findings that 5-year-olds working in dyads in which the children observed each other gained more skill in the task of Lego construction. Novice children whose performance improved spent three times longer observing their expert partners, and their partners spent five times longer monitoring and observing them, than members of dyads in which novices' performance did not improve.

(a)

(b)

Numerous studies in the social learning tradition have demonstrated that middle-class children in the United States learn from observation of modeled behavior (Aronfreed, 1968; Bandura, 1986; Zimmerman & Rosenthal, 1974). These studies have largely examined the benefits of observing models varying in personal characteristics or in modeling procedures (e.g., with or without rule statements; with highly organized or scrambled presentations). The research has not focused on how children go about observing, how participants in a situation in which children are observing communicate and foster or structure children's attention, or how children's observation of incidental activities may differ from their observation of purposefully modeled activities.

It is clear that children's active monitoring of events happening around them provides them with important information, even when the events are not staged for the children's benefit or adjusted to their viewing. Children pick up information from observing the interactions of other people (Hay, Murray, Cecire, & Nash, 1985; Lewis & Feiring, 1981). For example, toddlers appear to evaluate the character of a stranger by observing the reactions of others. Toddlers who watched their mothers interacting in a friendly manner with a stranger were less wary of the stranger and more comfortable accepting a toy from the stranger (Feiring, Lewis, & Starr, 1983).

I have argued throughout this book that it is not necessary for partners to attempt to teach for their roles to be considered supportive of children's learning. I have proposed that guided participation includes tacit structuring of communication and arrangement of the activities of children.

But what about the many occasions in which children are in the presence of others, but the others are not attempting to support the understanding of the children? How does such asymmetry fit with the overall picture of guided participation? There are many social opportunities for learning that are at least momentarily one-sided, with children observing adults or skilled peers. Although in such occasions caregivers may make some arrangements to facilitate the children's observations and may highlight some features of an activity, there is likely to be a much greater asymmetry of mutual involvement than that which has been a focus in most research on social interaction or intersubjectivity.

And in many situations, the observed people make no adjustment to facilitate or structure the observations of the children. Here the children take the responsibility for grasping essential features of the activity, molding to an understanding of the situation, and doing the work to match their understanding with that of others.

Figure 10.3 Observational opportunities for involvement in sociocultural activity. (a) A Mayan toddler in Guatemala accompanies his mother to market and watches with apparent concern (or appropriate disdain for the merchandise) as she bargains for a good price on a cabbage. (Photograph © B. Rogoff) (b) A 5-year-old boy from the United States looks on as his father tries to fix a fishing reel, learning about mechanics, fishing, and cursing. (Photograph courtesy of Salem Magarian)

Even in these situations, it is important to recognize the social and participatory nature of children's observations. Children's presence in any particular setting is by social arrangement. And children are actively involved in understanding the social world, paying special attention to the actions of people and the activities of value in the culture. Often their observations occur in contexts in which they are preparing to or already participate on other occasions. In this sense, children who are observing are working on a social curriculum. Their observations build on their current understanding based on participation in social activities with caregivers and peers in previous situations and on their projected roles in managing cultural activities using cultural tools of understanding and action.

In addition, children are seldom alone. As small children, they are usually near others, sometimes interacting with or observing them. As older children, they may amuse themselves alone for some time or be sent to do some solitary work. But their solitary amusement or work is likely to involve cultural materials and skills. For example, both watching television and chopping the family's firewood involve the use of cultural objects (television, ax) and cultural knowledge (language and visual conventions used on television, information about what wood is good to cut).

I am arguing here that children are, by virtue of being human, deeply involved in social contexts—in social interaction with others, observation of others, and use of sociocultural tools, skills, and perspectives.

Interdependence of Children and Caregivers in Human Development

Let us reverse the question about the importance of the social world in individual development, and ask if we can conceive of human development as an individual activity. My feeling is that a focus on the individual as an independent actor is very culturally determined, a product of middle-class Western striving for individualism and independence and emphasis on the individual as the most important (even sacred) unit of human functioning.

Some middle-class American children are regarded as little individuals even before they are born, to the point of having their portraits taken with ultrasound in utero so their parents can get to know them. Soon after birth, they sleep in separate rooms from their parents, with some parents arguing that this is necessary for the development of independence. Parents stress independence as the most important goal for their infants in the long term (Richman, Miller, & Solomon, 1988), and orient their children toward objects rather than toward other people. Infants are encouraged to rely not on people for comfort, but on pacifiers, blankets, and other "lovies." They and their parents engage in conflicts especially over independent nighttime sleeping, in which parents and infants are adversaries. Such conflicts reach a culturally recognized peak when the infants reach the "terrible twos" and they assert their independent wills. The children compete with their siblings and playmates early in life, and they compete in school and, later, in jobs for themselves, rather than for the honor or benefit of their family. When asked who they are, they are expected to respond with individual identification (name and age) rather than with relational information (name and parents' names), as do the Mayan children with whom I worked.

Child-rearing practices in many cultural groups contrast with the independence training of separate individuals in the U.S. middle class. Many communities seek an ideal of interdependence rather than independence. Children are socialized to responsiveness to the group and identification with the group, rather than encouraged to individualism. Infants are not separated from their mothers at birth, to spend 10 hours out of 24 fending for themselves. In a richly stimulating human environment, infants are socially involved; they seldom sit alone and play with objects. They spend most of their time in intimate contact with other people—being held, sleeping cuddled in arms, being carried on backs or hips—in relationships that Whiting has termed "symbiotic." Skilled caregivers know how to hold a baby as though "he's a part of you" (Heath, 1983, p. 75). Rather than facing the caregiver to learn from dyadic interaction, such infants face the same way as the caregiver and learn from her activities with the rest of the world and from interactions at her side with others. Rather than participating in battles of will as adversaries, infants and caregivers work together as a unit in which each is responsive to the other and goals are less likely to conflict, as caregivers support the needs of the babies as they carry out their other routine activities without a concern that the baby may "win" the battle of wills.

The differences in these models of child rearing have deep implications, involving not only the importance of children's efforts to observe and caregivers' tacit arrangements and communication with infants, which I have discussed, but also the nature of social interaction and support. Our cultural emphasis on independent individuality may keep us, as researchers, from seeing the interdependence that pervades child development in all cultures, with its form varying in accordance with cultural values of independence and interdependence. To understand the embeddedness of all individuals in their social context—to understand how we all appropriate our skills and understanding from guided participation in cultural activities—we must suspend our assumption that the basic unit of analysis is the individual.

The research literature on socialization and social interaction focuses on explicit interaction, aimed at children, largely through speech. We easily miss the adjustments that people who share goals and focus of attention make to each other without focusing directly on each other as targets of interaction. We miss the supports for children's development that go with shared participation in daily events. We miss the communication that is possible between people close to each other and facing the same direction. Research on communication focuses too exclusively on verbal and face-to-face interactions, with insufficient attention to the information that children and caregivers pick up from each others' movements, smells, and timing of actions and speech during shared activities.

Since we focus on infants as separate individuals, we assume that it is necessary for intersubjectivity to involve the relation between separate subjects, integrating their individual subjectivity. However, if we turn the question around, could we not regard intersubjectivity as involving the already existing ties and communication in which infants participate very intimately in utero (with links as explicit as the umbilical cord and postural adjustments between mother and child—innersubjectivity, if you will), which continue after birth in the intimacy of parent–child relationships?

There is evidence that before birth, infants learn about their mothers and the external world. Recent evidence demonstrates that the language experience of fetuses allows newborns to recognize their own mothers' voices, to distinguish unfamiliar from familiar stories that they heard repeatedly in their last weeks before birth (whether spoken by their mother or by another woman), and even to discriminate between an unfamiliar language and their "mother tongue" (Cooper & Aslin, in press; DeCasper & Fifer, 1980; DeCasper & Spence, 1986; Mehler et al., 1988).

Although the study of human development has focused on auditory and visual forms of communication, the links between young infants and their caregivers may be even more striking when we consider kinesthetic forms of communication, such as posture, patterns of gait and movement, and timing of movement. It is ironic that in studies of emotional development, research has so often studied emotion without motion. I doubt that static displays of facial expression are as communicative to infants as many forms of information available in movement and timing of changes of expression and other displays. Similarly, we have paid little attention to chemical forms of communication, the sorts of olfactory and other chemical cues that pass from person to person in situations of stress, attraction, and so on. As this form of communication has been pervasive for the infant throughout prenatal development, it would be surprising for it not to be important in the first months after birth. Such forms of communication may be less noticeable to adults (and especially American adults who stress distal forms of communication), but they may be central for babies, who are often credited with special skill in being able to "pick up on" the stress of a person holding them or of a whispered parental argument when they are in another room.

This view of interdependence, in which there is not an initial assumption of separateness of individuals, is an alternative to the view commonly held by cultural agreement among Euroamerican researchers. But such interdependence, I argue, is natural to being human and transforms with development through guided participation in cultural activities, as children become able to move away from the support of their caregivers to become involved with others distant in time or place, their ancestors or electronic-mail correspondents, according to the direction provided by their society.

FALKIRK COUNCIL
LIBRARY SUPPORT
FOR SCHOOLS

References

Adams, A. K. (1987, January). *"A penguin belongs to the bird family": Language games and the social transfer of categorical knowledge*. Paper presented at the Third International Conference on Thinking, Honolulu.

Adams, A. K., & Bullock, D. (1986). Apprenticeship in word use: Social convergence processes in learning categorically related nouns. In S. A. Kuczaj & M. D. Barrett (Eds.), *The development of word meaning: Progress in cognitive development research*. New York: Springer-Verlag.

Adamson, L. B., Bakeman, R., & Smith, C. B. (in press). Gestures, words, and early object sharing. In V. Volterra & C. Erting (Eds.), *From gesture to symbol in hearing and deaf children*. New York: Springer-Verlag.

Als, H. (1979). Social interaction: Dynamic matrix for developing behavioral organization. In I. C. Uzgiris (Ed.), *Social interaction and communication during infancy*. San Francisco: Jossey-Bass.

Altman, I., & Rogoff, B. (1987). World views in psychology: Trait, interactional, organismic, and transactional perspectives. In D. Stokols & I. Altman (Eds.), *Handbook of environmental psychology* (Vol. 1). New York: Wiley.

Angyal, A. (1941). *Foundations for a science of personality*. Cambridge, MA: Harvard University Press.

Aronfreed, J. (1968). *Conduct and conscience: The socialization of internalized control over behavior*. New York: Academic Press.

Aronson, E., Blaney, N., Stephan, C., Sikes, J., & Snapp, M. (1978). *The jigsaw classroom*. Beverly Hills, CA: Sage.

Azmitia, M. (1988). Peer interaction and problem solving: When are two heads better than one? *Child Development, 59*, 87–96.

Azmitia, M., & Perlmutter, M. (in press). Social influences on children's cognition: State of the art and future directions. In H. Reese (Ed), *Advances in child development and behavior*. San Diego, CA: Academic Press.

Bakeman, R., & Adamson, L. B. (1984). Coordinating attention to people and objects in mother–infant and peer–infant interaction. *Child Development, 55*, 1278–1289.

Bakhtin, M. M. (1981). *The dialogical imagination* (M. Holquist, Ed.). Austin: University of Texas Press.

Bakhurst, D. (1988). Activity, consciousness and communication. *Newsletter of the Laboratory for Comparative Human Cognition, 10*, 31–39.

Bandura, A. (1986). *Social foundations of thought and action: A social cognitive theory*. Englewood Cliffs, NJ: Prentice-Hall.

Barker, R. G. (1978). Behavior settings. In R. G. Barker & Associates (Eds.), *Habitats, environments, and human behavior*. San Francisco: Jossey-Bass.

Bartlett, F. C. (1932). *Remembering*. Cambridge: Cambridge University Press.

Bates, E. (1976). Pragmatics and sociolinguistics in child language. In D. M. Morehead & A. E. Morehead (Eds.), *Normal and deficient child language*. Baltimore: University Park Press.

Bates, E., Bretherton, I., Beeghly-Smith, M., & McNew, S. (1982). Social bases of language development. In H. W. Reese & L. P. Lipsitt (Eds.), *Advances in child development and behavior* (Vol. 16). New York: Academic Press.

211

Bearison, D. J. (in press). Interactional contexts of cognitive development: Piagetian approaches to sociogenesis. In L. Tolchinsky (Ed.), *Culture, cognition, and schooling*. Norwood, NJ: Ablex.

Bearison, D. J., Magzamen, S., & Filardo, E. K. (1986). Socio-cognitive conflict and cognitive growth in young children. *Merrill-Palmer Quarterly, 32*, 51–72.

Beebe, B., Jaffe, J., Feldstein, S., Mays, K., & Alson, D. (1985). Interpersonal timing: The application of an adult dialogue model to mother–infant vocal and kinesic interactions. In T. M. Field & N. Fox (Eds.), *Social perception in infants*. Norwood, NJ: Ablex.

Bellinger, D. (1979). Changes in the explicitness of mothers' directives as children age. *Journal of Child Language, 6*, 443–458.

Belsky, J., Goode, M. K., & Most, R. K. (1980). Maternal stimulation and infant exploratory competence: Cross-sectional, correlational, and experimental analyses. *Child Development, 51*, 1163–1178.

Benedict, R. (1955). Continuities and discontinuities in cultural conditioning. In M. Mead & M. Wolfenstein (Eds.), *Childhood in contemporary cultures*. Chicago: University of Chicago Press.

Berger, P. L., & Luckmann, T. (1966). *The social construction of reality*. New York: Doubleday.

Berkowitz, M. W., & Gibbs, J. C. (1985). The process of moral conflict resolution and moral development. In M. W. Berkowitz (Ed.), *Peer conflict and psychological growth*. San Francisco: Jossey-Bass.

Berland, J. C. (1982). *No five fingers are alike: Cognitive amplifiers in social context*. Cambridge, MA: Harvard University Press.

Bernstein, L. E. (1981). Language as a product of dialogue. *Discourse Processes, 4*, 117–147.

Bloom, K., Russell, A., & Wassenberg, K. (1985, April). *Turn taking affects the quality of infant vocalizations*. Paper presented at the meetings of the Society for Research in Child Development, Toronto.

Blount, B. G. (1972). Parental speech and language acquisition: Some Luo and Samoan examples. *Anthropological Linguistics. 14*, 119–130.

Bornstein, M. H. (1988). Mothers, infants, and the development of cognitive competence. In H. E. Fitzgerald, B. M. Lester, & M. W. Yogman (Eds.), *Theory and research in behavioral pediatrics* (Vol. 4). New York: Plenum Press.

Bos, M. C. (1937). Experimental study of productive collaboration. *Acta Psychologica, 3*, 315–426.

Bowers, K. S. (1973). Situationism in psychology: An analysis and critique. *Psychological Review, 80*, 307–336.

Bransford, J. D., McCarrell, N. S., Franks, J. J., & Nitsch, K. E. (1977). Toward unexplaining memory. In R. Shaw & J. D. Bransford (Eds.), *Perceiving, acting, and knowing: Toward an ecological psychology*. Hillsdale, NJ: Erlbaum.

Brazelton, T. B. (1982). Joint regulation of neonate–parent behavior. In E. Z. Tronick (Ed.), *Social interchange in infancy*. Baltimore: University Park Press.

Brazelton, T. B. (1983). Precursors for the development of emotions in early infancy. In R. Plutchik & H. Kellerman (Eds.), *Emotion: Theory, research, and experience* (Vol. 2). New York: Academic Press.

Bretherton, I. (1984a). Representing the social world in symbolic play: Reality and fantasy. In I. Bretherton (Ed.), *Symbolic play: The development of social understanding*. Orlando, FL: Academic Press.

Bretherton, I. (1984b). (Ed.), *Symbolic play: The development of social understanding*. Orlando, FL: Academic Press.

Bretherton, I., & Bates, E. (1979). The emergence of intentional communication. In I. C. Uzgiris (Ed.), *Social interaction and communication during infancy*. San Francisco: Jossey-Bass.

Bretherton, I., McNew, S., & Beeghly-Smith, M. (1981). Early person knowledge as expressed in gestural and verbal communication: When do infants acquire a "theory of mind"? In M. E. Lamb & L. R. Sherrod (Eds.), *Infant social cognition*. Hillsdale, NJ: Erlbaum.

Brody, G. H., Stoneman, Z., & Wheatley, P. (1984). Peer interaction in the presence and absence of observers. *Child Development, 55*, 1425–1428.

Bronfenbrenner, U. (1979). *The ecology of human development*. Cambridge, MA: Harvard University Press.

Brown, A. L., & Campione, J. C. (1984). Three faces of transfer: Implications for early competence, individual differences, and instruction. In M. E. Lamb, A. L. Brown, & B. Rogoff (Eds.), *Advances in developmental psychology* (Vol. 3). Hillsdale, NJ: Erlbaum.

Brown, A. L., & Reeve, R. A. (1987). Bandwidths of competence: The role of supportive contexts in learning and development. In L. S. Liben (Ed.), *Development and learning: Conflict or congruence?* Hillsdale, NJ: Erlbaum.

Brown, R. (1958). *Words and things*. New York: Free Press.

Bruner, J. S. (1981). Intention in the structure of action and interaction. In L. P. Lipsitt (Ed.), *Advances in infancy research* (Vol. 1). Norwood, NJ: Ablex.

Bruner, J. S. (1983). *Child's talk: Learning to use language*. New York: Norton.

Bruner, J. S. (1987). The transactional self. In J. Bruner & H. Haste (Eds.), *Making sense: The child's construction of the world*. London: Methuen.

Bruner, J. S., Jolly, A., & Sylva, K. (Eds.). (1976). *Play: Its role in development and evolution*. New York: Basic Books.

Buck-Morss, J. (1975). Socio-economic bias in Piaget's theory and its implications for cross-cultural studies. *Human Development, 18*, 35–49.

Budwig, N., Strage, A., & Bamberg, M. (1986). The construction of joint activities with an age-mate: The transition from caregiver–child to peer play. In J. Cook-Gumperz, W. Corsaro, & J. Streeck (Eds.), *Children's worlds and children's language*. Berlin: Mouton.

Burton, R. R., Brown, J. S., & Fischer, G. (1984). Skiing as a model of instruction. In B. Rogoff & J. Lave (Eds.), *Everyday cognition: Its development in social context*. Cambridge, MA: Harvard University Press.

Butterworth, G. (1987). Some benefits of egocentrism. In J. Bruner & H. Haste (Eds.), *Making sense: The child's construction of the world*. London: Methuen.

Butterworth, G., & Cochran, G. (1980). Towards a mechanism of joint visual attention in human infancy. *International Journal of Behavioral Development, 3*, 253–272.

Callanan, M. A. (1985). How parents label objects for young children: The role of input in the acquisition of category hierarchies. *Child Development, 56*, 508–523.

Camaioni, L., de Castro Campos, M. F. P., & DeLemos, C. (1984). On the failure of the interactionist paradigm in language acquisition: A re-evaluation. In W. Doise & A. Palmonari (Eds.), *Social interaction in individual development*. Cambridge: Cambridge University Press.

Campbell, D. T., & Levine, R. A. (1961). A proposal for cooperative cross-cultural research on ethnocentrism. *Journal of Conflict Resolution, 5*, 82–108.

Carew, J. V. (1980). Experience and the development of intelligence in young children at home and in day care. *Monographs of the Society for Research in Child Development, 45* (6–7, Serial No. 187).

Carpenter, I. (1976). The tallest Indian. *American Education, 12*, 23–25.

Carraher, T. N., Carraher, D. W., & Schliemann, A. D. (1985). Mathematics in the streets and in schools. *British Journal of Developmental Psychology, 3*, 21–29.

Cazden, C. B. (1979). Peek-a-boo as an instructional model: Discourse development at home and at school. *Papers and reports on child language development* (No. 17). Stanford, CA: Stanford University, Department of Linguistics.

Cazden, C. B. (1988). *Classroom discourse*. Portsmouth, NH: Heinemann.

Cazden, C. B., & John, V. P. (1971). Learning in American Indian children. In M. L. Wax, S. Diamond, & F. O. Gearing (Eds.), *Anthropological perspectives in education*. New York: Basic Books.

Chapman, M. (1986). The structure of exchange: Piaget's sociological theory. *Human Development, 29,* 181–194.

Chapman, M. (1988). Contextuality and directionality of cognitive development. *Human Development, 31,* 92–106.

Chen, M. J., Braithwaite, V., & Huang, S. T. (1982). Attributes of intelligent behavior: Perceived relevance and difficulty by Australian and Chinese students. *Journal of Cross-Cultural Psychology, 13,* 139–156.

Churcher, J., & Scaife, M. (1982). How infants see the point. In G. Butterworth & P. Light (Eds.), *Social cognition: Studies of the development of understanding.* Chicago: University of Chicago Press.

Clark, H. H., & Haviland, S. E. (1977). Comprehension and the given-new contract. In R. O. Freedle (Ed.), *Discourse production and comprehension.* Norwood, N.J.: Ablex.

Cole, M. (1985). The zone of proximal development: Where culture and cognition create each other. In J. V. Wertsch (Ed.), *Culture, communication, and cognition: Vygotskian perspectives.* Cambridge: Cambridge University Press.

Cole, M. (1988). Cross-cultural research in the sociohistorical tradition. *Human Development, 31,* 137–157.

Cole, M., Gay, J., Glick, J. A., & Sharp, D. W. (1971). *The cultural context of learning and thinking.* New York: Basic Books.

Cole, M., & Griffin, P. (1980). Cultural amplifiers reconsidered. In D. R. Olson (Ed.), *The social foundations of language and thought.* New York: Norton.

Cole, M., & Scribner, S. (1977). Cross-cultural studies of memory and cognition. In R. V. Kail, Jr., & J. W. Hagen (Eds.), *Perspectives on the development of memory and cognition.* Hillsdale, NJ: Erlbaum.

Cole, M., Sharp, D. W., & Lave, C. (1976). The cognitive consequences of education. *Urban Review, 9,* 218–233.

Collins, A., Brown, J. S., & Newman, S. E. (in press). Cognitive apprenticeship: Teaching the craft of reading, writing, and mathematics. In L. B. Resnick (Ed.), *Knowing, learning, and instruction: Essays in honor of Robert Glaser.* Hillsdale, NJ: Erlbaum.

Condon, W. S. (1977). A primary phase in the organization of infant responding behavior. In H. R. Schaffer (Ed.), *Studies in mother–infant interaction.* New York: Academic Press.

Cooper, C. R., Marquis, A., & Edward, D. (1986). Four perspectives on peer learning among elementary school children. In E. C. Mueller & C. R. Cooper (Eds.), *Process and outcome in peer relationships.* San Diego, CA: Academic Press.

Cooper, R. P., & Aslin, R. N. (in press). The language environment of the young infant: Implications for early perceptual development. *Canadian Journal of Psychology.*

Corsaro, W. A., & Rizzo, T. A. (1988). *Discussione* and friendship: Socialization processes in the peer culture of Italian nursery school children. *American Sociological Review, 53,* 879–894.

Cronbach, L. J. (1975). Beyond the two disciplines of scientific psychology. *American Psychologist, 30,* 116–127.

Damon, W. (1984). Peer education: The untapped potential. *Journal of Applied Developmental Psychology, 5,* 331–343.

Damon, W., & Killen, M. (1982). Peer interaction and the process of change in children's moral reasoning. *Merrill-Palmer Quarterly, 28,* 347–378.

Damon, W., & Phelps, E. (1987, June). *Peer collaboration as a context for cognitive growth.* Paper presented at Tel Aviv University School of Education, Tel Aviv.

D'Andrade, R. G. (1981). The cultural part of cognition. *Cognitive Science, 5,* 179–195.

Dasen, P. (1984). The cross-cultural study of intelligence: Piaget and the Baoulé. *International Journal of Psychology, 19*, 407–434.

DeCasper, A. J., & Fifer, W. P. (1980). Of human bonding: Newborns prefer their mothers' voices. *Science, 208*, 1174–1176.

DeCasper, A. J., & Spence, M. (1986). Prenatal maternal speech influences newborns' perception of speech sounds. *Infant Behavior and Development, 9*, 133–150.

DeLoache, J. S. (1983, April). *Joint picture book reading as memory training for toddlers.* Paper presented at the meetings of the Society for Research in Child Development, Detroit.

DeLoache, J. S. (1984). What's this? Maternal questions in joint picturebook reading with toddlers. *Quarterly Newsletter of the Laboratory for Comparative Human Cognition, 6*, 87–95.

Demetras, M. J., Post, K. N., & Snow, C. E. (1986). Feedback to first language learners: The role of repetitions and clarification questions. *Journal of Child Language, 13*, 275–292.

Dewey, J., & Bentley, A. F. (1949). *Knowing and the known.* Boston: Beacon Press.

Dixon, S. D., LeVine, R. A., Richman, A., & Brazelton, T. B. (1984). Mother–child interaction around a teaching task: An African–American comparison. *Child Development, 55*, 1252–1264.

Doise, W. (1985). Social regulations in cognitive development. In R. A. Hinde, A.-N. Perret-Clermont, & J. Stevenson-Hinde (Eds.), *Social relationships and cognitive development.* Oxford: Clarendon Press.

Doise, W., & Mackie, D. (1981). On the social nature of cognition. In J. P. Forgas (Ed.), *Social cognition: Perspectives on everyday understanding.* London: Academic Press.

Donaldson, M. (1978). *Children's minds.* New York: Norton.

Drake, S. G. (1834). *Biography and history of the Indians of North America.* Boston: Perkins and Hilliard, Gray.

Draper, P., & Harpending, H. (1987). Parent investment and the child's environment. In J. B. Lancaster, J. Altmann, A. S. Rossi, & L. R. Sherrod (Eds.), *Parenting across the lifespan: Biosocial dimensions.* New York: Aldine de Gruyter.

Dube, E. F. (1982). Literacy, cultural familiarity, and "intelligence" as determinants of story recall. In U. Neisser (Ed.), *Memory observed: Remembering in natural contexts.* San Francisco: Freeman.

Dunn, J., & Dale, N. (1984). I a daddy: 2-year-olds' collaboration in joint pretend with sibling and with mother. In I. Bretherton (Ed.), *Symbolic play: The development of social understanding.* Orlando, FL: Academic Press.

Eckerman, C. O., Whatley, J. L., & McGhee, L. J. (1979). Approaching and contacting the object another manipulates: A social skill of the one-year-old. *Developmental Psychology, 15*, 585–593.

Edwards, C. P. (1981). The comparative study of the development of moral judgment and reasoning. In R. H. Munroe, R. L. Munroe, & B. B. Whiting (Eds.), *Handbook of cross-cultural human development.* New York: Garland.

Edwards, D. (1978). Social relations and early language. In A. Lock (Ed.), *Action, gesture and symbol: The emergence of language.* New York: Academic Press.

Egeland, B., Jacobvitz, D., & Sroufe, L. A. (1988). Breaking the cycle of abuse. *Child Development, 59*, 1080–1088.

Eisenberg, A. R. (1985). Learning to describe past experiences in conversation. *Discourse Processes, 8*, 177–204.

Ekehammar, B. (1974). Interactionism in personality from a historical perspective. *Psychological Bulletin, 81*, 1026–1048.

Ellis, S., & Rogoff, B. (1982). The strategies and efficacy of child versus adult teachers. *Child Development, 53*, 730–735.

Ellis, S., & Rogoff, B. (1986). Problem solving in children's management of instruction.

In E. Mueller & C. Cooper (Eds.), *Process and outcome in peer relationships.* Orlando, FL: Academic Press.

Ellis, S., Rogoff, B., & Cromer, C. C. (1981). Age segregation in children's social interactions. *Developmental Psychology, 17,* 399–407.

Endler, N. S., & Edwards, J. (1978). Person by treatment interactions in personality research. In L. A. Pervin & M. Lewis (Eds.), *Perspectives in interactional psychology.* New York: Plenum Press.

Erickson, F. (1982). Taught cognitive learning in its immediate environments: A neglected topic in the anthropology of education. *Anthropology & Education Quarterly, 13,* 149–180.

Erickson, F. (1987). Transformation and school success: The politics and culture of educational achievement. *Anthropology & Education Quarterly, 18,* 335–356.

Evans, M. A., & Bienert, H. (1987, April). *Asking less may gather more: The effect of teacher interactive styles on reticent children.* Paper presented at the meetings of the Society for Resarch in Child Development, Baltimore.

Feinman, S. (1982). Social referencing in infancy. *Merrill-Palmer Quarterly, 28,* 445–470.

Feinman, S., & Lewis, M. (1983). Is there social life beyond the dyad? A social psychological view of social connections in infancy. In M. Lewis (Ed.), *Beyond the dyad.* New York: Plenum Press.

Feiring, C., Lewis, M., & Starr, M. D. (1983, April). *Indirect effects and infants' reaction to strangers.* Paper presented at the meetings of the Society for Research in Child Development, Detroit.

Feldman, D. H. (1980). *Beyond universals in cognitive development.* Norwood, NJ: Ablex.

Fernald, A. (1988, November). *The universal language: Infants' responsiveness to emotion in the voice.* Paper presented at the Developmental Psychology Program, Stanford University, Stanford, CA.

Ferrier, L. (1978). Word, context and imitation. In A. Lock (Ed.), *Action, gesture and symbol: The emergence of language.* New York: Academic Press.

Field, T. M., Sostek, A. M., Vietze, P., & Leiderman, P. H. (Eds.). (1981). *Culture and early interactions.* Hillsdale, NJ: Erlbaum.

Fischer, K. W. (1980). A theory of cognitive development: The control and construction of hierarchies of skills. *Psychological Review, 87,* 477–531.

Fivush, R. (1988). *Form and function in early autobiographical memory.* Unpublished manuscript, Emory University, Atlanta.

Fivush, R., & Fromhoff, F. A. (1988). Style and structure in mother–child conversations about the past. *Discourse Processes, 11,* 337–355.

Flavell, J. H., Beach, D. R., & Chinsky, J. M. (1966). Spontaneous verbal rehearsal in a memory task as a function of age. *Child Development, 37,* 283–299.

Fobih, D. K. (1979). *The influence of different educational experiences on classificatory and verbal reasoning behavior of children in Ghana.* Unpublished doctoral dissertation, University of Alberta, Edmonton.

Fogel, A., & Thelen, E. (1987). Development of early expressive and communicative action: Reinterpreting the evidence from a dynamic systems perspective. *Developmental Psychology, 23,* 747–761.

Forbes, D., Katz, M. M., & Paul, B. (1986). "Frame talk": A dramatistic analysis of children's fantasy play. In E. S. Mueller & C. R. Cooper (Eds.), *Process and outcome in peer relationships.* San Diego, CA: Academic Press.

Forman, E. A. (1987). Learning through peer interaction: A Vygotskian perspective. *Genetic Epistemologist, 15,* 6–15.

Forman, E. A., & Cazden, C. B. (1985). Exploring Vygotskian perspectives in education: The cognitive value of peer interaction. In J. V. Wertsch (Ed.), *Culture, communication, and cognition: Vygotskian perspectives.* Cambridge: Cambridge University Press.

Forman, E. A., & Kraker, M. J. (1985). The social origins of logic: The contributions of Piaget and Vygotsky. In M. W. Berkowitz (Ed.), *Peer conflict and psychological growth*. San Francisco: Jossey-Bass.

Fortes, M. (1938). *Social and psychological aspects of education in Taleland*. Oxford: Oxford University Press.

Fox, B. A. (1988a). *Interaction as a diagnostic resource in tutoring* (Tech. Rep. No. 88–3). Boulder: University of Colorado, Institute of Cognitive Science.

Fox, B. A. (1988b). *Cognitive and interactional aspects of correction in tutoring* (Tech. Rep. No. 88–2). Boulder: University of Colorado, Institute of Cognitive Science.

Fraiberg, S., Adelson, E., & Shapiro, V. (1975). Ghosts in the nursery: A psychoanalytic approach to the problems of impaired infant–mother relationships. *Journal of the American Academy of Child Psychiatry, 14*, 387–421.

Freed, R. S., & Freed, S. A. (1981). *Enculturation and education in Shanti Nagar* (Volume 57, Part 2). *Anthropological Papers of the American Museum of Natural History*. New York.

Freedman, R. (1988). Newbery medal acceptance. *Horn Book Magazine, 64*, 444–451.

French, L. (1987). *Effects of partner and setting on young children's discourse: A case study*. Unpublished manuscript, University of Rochester.

Friedman, A. (1979). Framing pictures: The role of knowledge in automated encoding and memory for gist. *Journal of Experimental Psychology, 108*, 316–355.

Furth, H. G. (1974). Two aspects of experience in ontogeny: Development and learning. In H. Reese (Ed.), *Advances in child development and behavior* (Vol. 9). New York: Academic Press.

Gardner, W. P., & Rogoff, B. (1988). *Children's adjustment of deliberateness of planning to task circumstances*. Unpublished manuscript, University of Virginia, Charlottesville.

Garvey, C. (1986). Peer relations and the growth of communication. In E. C. Mueller & C. R. Cooper (Eds.), *Process and outcome in peer relationships*. San Diego, CA: Academic Press.

Gaskins, S., & Lucy, J. A. (1987, May). *The role of children in the production of adult culture: A Yucatec case*. Paper presented at the meeting of the American Ethnological Society, San Antonio, TX.

Gauvain, M., & Rogoff, B. (1989). Collaborative problem solving and children's planning skills. *Developmental Psychology, 25*, 139–151.

Gearhart, M. (1979, March). *Social planning: Role play in a novel situation*. Paper presented at the meetings of the Society for Research in Child Development, San Francisco.

Gellatly, A. R. H. (1987). Acquisition of a concept of logical necessity. *Human Development, 30*, 32–47.

Gibson, E. J. (1982). The concept of affordances in development: The renascence of functionalism. In W. A. Collins (Ed.), *Minnesota Symposia on Child Psychology* (Vol. 15). Hillsdale, NJ: Erlbaum.

Gibson, J. J. (1979). *The ecological approach to visual perception*. Boston: Houghton Mifflin.

Gill, R., & Keats, D. M. (1980). Elements of intellectual competence: Judgments by Australian and Malay university students. *Journal of Cross-Cultural Psychology, 11*, 233–243.

Glachan, N. M., & Light, P. H. (1982). Peer interaction and learning. In G. E. Butterworth & P. H. Light (Eds.), *Social cognition: Studies of the development of understanding*. Brighton: Harvester Press.

Glick, J. (1975). Cognitive development in cross-cultural perspective. In F. Horowitz et al. (Eds.), *Review of child development research* (Vol. 4). Chicago: University of Chicago Press.

Goffman, E. (1964). The neglected situation. In J. J. Gumperz & D. Hymes (Eds.), *The ethnography of communication*. Special Publication of the *American Anthropologist, 66* (No. 6, Part 2), 133–136.

Gollin, E. S. (1981). Development and plasticity. In E. S. Gollin (Ed.), *Developmental plasticity*. New York: Academic Press.

Göncü, A. (1987). Toward an interactional model of developmental changes in social pretend play. In L. Katz (Ed.), *Current topics in early childhood education*. Norwood, NJ: Ablex.

Göncü, A., & Rogoff, B. (1987, April). *Adult guidance and children's participation in learning*. Paper presented at the meetings of the Society for Research in Child Development, Baltimore.

Goodnow, J. J. (1976). The nature of intelligent behavior: Questions raised by cross-cultural studies. In L. B. Resnick (Ed.), *The nature of intelligence*. Hillsdale, NJ: Erlbaum.

Goodnow, J. J. (1980). Everyday concepts of intelligence and its development. In N. Warren (Ed.), *Studies in cross-cultural psychology* (Vol. 2). London: Academic Press.

Goodnow, J. J. (1987, November). *The socialization of cognition: What's involved?* Paper presented at the conference on Culture and Human Development, Chicago.

Goody, E. N. (1978). Towards a theory of questions. In E. N. Goody, (Ed.), *Questions and politeness*. Cambridge: Cambridge University Press.

Goody, J. (1977). *The domestication of the savage mind*. Cambridge: Cambridge University Press.

Goody, J., & Watt, I. (1968). The consequences of literacy. In J. R. Goody (Ed.), *Literacy in traditional societies*. Cambridge: Cambridge University Press.

Graves, Z. R., & Glick, J. (1978). The effect of context on mother–child interaction. *Quarterly Newsletter of the Institute for Comparative Human Development, 2,* 41–46.

Greenfield, P. M. (1966). On culture and conservation. In J. S. Bruner, R. R. Olver, & P. M. Greenfield (Eds.), *Studies in cognitive growth*. New York: Wiley.

Greenfield, P. M. (1984). A theory of the teacher in the learning activities of everyday life. In B. Rogoff & J. Lave (Eds.), *Everyday cognition: Its development in social context*. Cambridge, MA: Harvard University Press.

Greenfield, P. M., & Lave, J. (1982). Cognitive aspects of informal education. In D. Wagner & H. Stevenson (Eds.), *Cultural perspectives on child development*. San Francisco: Freeman.

Greenfield, P. M., & Smith, J. (1976). *The structure of communication in early language development*. New York: Academic Press.

Guilmet, G. M. (1979). Navajo and Caucasian children's verbal and nonverbal-visual behavior in the urban classroom. *Anthropology and Education Quarterly, 9,* 196–215.

Gunnar, M. R., & Stone, C. (1984). The effects of positive maternal affect on infant responses to pleasant, ambiguous, and fear-provoking toys. *Child Development, 55,* 1231–1236.

Halliday, M. A. K. (1979). One child's protolanguage. In M. Bullowa (Ed.), *Before speech: The beginning of interpersonal communication*. Cambridge: Cambridge University Press.

Harding, C. G. (1982). *Prelanguage vocalizations and words*. Paper presented at the International Conference on Infant Studies, Austin, TX.

Hardy-Brown, K., Plomin, R., & DeFries, J. C. (1981). Genetic and environmental influences on the rate of communicative development in the first year of life. *Developmental Psychology, 17,* 704–717.

Harkness, S., & Super, C. M. (1977). Why African children are so hard to test. In L. L. Adler (Ed.), *Issues in cross-cultural research. Annals of the New York Academy of Sciences, 285,* 326–331.

Harlow, H. F. (1963). The maternal affectional system. In B. M. Foss (Ed.), *Determinants of infant behavior II*. London: Methuen.

Hart, S. S., Leal, L., Burney, L., & Santulli, K. A. (1985, April). *Memory in the ele-*

mentary school classroom: How teachers encourage strategy use. Paper presented at the meetings of the Society for Research in Child Development, Toronto.

Hartup, W. W. (1977, Fall). Peers, play, and pathology: A new look at the social behavior of children. *Newsletter of the Society for Research in Child Development.*

Hartup, W. (1985). Relationships and their significance in cognitive development. In R. Hinde & A. Perret-Clermont (Eds.), *Relationships and cognitive development.* Oxford: Oxford University Press.

Hatano, G. (1982). Cognitive consequences of practice in culture specific procedural skills. *Quarterly Newsletter of the Laboratory of Comparative Human Cognition, 4,* 15–17.

Hay, D. F. (1980). Multiple functions of proximity seeking in infancy. *Child Development, 51,* 636–645.

Hay, D. F., Murray, P., Cecire, S., & Nash, A. (1985). Social learning of social behavior in early life. *Child Development, 56,* 43–57.

Heath, S. B. (1982). What no bedtime story means: Narrative skills at home and school. *Language in Society, 11,* 49–76.

Heath, S. B. (1983). *Ways with words: Language, life, and work in communities and classrooms.* Cambridge: Cambridge University Press.

Heber, M. (1981). Instruction *versus* conversation as opportunities for learning. In W. P. Robinson (Ed.), *Communications in development.* London: Academic Press.

Heckhausen, J. (1984). *Mother–infant dyads in joint object-centered action.* Unpublished doctoral dissertation, University of Strathclyde, Glasgow.

Henderson, B. B. (1984a). Parents and exploration: The effect of context on individual differences in exploratory behavior. *Child Development, 55,* 1237–1245.

Henderson, B. B. (1984b). Social support and exploration. *Child Development, 55,* 1246–1251.

Hodapp, R. M., Goldfield, E. C., & Boyatzis, C. J. (1984). The use and effectiveness of maternal scaffolding in mother–infant games. *Child Development, 55,* 772–781.

Hoff-Ginsberg, E. (1986). Function and structure in maternal speech: Their relation to the child's development of syntax. *Developmental Psychology, 22,* 155–163.

Hoff-Ginsberg, E., & Shatz, M. (1982). Linguistic input and the child's acquisition of language. *Psychological Bulletin, 92,* 3–26.

Hollos, M. (1980). Collective education in Hungary: The development of competitive, cooperative and role-taking behaviors. *Ethos, 8,* 3–23.

Howard, A. (1970). *Learning to be Rotuman.* New York: Teachers College Press.

Howes, C., & Farver, J. (1987). Social pretend play in 2-year-olds: Effects of age of partner. *Early Childhood Research Quarterly, 2,* 305–314.

Hubley, P., & Trevarthen, C. (1979). Sharing a task in infancy. In I. C. Uzgiris (Ed.), *Social interaction and communication during infancy.* San Francisco: Jossey-Bass.

Irvine, J. T. (1978). Wolof "magical thinking": Culture and conservation revisited. *Journal of Cross-Cultural Psychology, 9,* 300–310.

Isaacs, E. A., & Clark, H. H. (1987). References in conversation between experts and novices. *Journal of Experimental Psychology: General, 116,* 26–37.

John-Steiner, V. (1984). Learning styles among Pueblo children. *Quarterly Newsletter of the Laboratory of Comparative Human Cognition, 6,* 57–62.

John-Steiner, V. (1985). *Notebooks of the mind: Explorations of thinking.* Albuquerque: University of New Mexico Press.

John-Steiner, V., & Tatter, P. (1983). An interactionist model of language development. In B. Bain (Ed.), *The sociogenesis of language and human conduct.* New York: Plenum Press.

Johnston, T. D., and Turvey, M. T. (1980). A sketch of an ecological metatheory for theories of learning. In G. H. Bower (Ed.), *The psychology of learning and motivation* (Vol. 14). New York: Academic Press.

Jones, C. P., & Adamson, L. B. (1987). Language use in mother–child and mother–child–sibling interactions. *Child Development, 58,* 356–366.

Jordan, C. (1977, February). *Maternal teaching, peer teaching, and school adaptation in an urban Hawaiian population.* Paper presented at the meetings of the Society for Cross-Cultural Research, East Lansing, MI.

Kagan, J., Klein, R. E., Finley, G. E., Rogoff, B., & Nolan, E. (1979). A cross-cultural study of cognitive development. *Monographs of the Society for Research in Child Development, 44* (5, Serial No. 180).

Kantor, J. R. (1946). The aim and progress of psychology. *American Psychologist, 22,* 131–142.

Katz, R. (1982). *Boiling energy.* Cambridge, MA: Harvard University Press.

Kaye, K. (1977a). Infants' effects upon their mothers' teaching strategies. In J. D. Glidewell (Ed.), *The social context of learning and development.* New York: Gardner Press.

Kaye, K. (1977b). Toward the origin of dialogue. In H. R. Schaffer (Ed.), *Studies in mother–infant interaction.* New York: Academic Press.

Kaye, K. (1979a). The development of skills. In G. Whitehurst & B. Zimmerman (Eds.), *The functions of language and cognition.* New York: Academic Press.

Kaye, K. (1979b). Thickening thin data: The maternal role in developing communication and language. In M. Bullowa (Ed.), *Before speech: The beginning of interpersonal communication.* Cambridge: Cambridge University Press.

Kaye, K. (1982). Organism, apprentice, and person. In E. Z. Tronick (Ed.), *Social interchange in infancy.* Baltimore: University Park Press.

Kaye, K., & Charney, R. (1980). How mothers maintain "dialogue" with two-year-olds. In D. Olson (Ed.), *The social foundations of language and thought.* New York: Norton.

Kearins, J. M. (1981). Visual spatial memory in Australian aboriginal children of desert regions. *Cognitive Psychology, 13,* 434–460.

Keller-Cohen, D. (1978). Context in child language. *Annual Review of Anthropology, 7,* 453–482.

Kerwin, M. L. E., & Day, J. D. (1985). Peer influences on cognitive development. In J. B. Pryor & J. D. Day (Eds.), *The development of social cognition.* New York: Springer-Verlag.

Kessel, F. S., & Siegel, A. W. (1985). *The child and other cultural inventions.* New York: Praeger.

Kessen, W. (1979). The American child and other cultural inventions. *American Psychologist, 34,* 815–820.

Kilbride, P. L. (1980). Sensorimotor behavior of Baganda and Samai infants. *Journal of Cross-Cultural Psychology, 11,* 131–152.

Kitchener, R. F. (1985). Holistic structuralism, elementarism and Piaget's theory of "relationalism." *Human Development, 28,* 281–294.

Koester, L. S., & Bueche, N. A. (1980). Preschoolers as teachers: When children are seen but not heard. *Child Study Journal, 10,* 107–118.

Kohn, M. L., & Schooler, C. (1973). Occupational experience and psychological functioning: An assessment of reciprocal effects. *American Sociological Review, 38,* 97–118.

Konner, M. (1975). Relations among infants and juveniles in comparative perspective. In M. Lewis & L. A. Rosenblum (Eds.), *Friendship and peer relations.* New York: Wiley.

Kontos, S. (1983). Adult–child interaction and the origins of metacognition. *Journal of Educational Research, 77,* 43–54.

Kruger, A. C. (1988, March). *The effect of peer and adult–child transactive discussions on moral reasoning.* Papers presented at the meeting of the Conference on Human Development, Charleston, SC.

Kruger, A. C., & Tomasello, M. (1986). Transactive discussions with peers and adults. *Developmental Psychology, 22,* 681–685.

Kruper, J. C., & Uzgiris, I. C. (1985, April). *Fathers' and mothers' speech to infants.* Paper presented at the meetings of the Society for Research in Child Development, Toronto.

Kuhn, D. (1972). Mechanisms of change in the development of cognitive structures. *Child Development, 43,* 833–842.

Laboratory of Comparative Human Cognition. (1983). Culture and cognitive development. In W. Kessen (Ed.), *History, theory, and methods,* Vol. 1 of P. H. Mussen (Ed.), *Handbook of child psychology.* New York: Wiley.

Lancaster, J., Altmann, J., Rossi, A. S., & Sherrod, L. R. (Eds.). (1987). *Parenting across the life span: Biosocial dimensions.* New York: Aldine de Gruyter.

Lancy, D. F. (1980). Play in species adaptation. *Annual Review of Anthropology, 9,* 471–495.

Lave, J. (1988, May). *The culture of acquisition and the practice of understanding* (Report No. IRL 88–0007). Palo Alto, CA: Institute for Research on Learning.

Leiderman, P. H., Tulkin, S. R., & Rosenfeld, A. (Eds.). (1977). *Culture and infancy: Variations in the human experience.* New York: Academic Press.

Lempers, J. D. (1979). Young children's production and comprehension of nonverbal deictic behaviors. *Journal of Genetic Psychology, 135,* 93–102.

Leont'ev, A. N. (1981). The problem of activity in psychology. In J. V. Wertsch (Ed.), *The concept of activity in Soviet psychology.* Armonk, NY: Sharpe.

Lerner, R. M. (1978). Nature, nurture, and dynamic intractionism. *Human Development, 21,* 1–20.

Lerner, R. M., & Kauffman, M. B. (1985). The concept of development in contextualism. *Developmental Review, 5,* 309–333.

LeVine, R. A. (1977). Child rearing as cultural adaptation. In P. H. Leiderman, S. R. Tulkin, & A. Rosenfeld (Eds.), *Culture and infancy: Variations in the human experience.* New York: Academic Press.

LeVine, R. A. (1989). Environments in child development: An anthropological perspective. In W. Damon (Ed.), *Child development today and tomorrow.* San Francisco: Jossey-Bass.

Lewis, M., & Feiring, C. (1981). Direct and indirect interactions in social relationships. In L. P. Lipsett (Ed.), *Advances in infancy research* (Vol. 1). Norwood, NJ: Ablex.

Light, P. H. (1986). Context, conservation and conversation. In M. Richards and P. Light (Eds.), *Children of social worlds.* Cambridge, MA: Harvard University Press.

Light, P. H., Buckingham, N., & Robbins, A. M. (1979). The conservation task as an interactional setting. *British Journal of Educational Psychology, 49,* 304–310.

Light, P., Foot, T., Colbourn, C., & McClelland, I. (1987). Collaborative interactions at the microcomputer keyboard. *Educational Psychology, 7,* 13–21.

Light, P., & Glachan, M. (1985). Facilitation of individual problem solving through peer interaction. *Educational Psychology, 5,* 217–225.

Light, P., Gorsuch, C., & Newman, J. (1987). Why do you ask? Context and communication in the conservation task. *European Journal of Psychology of Education, 2,* 73–82.

Light, P., & Perret-Clermont, A.-N. (1989). Social context effects in learning and testing. In A. Gellatly, D. Rogers, & J. Sloboda (Eds.), *Cognition and social worlds.* Oxford: Clarendon Press.

Lock, A. (1978). The emergence of language. In A. Lock (Ed.), *Action, gesture and symbol: The emergence of language.* London: Academic Press.

Lomov, B. F. (1978). Psychological processes and communication. *Soviet Psychology, 17,* 3–22.

Lucy, J. A., & Wertsch, J. V. (1987). Vygotsky and Whorf: A comparative analysis. In M. Hickmann (Ed.), *Social and functional approaches to language and thought*. San Diego, CA: Academic Press.

Luria, A. R. (1971). Towards the problem of the historical nature of psychological processes. *International Journal of Psychology, 6*, 259–272.

Luria, A. R. (1976). *Cognitive development: Its cultural and social foundations*. Cambridge, MA: Harvard University Press.

Luria, A. R. (1987). Afterword to the Russian edition. In R. W. Rieber & A. S. Carton (Eds.), *The collected works of L. S. Vygotsky: Vol. 1. Problems of general psychology*. New York: Plenum Press.

Lutz, C., & LeVine, R. A. (1982). Culture and intelligence in infancy: An ethnopsychological view. In M. Lewis (Ed.), *Origins of intelligence: Infancy and early childhood*. New York: Plenum Press.

Magkaev, V. K. (1977). An experimental study of the planning function of thinking in young school children. In M. Cole (Ed.), *Soviet developmental psychology: An anthology*. White Plains, NY: Sharpe.

Mandler, J. M. (1979). Categorical and schematic organization in memory. In C. R. Puff (Ed.), *Memory organization and structure*. New York: Academic Press.

Mandler, J. M., Scribner, S., Cole, M., & DeForest, M. (1980). Cross-cultural invariance in story recall. *Child Development, 51*, 19–26.

Mannle, S., & Tomasello, M. (1989). Fathers, siblings, and the Bridge Hypothesis. In K. Nelson & A. van Kleeck (Eds.), *Children's language* (Vol. 6). Hillsdale, NJ: Erlbaum.

Martin, L. (1985). The role of social interaction in children's problem solving. *Quarterly Newsletter of the Laboratory for Comparative Human Cognition, 7*, 40–45.

Martinez, M. A. (1987). Dialogues among children and between children and their mothers. *Child Development, 58*, 1035–1043.

Martini, M., & Kirkpatrick, J. (1981). Early interactions in the Marquesas Islands. In T. M. Field, A. M. Sostek, P. Vietze, & P. H. Leiderman (Eds.), *Culture and early interactions*. Hillsdale, NJ: Erlbaum.

Masur, E. F. (1982). Mothers' responses to infants' object-related gestures: Influences on lexical development. *Journal of Child Language, 9*, 23–30.

Matsuyama, U. K. (1983). Can story grammar speak Japanese? *Reading Teacher, 36*, 666–669.

McGarrigle, J., & Donaldson, M. (1975). Conservation accidents. *Cognition, 3*, 341–350.

McLane, J. B. (1987). Interaction, context, and the zone of proximal development. In M. Hickmann (Ed.), *Social and functional approaches to language and thought*. San Diego, CA: Academic Press.

McNamee, G. D. (1980). *The social origins of narrative skills*. Unpublished doctoral dissertation, Northwestern University, Evanston, IL.

Meacham, J. A. (1977). A transactional model of remembering. In N. Datan & H. W. Reese (Eds.), *Life-span developmental psychology*. New York: Academic Press.

Mead, G. H. (1934). *Mind, self, and society* (C. W. Morris, Ed.). Chicago: University of Chicago Press.

Mehan, H. (1976). Assessing children's school performance. In J. Beck, C. Jenks, N. Keddie, & M. F. D. Young (Eds.), *World apart*. London: Collier Macmillan.

Mehler, J., Jusczyk, P. W., Lambertz, G., Halsted, N., Bertoncini, J., & Amiel-Tison, C. (1988). A precursor of language acquisition in young infants. *Cognition, 29*, 143–178.

Mervis, C. B. (1984). Early lexical development: The contributions of mother and child. In C. Sophian (Ed.), *Origins of cognitive skills*. Hillsdale, NJ: Erlbaum.

Messer, D. J. (1980). The episodic structure of maternal speech to young children. *Journal of Child Language, 7*, 29–40.

Michaels, C. F., & Carello, C. (1981). *Direct perception.* Englewood Cliffs, NJ: Prentice-Hall.

Michaels, S., & Cazden, C. B. (1986). Teacher/child collaboration as oral preparation for literacy. In B. B. Schieffelin & P. Gilmore (Eds.), *The acquisition of literacy: Ethnographic perspectives.* Norwood, NJ: Ablex.

Miller, G. (1977). *Spontaneous apprentices.* New York: Seabury Press.

Miller, M. (1987). Argumentation and cognition. In M. Hickmann (Ed.), *Social and functional approaches to language and thought.* San Diego, CA: Academic Press.

Miller, P. J. (1979). *Amy, Wendy, and Beth: Learning language in South Baltimore.* Austin: University of Texas Press.

Mischel, W. (1979). On the interface of cognition and personality: Beyond the person–situation debate. *American Psychologist, 34,* 740–754.

Mistry, J., Goncu, A., & Rogoff, B. (1988, April). *Cultural variations in role relations in the socialization of toddlers.* Paper presented at the International Conference of Infant Studies, Washington, D.C.

Mistry, J., & Rogoff, B. (1987, April). *Influence of purpose and strategic assistance on preschool children's remembering.* Paper presented at the meetings of the Society for Research in Child Development, Baltimore.

Moerk, E. L. (1983). *The mother of Eve—as a first language teacher.* Norwood, NJ: Ablex.

Moerk, E. L. (1985). A differential interactive analysis of language teaching and learning. *Discourse Processes, 8,* 113–142.

Morelli, G. A., Fitz, D., Oppenheim, D., Nash, A., Nakagawa, M., & Rogoff, B. (1988, November). *Social relations in infants' sleeping arrangements.* Paper presented at the meetings of the American Anthropological Association, Phoenix.

Mueller, J. H., Rankin, J. L., & Carlomusto, M. (1979). Adult age differences in free recall as a function of basis of organization and method of presentation. *Journal of Gerontology, 34,* 375–385.

Mugny, G., & Doise, W. (1978). Socio-cognitive conflict and structure of individual and collective performances. *European Journal of Social Psychology, 8,* 181–192.

Mugny, G., Perret-Clermont, A.-N., & Doise, W. (1981). Interpersonal coordinations and social differences in the construction of the intellect. In G. M. Stephenson & J. M. Davis (Eds.), *Progress in applied psychology* (Vol. 1). New York: Wiley.

Munroe, R. L., & Munroe, R. M. (1975). *Cross-cultural human development.* Monterey, CA: Brooks/Cole.

Murray, F. B. (1982). Teaching through social conflict. *Contemporary Educational Psychology, 7,* 257–271.

Murray, H. A. (1938). *Explorations in personality.* New York: Oxford University Press.

Murray, L., & Trevarthen, C. (1985). Emotional regulation of interactions between two-month-olds and their mothers. In T. M. Field & N. Fox (Eds.), *Social perception in infants.* Norwood, NJ: Ablex.

Nash, M. (1967). *Machine age Maya.* Chicago: University of Chicago Press.

Neisser, U. (1976). General, academic, and artificial intelligence. In L. B. Resnick (Ed.), *The nature of intelligence.* Hillsdale, NJ: Erlbaum.

Neisser, U. (Ed.). (1982). *Memory observed: Remembering in natural contexts.* San Francisco: Freeman.

Nelson, K. E. (1977). Facilitating children's syntax acquisition. *Developmental Psychology, 13,* 101–107.

Nelson, K. E., Denninger, M. S., Bonvillian, J. D., Kaplan, B. J., & Baker, N. D. (1984). Maternal input adjustments and non-adjustments as related to children's linguistic advances and to language acquisition theories. In A. D. Pellegrini & T. D. Yawkey (Eds.), *The development of oral and written language in social contexts.* Norwood, NJ: Ablex.

Nelson-LeGall, S. (1985). Help-seeking behavior in learning. In E. W. Gordon (Ed.),

Review of research in education (Vol. 12). Washington, DC: American Educational Research Association.

Newman, D. (1982). Perspective-taking versus content in understanding lies. *Quarterly Newsletter of the Laboratory of Comparative Human Cognition, 4,* 26–29.

Newman, D., Riel, M., & Martin, L. M. W. (1983). Cultural practices and Piagetian theory: The impact of a cross-cultural research program. *Contributions to Human Development, 8,* 135–154.

Newson, J. (1977). An intersubjective approach to the systematic description of mother–infant interaction. In H. R. Schaffer (Ed.), *Studies in mother–infant interaction.* New York: Academic Press.

Newson, J., & Newson, E. (1974). Cultural aspects of childrearing in the English speaking world. In M. P. M. Richards (Ed.), *The integration of the child into a social world.* Cambridge: Cambridge University Press.

Newson, J., & Newson, E. (1975). Intersubjectivity and the transmission of culture: On the social origins of symbolic functioning. *Bulletin of the British Psychological Society, 28,* 437–446.

Ochs, E. (1979). Introduction: What child language can contribute to pragmatics. In E. Ochs & B. Schieffelin (Eds.), *Developmental pragmatics.* New York: Academic Press.

Ochs, E., & Schieffelin, B. B. (1984). Language acquisition and socialization: Three developmental stories and their implications. In R. Schweder & R. LeVine (Eds.), *Culture and its acquisition.* Chicago: University of Chicago Press.

Olson, D. R. (1976). Culture, technology, and intellect. In L. B. Resnick (Ed.), *The nature of intelligence.* Hillsdale, NJ: Erlbaum.

Olson, S. L., Bates, J. E., & Bayles, K. (1984). Mother–infant interaction and the development of individual differences in children's cognitive competence. *Developmental Psychology, 20,* 166–179.

Overton, W. F., & Reese, H. W. (1973). Models of development: Methodological implications. In J. R. Nesselroade & H. W. Reese (Eds.), *Life-span developmental psychology: Methodological issues.* New York: Academic Press.

Packer, M. J. (1983). Communication in early infancy: Three common assumptions examined and found inadequate. *Human Development, 26,* 233–248.

Papert, S. (1980). *Mindstorms: Children, computers, and powerful ideas.* New York: Basic Books.

Papousek, H., & Papousek, M. (1983). The psychobiology of the first didactic programs and toys in human infants. In A. Oliverio & M. Zappella (Eds.), *The behavior of human infants.* New York: Plenum Press.

Papousek, M., Papousek, H., & Bornstein, M. H. (1985). The naturalistic vocal environment of young infants. In T. M. Field & N. Fox (Eds.), *Social perception in infants.* Norwood, NJ: Ablex.

Parke, R. D., & O'Leary, S. E. (1976). Family interaction in the newborn period: Some findings, some observations and some unresolved issues. In K. F. Riegel & J. A. Meacham (Eds.), *The developing individual in a changing world* (Vol. 2). The Hague: Mouton.

Parrinello, R. M., & Ruff, H. A. (1988). The influence of adult intervention on infants' level of attention. *Child Development, 59,* 1125–1135.

Pearson, P. D., & Gallagher, M. C. (1983). The instruction of reading comprehension. *Contemporary Educational Psychology, 8,* 317–344.

Penner, S. G. (1987). Parental responses to grammatical and ungrammatical child utterances. *Child Development, 58,* 376–384.

Pepper, S. C. (1942). *World hypotheses: A study in evidence.* Berkeley: University of California Press.

Perlmutter, M. (1979). Age differences in adults' free recall, cued recall, and recognition. *Journal of Gerontology, 34,* 533–539.

Perret-Clermont, A.-N., Brun, J., Saada, E. H., & Schubauer-Leoni, M.-L. (1984). Psychological processes, operatory level and the acquisition of knowledge. *Interactions didactiques* (No. 2 bis). Universities of Geneva and of Neuchâtel.

Perret-Clermont, A.-N., & Schubauer-Leoni, M.-L. (1981). Conflict and cooperation as opportunities for learning. In P. Robinson (Ed.), *Communication in development*. London: Academic Press.

Peters, A. M., (1986). *I wanna tell story: The development of collaborative story telling by a 2-year old blind child and his father*. Unpublished manuscript, University of Hawaii, Honolulu.

Petitto, A. L. (1983). *Long division of labor: In support of an interactive learning theory*. Unpublished manuscript, University of Rochester.

Philips, S. U. (1972). Participant structures and communicative competence: Warm Springs children in community and classroom. In C. B. Cazden, V. P. John & D. Hymes (Eds.), *Functions of language in the classroom*. New York: Teachers College Press.

Piaget, J. (1926). *The language and thought of the child*. New York: Harcourt, Brace.

Piaget, J. (1952). *The origins of intelligence in children*. New York: Norton.

Piaget, J. (1972). Intellectual evolution from adolescence to adulthood. *Human Development, 15*, 1–12.

Piaget, J. (1977). Logique génétique et sociologie. In *Etudes sociologiques*. Geneva: Librairie Droz. (Reprinted from *Revue Philosophique de la France et de l'Etranger*, 1928, *53*, 161–205)

Piaget, J. (1977). Les operations logiques et la vie sociale. In *Etudes sociologiques*. Geneva: Librairie Droz.

Piaget, J. (1977). Problèmes de la psycho-sociologie de l'enfance. In *Etudes sociologiques*. Geneva: Librairie Droz. (Reprinted from *Traité de sociologie*, G. Gurvitch, Paris: Presses Universitaires de France, 1963, pp. 229–254)

Pick, A. D. (1979). Listening to melodies: Perceiving events. In A. D. Pick (Ed.), *Perception and its development: A tribute to Eleanor J. Gibson*. Hillsdale, NJ: Erlbaum.

Poe, P. (1982). Beginning in the bathtub. *American Baby, 44*, 12–20.

Pressley, M., Heisel, B. E., McCormick, C. B., & Nakamura, G. (1982). Memory strategy instruction with children. In C. J. Brainerd & M. Pressley (Eds.), *Progress in cognitive development research: Vol. 2. Verbal processes in children*. New York: Springer-Verlag.

Prindle, S. S., Carello, C., & Turvey, M. T. (1980). Animal–environment mutuality and direct perception. *Behavioral and Brain Sciences, 3*, 395–397.

Radziszewska, B., & Rogoff, B. (1988). Influence of adult and peer collaborators on children's planning skills. *Developmental Psychology, 24*, 840–848.

Ratner, H. H. (1984). Memory demands and the development of young children's memory. *Child Development, 55*, 2173–2191.

Reed, E. S., & Jones, R. K. (1977). Towards a definition of living systems: A theory of ecological support for behavior. *Acta Biotheoretica, 26*, 153–163.

Resnick, D. P., & Resnick, L. B. (1977). The nature of literacy: An historical exploration. *Harvard Educational Review, 47*, 370–385.

Rheingold, H. L. (1969). The social and socializing infant. In D. A. Goslin (Ed.), *Handbook of socialization theory and research*. Chicago: Rand McNally.

Rheingold, H. L. (1982). Little children's participation in the work of adults, a nascent prosocial behavior. *Child Development, 53*, 114–125.

Rheingold, H. L. (1985). Development as the acquisition of familiarity. *Annual Review of Psychology, 36*, 1–17.

Rice, G. E. (1980). On cultural schemata. *American Ethnologist, 7*, 152–171.

Richards, M. P. M. (1978). The biological and the social. In A. Lock (Ed.), *Action, gesture and symbol: The emergence of language*. London: Academic Press.

Richman, A. L., Miller, P. M., & Solomon, M. J. (1988). The socialization of infants in suburban Boston. In R. A. LeVine, P. M. Miller, & M. M. West (Eds.), *Parental behavior in diverse societies.* San Francisco: Jossey-Bass.

Ricks, M. H. (1985). The social transmission of parental behavior: Attachment across generations. In I. Bretherton & E. Waters (Eds.), *Growing points of attachment theory and research. Monographs of the Society for Research in Child Development, 50* (1–2, Serial No. 209).

Riegel, K. F. (1972). The influence of economic and political ideology upon the development of developmental psychology. *Psychological Bulletin, 78,* 129–141.

Riegel, K. F. (1973). Developmental psychology and society: Some historical and ethical considerations. In J. R. Nesselroade & H. W. Reese (Eds.), *Life-span developmental psychology: Methodological issues.* New York: Academic Press.

Riegel, K. F. (1979). *Foundations of dialectical psychology.* New York: Academic Press.

Rogoff, B. (1981a). Adults and peers as agents of socialization: A Highland Guatemalan profile. *Ethos, 9,* 18–36.

Rogoff, B. (1981b). Schooling and the development of cognitive skills. In H. C. Triandis & A. Heron (Eds.), *Handbook of cross-cultural psychology* (Vol. 4). Rockleigh, NJ: Allyn & Bacon.

Rogoff, B. (1982a). Mode of instruction and memory test performance. *International Journal of Behavioral Development, 5,* 33–48.

Rogoff, B. (1982b). Integrating context and cognitive development. In M. E. Lamb & A. L. Brown (Eds.), *Advances in developmental psychology* (Vol. 2). Hillsdale, NJ: Erlbaum.

Rogoff, B. (1986). Adult assistance of children's learning. In T. E. Raphael (Ed.), *The contexts of school based literacy.* New York: Random House.

Rogoff, B., Ellis, S., & Gardner, W. (1984). Adjustment of adult–child instruction according to child's age and task. *Developmental Psychology, 20,* 193–199.

Rogoff, B., & Gardner, W. P. (1984). Guidance in cognitive development: An examination of mother–child instruction. In B. Rogoff & J. Lave (Eds.), *Everyday cognition: Its development in social context.* Cambridge, MA: Harvard University Press.

Rogoff, B., & Gauvain, M. (1986). A method for the analysis of patterns illustrated with data on mother–child instructional interaction. In J. Valsiner (Ed.), *The role of the individual subject in scientific psychology.* New York: Plenum Press.

Rogoff, B., Gauvain, M., & Ellis, S. (1984). Development viewed in its cultural context. In M. H. Bornstein & M. E. Lamb (Eds.), *Developmental psychology.* Hillsdale, NJ: Erlbaum.

Rogoff, B., Malkin, C., & Gilbride, K. (1984). Interaction with babies as guidance in development. In B. Rogoff & J. V. Wertsch (Eds.), *Children's learning in the "zone of proximal development."* San Francisco: Jossey-Bass.

Rogoff, B., & Mistry, J. (1985). Memory development in cultural context. In M. Pressley & C. Brainerd (Eds.), *Cognitive learning and memory in children.* New York: Springer-Verlag.

Rogoff, B., Mistry, J., Radziszewska, B., & Germond, J. (in press). Infants' instrumental social interaction with adults. In S. Feinman (Ed.), *Social referencing and the social construction of reality in infancy.* New York: Plenum Press.

Rogoff, B., Mosier, C., Mistry, J., & Göncü, A. (in press). Toddlers' guided participation in cultural activity. *Cultural Dynamics.*

Rogoff, B., Sellers, M. J., Pirotta, S., Fox, N., & White, S. H. (1975). Age of assignment of roles and responsibilities to children: A cross-cultural survey. *Human Development, 18,* 353–369.

Rogoff, B., & Waddell, K. J. (1982). Memory for information organized in a scene by children from two cultures. *Child Development, 53,* 1224–1228.

Rommetveit, R. (1976). On Piagetian cognitive operations, semantic competence and message structure in adult–child communication. In I. Markova (Ed.), *The social context of language.* London: Wiley.

Rommetveit, R. (1985). Language acquisition as increasing linguistic structuring of experience and symbolic behavior control. In J. V. Wertsch (Ed.), *Culture, communication, and cognition: Vygotskian perspectives*. Cambridge: Cambridge University Press.

Ross, B. M., & Millsom, C. (1970). Repeated memory of oral prose in Ghana and New York. *International Journal of Psychology, 5*, 173–181.

Rubtsov, V. V. (1981). The role of cooperation in the development of intelligence. *Soviet Psychology, 19*, 41–62.

Rubtsov, V. V., & Guzman, R. Ya. (1984–1985). Psychological characteristics of the methods pupils use to organize joint activity in dealing with a school task. *Soviet Psychology, 23*, 65–84.

Ruddle, K., & Chesterfield, R. (1978). Traditional skill training and labor in rural societies. *Journal of Developing Areas, 12*, 389–398.

Sartre, J.-P. (1964). *The words.* New York: Braziller.

Saxe, G. B. (1988). *Mathematics in and out of school.* Unpublished manuscript, University of California, Los Angeles.

Saxe, G. B., Gearhart, M., & Guberman, S. B. (1984). The social organization of early number development. In B. Rogoff & J. V. Wertsch (Eds.), *Children's learning in the "zone of proximal development."* San Francisco: Jossey-Bass.

Scaife, M., & Bruner, J. (1975). The capacity for joint visual attention in the infant. *Nature, 253*, 265–266.

Schaffer, H. R. (1977a). *Mothering.* London: Fontana/Open Books.

Schaffer, H. R. (Ed.). (1977b). *Studies in mother–infant interaction.* New York: Academic Press.

Schaffer, H. R. (1984). *The child's entry into a social world.* London: Academic Press.

Schaffer, H. R., Hepburn, A., & Collis, G. M. (1983). Verbal and nonverbal aspects of mothers' directives. *Journal of Child Language, 10*, 337–355.

Schallert, D. L., & Kleiman, G. M. (1979, June). *Some reasons why teachers are easier to understand than textbooks* (Reading Education Report No. 9). Urbana-Champaign: University of Illinois, Center for Study of Reading. (ERIC Report No. ED 172 189)

Shieffelin, B. B., & Eisenberg, A. R. (1984). Cultural variation in children's conversations. In R. Schiefelbusch & J. Pickar (Eds.), *The acquisition of communicative competence*. Baltimore: University Park Press.

Schneiderman, M. H. (1983). "Do what I mean, not what I say!" Changes in mothers' action directives to young children. *Journal of Child Language, 10*, 357–367.

Scollon, R. (1976). *Conversations with a one-year-old.* Honolulu: University Press of Hawaii.

Scribner, S. (1974). Developmental aspects of categorized recall in a West African society. *Cognitive Psychology, 6*, 475–494.

Scribner, S. (1975). Recall of classical syllogisms: A cross-cultural investigation of error on logical problems. In R. J. Falmagne (Ed.), *Reasoning: Representation and process in children and adults.* New York: Wiley.

Scribner, S. (1977). Modes of thinking and ways of speaking: Culture and logic reconsidered. In P. N. Johnson-Laird & P. C. Wason (Eds.), *Thinking.* Cambridge: Cambridge University Press.

Scribner, S. (1985). Vygotsky's uses of history. In J. V. Wertsch (Ed.), *Culture, communication, and cognition: Vygotskian perspectives*. Cambridge: Cambridge University Press.

Scribner, S., & Cole, M. (1973). Cognitive consequences of formal and informal education. *Science, 182*, 553–559.

Scribner, S., & Cole, M. (1981). *The psychology of literacy.* Cambridge, MA: Harvard University Press.

Serpell, R. (1977). Strategies for investigating intelligence in its cultural context. *Quarterly Newsletter of the Institute for Comparative Human Development, 1*, 11–15.

Serpell, R. (1982). Measures of perception, skills and intelligence. In W. W. Hartup (Ed.), *Review of child development research* (Vol. 6). Chicago: University of Chicago Press.

Sharp, D., Cole, M., & Lave, C. (1979). Education and cognitive development: The evidence from experimental research. *Monographs of the Society for Research in Child Development, 44* (Serial No. 178).

Shatz, M. (1987). Bootstrapping operations in child language. In K. E. Nelson & A. van Kleeck (Eds.), *Children's language* (Vol. 6). Hillsdale, NJ: Erlbaum.

Shaw, R., & Bransford, J. D. (Eds.). (1977). *Perceiving, acting and knowing: Toward an ecological psychology.* Hillsdale, NJ: Erlbaum.

Shore, B. (1988, November). *Interpretation under fire.* Paper presented at the meetings of the American Anthropological Association, Phoenix.

Shotter, J. (1978). The cultural context of communication studies: Theoretical and methodological issues. In A. Lock (Ed.), *Action, gesture and symbol: The emergence of language.* London: Academic Press.

Shotter, J., & Newson, J. (1982). An ecological approach to cognitive development: Implicate orders, joint action, and intentionality. In G. Butterworth & P. Light (Eds.), *Social cognition studies in the development of understanding.* Brighton: Harvester Press.

Siegler, R. S. (1981). Developmental sequences within and between concepts. *Monographs of the Society for Research in Child Development, 46* (2, Serial No. 189).

Sigel, I. E., & Cocking, R. R. (1977). Cognition and communication: A dialectic paradigm for development. In M. Lewis & L. A. Rosenblum (Eds.), *Interaction, conversation, and the development of language: The origins of behavior* (Vol. 5). New York: Wiley.

Skeat, W. W. (1974). *An etymological dictionary of the English language.* Oxford: Clarendon Press.

Skeen, J., & Rogoff, B. (1987). Children's difficulties in deliberate memory for spatial relationships: Misapplication of verbal mnemonic strategies? *Cognitive Development, 2,* 1–19.

Slavin, R. E. (1987). Developmental and motivational perspectives on cooperative learning: A reconciliation. *Child Development, 58,* 1161–1167.

Slobin, D. I. (1973). Cognitive prerequisites for the development of grammar. In C. A. Ferguson & D. I. Slobin (Eds.), *Studies of child language development.* New York: Holt, Rinehart and Winston.

Smedslund, J. (1984). The invisible obvious: Culture in psychology. In K. M. J. Lagerspetz & P. Niemi (Eds.), *Psychology in the 1990's.* Amsterdam: Elsevier.

Smollett, E. W. (1975). Differential enculturation and social class in Canadian schools. In T. R. Williams (Ed.), *Socialization and communication in primary groups.* The Hague: Mouton.

Snow, C. (1977). Mother's speech research: From input to interaction. In C. Snow & C. Ferguson, *Talking to children.* New York: Cambridge University Press.

Snow, C. E. (1982a). Are parents language teachers? In K. Borman (Ed.), *Social life of children in a changing society.* Hillsdale, NJ: Erlbaum.

Snow, C. E. (1982b, March). *Literacy and language: Relationships during the preschool years.* Paper presented at the meetings of the American Educational Research Association, New York.

Snow, C. E. (1984). Parent–child interaction and the development of communicative ability. In R. Schiefelbusch & J. Pickar (Eds.), *The acquisition of communicative competence.* Baltimore: University Park Press.

Sorce, J. F., Emde, R. N., Campos, J., & Klinnert, M. D. (1985). Maternal emotional signaling: Its effect on the visual cliff behavior of 1-year-olds. *Developmental Psychology, 21,* 195–200.

Sorenson, E. R. (1979). Early tactile communication and the patterning of human organization: A New Guinea case study. In M. Bullowa (Ed.), *Before speech: The beginning of interpersonal communication.* Cambridge: Cambridge University Press.

Sostek, A. M., Vietze, P., Zaslow, M., Kreiss, L., van der Waals, F., & Rubinstein, D. (1981). Social context in caregiver–infant interaction: A film study of Fais and the United States. In T. M. Field, A. M. Sostek, P. Vietze, & P. H. Leiderman (Eds.), *Culture and early interactions.* Hillsdale, NJ: Erlbaum.

Stigler, J. W., Barclay, C., & Aiello, P. (1982). Motor and mental abacus skill: A preliminary look at an expert. *Quarterly Newsletter of the Laboratory of Comparative Human Cognition, 4,* 12–14.

Subbotskii, E. V. (1987). Communicative style and the genesis of personality in preschoolers. *Soviet Psychology, 25,* 38–58.

Sugarman-Bell, S. (1978). Some organizational aspects of pre-verbal communication. In I. Markova (Ed.), *The social context of language.* New York: Wiley.

Super, C. M. (1981). Behavioral development in infancy. In R. H. Munroe, R. L. Munroe, & B. B. Whiting (Eds.), *Handbook of cross-cultural human development.* New York: Garland.

Super, C. M., & Harkness, S. (1983). *Looking across at growing up: The cultural expression of cognitive development in middle childhood.* Unpublished manuscript, Harvard University.

Sutter, B. & Grensjo, B. (1988). Explorative learning in the school? Experiences of local historical research by pupils. *Quarterly Newsletter of the Laboratory of Comparative Human Cognition, 10,* 39–54.

Sylva, K., Bruner, J. S., & Genova, P. (1976). The role of play in the problem-solving of children 3–5 years old. In J. S. Bruner, A. Jolly, & K. Sylva (Eds.), *Play: Its role in development and evolution.* New York: Basic Books.

Taylor, D. (1983). *Family literacy.* Exeter, NH: Heinemann Educational Books.

Tomasello, M., & Farrar, M. J. (1986). Joint attention and early language. *Child Development, 57,* 1454–1463.

Tomasello, M., Mannle, S., & Kruger, A. C. (1986). Linguistic environment of 1- to 2-year-old twins. *Developmental Psychology, 22,* 169–176.

Trevarthen, C. (1980). Instincts for human understanding and for cultural cooperation: Their development in infancy. In M. von Cranach, K. Foppa, W. Lepenies, & D. Ploog (Eds.), *Human ethology: Claims and limits of a new discipline.* Cambridge: Cambridge University Press.

Trevarthen, C. (1988). Universal co-operative motives: How infants begin to know the language and culture of their parents. In G. Jahoda & I. M. Lewis (Eds.), *Acquiring culture: Cross cultural studies in child development.* London: Croom Helm.

Trevarthen, C., & Hubley, P. (1978). Secondary intersubjectivity: Confidence, confiding and acts of meaning in the first year. In A. Lock (Ed.), *Action, gesture and symbol: The emergence of language.* London: Academic Press.

Trevarthen, C., Hubley, P., & Sheeran, L. (1975). Les activités innées du nourrisson. *La Recherche, 6,* 447–458.

Tronick, E. Z. (1982). *Social interchange in infancy: Affect, cognition, and communication.* Baltimore: University Park Press.

Tronick, E., Als, H., & Adamson, L. (1979). Structure of early face-to-face communicative interactions. In M. Bullowa (Ed.), *Before speech: The beginning of interpersonal communication.* Cambridge: Cambridge University Press.

Tronick, E. Z., & Field, T. (Eds.). (1986). *Maternal depression and infant disturbance.* San Francisco: Jossey-Bass.

Tudge, J. R. H. (1985). The effect of social interaction on cognitive development: How creative is conflict? *Quarterly Newsletter of the Laboratory of Comparative Human Cognition, 7,* 33–40.

Tudge, J. R. H., & Rogoff, B. (1989). Peer influences on cognitive development: Piagetian and Vygotskian perspectives. In M. Bornstein & J. Bruner (Eds.), *Interaction in human development*. Hillsdale, NJ: Erlbaum.

Turvey, M. T., & Shaw, R. E. (1979). The primacy of perceiving: An ecological reformulation of perception for understanding memory. In L. G. Nilsson (Ed.), *Prospectus on memory research: Essays in honor of Uppsala University's 500th Anniversary*. Hillsdale, NJ: Erlbaum.

Valdez-Menchaca, M. C. (1987, April). *The effects of incidental teaching on vocabulary acquisition by young children*. Paper presented at the meetings of the Society for Research in Child Development, Baltimore.

Valsiner, J. (1984). Construction of the zone of proximal development in adult–child joint action: The socialization of meals. In B. Rogoff & J. V. Wertsch (Eds.), *Children's learning in the "zone of proximal development."* San Francisco: Jossey-Bass.

Valsiner, J. (1987). *Culture and the development of children's action*. Chichester: Wiley.

Vandell, D. L., & Wilson, K. S. (1987). Infants' interactions with mother, sibling, and peer: Contrasts and relations between interaction systems. *Child Development, 58*, 176–186.

Vandenberg, B. (1980). Play, problem-solving, and creativity. In K. H. Rubin (Ed.), *Children's play*. San Francisco: Jossey-Bass.

Van Valin, R. D., Jr. (1980). Meaning and interpretation. *Journal of Pragmatics, 4*, 213–231.

Voneche, J. (1984). Introduction to issues on phylogeny and ontogeny. *Human Development, 27*, 227–232.

Vygotsky, L. S. (1967). Play and its role in the mental development of the child. *Soviet Psychology, 5*, 6–18.

Vygotsky, L. S. (1978). *Mind in society: The development of higher psychological processes*. Cambridge, MA: Harvard University Press.

Vygotsky, L. S. (1981). The genesis of higher mental functions. In J. V. Wertsch (Ed.), *The concept of activity in Soviet psychology*. New York: Sharpe.

Vygotsky, L. S. (1987). *Thinking and speech*. In R. W. Rieber & A. S. Carton (Eds.), *The collected works of L. S. Vygotsky* (N. Minick, Trans.). New York: Plenum Press.

Waddell, K. J., & Rogoff, B. (1987). Contextual organization and intentionality in adults' spatial memory. *Developmental Psychology, 23*, 514–520.

Wagner, D. A., & Spratt, J. E. (1987). Cognitive consequences of contrasting pedagogies: The effects of Quranic preschooling in Morocco. *Child Development, 58*, 1207–1219.

Ward, M. C. (1971). *Them children: A study in language learning*. New York: Holt, Rinehart and Winston.

Wartofsky, M. (1984). The child's construction of the world and the world's construction of the child. In F. S. Kessel & A. W. Siegel (Eds.), *The child and other cultural inventions*. New York: Praeger.

Watson-Gegeo, K. A., & Gegeo, D. W. (1986a). The social world of Kwara'ae children: Acquisition of language and values. In J. Cook-Gumperz, W. Corsaro, & J. Streeck (Eds.), *Children's language and children's worlds*. The Hague: Mouton.

Watson-Gegeo, K. A., & Gegeo, D. W. (1986b). *Communicative routines in Kwara'ae children's language socialization*. Final report to the National Science Foundation.

Watson-Gegeo, K. A., & Gegeo, D. W. (1989). The role of sibling interaction in child socialization. In P. Zukow (Ed.), *Sibling interaction across cultures: Theoretical and methodological issues*. New York: Springer-Verlag.

Waxman, S., & Gelman, R. (1986). Preschoolers' use of superordinate relations in classification and language. *Cognitive Development, 1*, 139–156.

Weisner, T. S., & Gallimore, R. (1977). My brother's keeper: Child and sibling caretaking. *Current Anthropology, 18*, 169–190.

Wellen, C. J. (1985). Effects of older siblings on the language young children hear and produce. *Journal of Speech and Hearing Disorders, 50,* 84–99.

Wells, G. (1975). The contexts of children's early language experience. *Educational Review, 27,* 114–125.

Wells, G. (1979). Apprenticeship in meaning. In K. Nelson (Ed.), *Children's language* (Vol. 2). New York: Halsted Press.

Wenger, M. (1983). *Gender role socialization in an East African community: Social interaction between 2- to 3-year-olds and older children in social ecological perspective.* Unpublished doctoral dissertation, Harvard University.

Wertsch, J. V. (1978). Adult–child interaction and the roots of metacognition. *Quarterly Newsletter of the Institute for Comparative Human Development, 2,* 15–18.

Wertsch, J. V. (1979a). From social interaction to higher psychological processes. *Human Development, 22,* 1–22.

Wertsch, J. V. (1979b, March). *The social interactional origins of metacognition.* Paper presented at the meetings of the Society for Research in Child Development, San Francisco.

Wertsch, J. V. (1984). The zone of proximal development: Some conceptual issues. In B. Rogoff & J. V. Wertsch (Eds.), *Children's learning in the "zone of proximal development."* San Francisco: Jossey-Bass.

Wertsch, J. V. (1985). *Vygotsky and the social formation of mind.* Cambridge, MA: Harvard University Press.

Wertsch, J. V. (1987). Collective memory: Issues from a sociohistorical perspective. *Quarterly Newsletter of the Laboratory of Comparative Human Cognition, 9,* 19–22.

Wertsch, J. V., & Hickmann, M. (1987). Problem solving in social interaction: A microgenetic analysis. In M. Hickmann (Ed.), *Social and functional approaches to language and thought.* San Diego, CA: Academic Press.

Wertsch, J. V., Minick, N., & Arns, F. J. (1984). The creation of context in joint problem-solving. In B. Rogoff & J. Lave (Eds.), *Everyday cognition: Its development in social context.* Cambridge: MA: Harvard University Press.

Wertsch, J. V., & Stone, C. A. (1979, February). *A social interactional analysis of learning disabilities remediation.* Paper presented at the International Conference of the Association for Children with Learning Disabilities, San Francisco.

Wertsch, J. V., & Youniss, J. (1987). Contextualizing the investigator: The case of developmental psychology. *Human Development, 30,* 18–31.

West, M. J., & King, A. P. (1985, April). *A niche for nature and nurture.* Paper presented at the meetings of the Society for Research in Child Development, Toronto.

White, S. H. (1965). Evidence for a hierarchical arrangement of learning processes. In L. P. Lipsitt & C. C. Spiker (Eds.), *Advances in child development and behavior* (Vol. 2). New York: Academic Press.

White, S. H., & Siegel, A. W. (1984). Cognitive development in time and space. In B. Rogoff & J. Lave (Eds.), *Everyday cognition: Its development in social context.* Cambridge, MA: Harvard University Press.

Whiting, B. B. (1979). *Maternal behavior in cross-cultural perspective.* Paper presented at the meeting of the Society for Cross-Cultural Research, Charlottesville, VA.

Whiting, B. B. (1980). Culture and social behavior: A model for the development of social behavior. *Ethos, 8,* 95–116.

Whiting, B. B., & Edwards, C. P. (1988). *Children of different worlds: The formation of social behavior.* Cambridge, MA: Harvard University Press.

Whiting, B. B., & Whiting, J. W. M. (1975). *Children of six cultures: A psycho-cultural analysis.* Cambridge, MA: Harvard University Press.

Whiting, J. W. M. (1981). Environmental constraints on infant care practices. In R. H. Munroe, R. L. Munroe, & B. B. Whiting (Eds.), *Handbook of cross-cultural human development.* New York: Garland.

Wober, M. (1972). Culture and the concept of intelligence: A case in Uganda. *Journal of Cross-Cultural Psychology, 3,* 327–328.

Wolf, D. P. (1988). Becoming literate: One reader reading. *Academic connections* (The College Board), 1–4.

Wolff, P. H. (1963). The natural history of a family. In B. M. Foss (Ed.), *Determinants of infant behavior II*. London: Methuen.

Wood, D. (1986). Aspects of teaching and learning. In M. Richards & P. Light (Eds.), *Children of social worlds*. Cambridge: Polity Press.

Wood, D., Bruner, J. S., & Ross, G. (1976). The role of tutoring in problem-solving. *Journal of Child Psychology and Psychiatry, 17,* 89–100.

Wood, D. J., & Middleton, D. (1975). A study of assisted problem-solving. *British Journal of Psychology, 66,* 181–191.

Wood, D., Wood, H., & Middleton, D. (1978). An experimental evaluation of four face-to-face teaching strategies. *International Journal of Behavioral Development, 2,* 131–147.

Youniss, J. (1987). Social construction and moral development: Update and expansion of an idea. In W. M. Kurtines & J. L. Gewirtz (Eds.), *Moral development through social interaction*. New York: Wiley.

Zborowski, M. (1955). The place of book-learning in traditional Jewish culture. In M. Mead & M. Wolfenstein (Eds.), *Childhood in contemporary cultures*. Chicago: University of Chicago Press.

Zimmerman, B. J., & Rosenthal, T. L. (1974). Observational learning of rule-governed behavior by children. *Psychological Bulletin, 81,* 29–42.

Zinchenko, V. P. (1985). Vygotsky's ideas about units for the analysis of mind. In J. V. Wertsch (Ed.), *Culture, communication and cognition: Vygotskian perspectives*. Cambridge, MA: Cambridge University Press.

Zukow, P. G., Reilly, J., & Greenfield, P. M. (1982). Making the absent present: Facilitating the transition from sensorimotor to linguistic communication. In K. Nelson (Ed.), *Children's language* (Vol. 3). New York: Gardner Press.

Index